OXFOR

AND (..... .... INGS

Blaise Pascal (1623–62), sickly as a youth and in poor health throughout his life, was precociously gifted as a mathematician and scientist, but is now chiefly remembered for his commitment to the religious group associated with the monastery of Port-Royal, generally if inappropriately referred to as 'Jansenist'. He never wrote a book, but did compose a brilliant series of satirical and polemical flysheets, subsequently known as the *Lettres provinciales*, against the relaxation of strict and immutable moral norms, and left a series of abandoned texts, of which the most important were post-humously published after heavy editing by his family and admirers for purposes of religious edification. They have ever since been known after their modish seventeenth-century title as the *Pensées*. Some of the texts were notes produced in the context of preparing a religious apologetic.

Pascal mixed in the upper bourgeois society of his time, was on friendly terms with important scientists, administrators, legal officials, and some of the higher nobility. In the expression of his religious views, Pascal brought French prose writing to new peaks of lyrical, satirical, and polemical brilliance. Although he failed to resolve the religious problems which confronted him, he was the most brilliant religious philosopher of his century and the author of the finest satirical work written in seventeenth-century France.

Anthony Levi took premature retirement as Buchanan Professor of French Language and Literature in the University of Saint Andrews in order to undertake full-time research. His books include a two-volume *Guide to French Literature*, 1992 and 1994, and an annotated edition of Erasmus' *Praise of Folly*.

Honor Levi read French at Warwick, discovered and published for her Edinburgh Ph.D. the legal inventory of Richelieu's possessions at death, and reconstituted the original layout of what is now the Palais-Royal in Paris. She taught French, published papers given in France at historical symposia, wrote on French art history and literature, and published a series of encyclopedia articles on historic French towns.

OXFORD WORLD'S CLASSICS

*For over 100 years Oxford World's Classics have brought
readers closer to the world's great literature. Now with over 700
titles—from the 4,000-year-old myths of Mesopotamia to the
twentieth century's greatest novels—the series makes available
lesser-known as well as celebrated writing.*

*The pocket-sized hardbacks of the early years contained
introductions by Virginia Woolf, T. S. Eliot, Graham Greene,
and other literary figures which enriched the experience of reading.
Today the series is recognized for its fine scholarship and
reliability in texts that span world literature, drama and poetry,
religion, philosophy and politics. Each edition includes perceptive
commentary and essential background information to meet the
changing needs of readers.*

OXFORD WORLD'S CLASSICS

BLAISE PASCAL

Pensées
and Other Writings

Translated by
HONOR LEVI

Edited with an Introduction and Notes by
ANTHONY LEVI

OXFORD
UNIVERSITY PRESS

OXFORD
UNIVERSITY PRESS

Great Clarendon Street, Oxford OX2 6DP

Oxford University Press is a department of the University of Oxford.
It furthers the University's objective of excellence in research, scholarship,
and education by publishing worldwide in

Oxford New York

Athens Auckland Bangkok Bogotá Buenos Aires Cape Town
Chennai Dar es Salaam Delhi Florence Hong Kong Istanbul Karachi
Kolkata Kuala Lumpur Madrid Melbourne Mexico City Mumbai Nairobi
Paris São Paulo Shanghai Singapore Taipei Tokyo Toronto Warsaw

with associated companies in Berlin Ibadan

Oxford is a registered trade mark of Oxford University Press
in the UK and in certain other countries

Published in the United States
by Oxford University Press Inc., New York

Translation © Honor Levi 1995
Editorial material © Anthony Levi 1995

First published as a World's Classics paperback 1995
Reissued as an Oxford World's Classics paperback 1999
Reissued 2008

British Library Cataloguing in Publication Data

Data available

Library of Congress Cataloging in Publication Data

Pascal, Blaise, 1623–1662.
[Pensées. English]
Pensées and other writings / Blaise Pascal ; translated by Honor
Levi ; with an introduction and notes by Anthony Levi.
p. cm.—(Oxford world's classics)
Chiefly a translation of: Pensées.
Includes bibliographical references and index.
1. Apologetics. 2. Catholic Church—Apologetic works. 3. Grace
(Theology). 4. Predestination. I. Levi, Honor. II. Levi, Anthony.
III. Pascal, Blaise, 1623–1662. Selection. English. IV. Title.
V. Series
B1901.P413 1995 230.2—dc20 94–33572

ISBN 978-0-19-954036-5

20

Printed in Great Britain by
Clays Ltd, Elcograf S.p.A.

CONTENTS

Introduction   vii

Note on the Text   xxxviii

Select Bibliography   xlii

A Chronology of Blaise Pascal   xliv

PENSÉES   I

DISCUSSION WITH MONSIEUR DE SACY   182

THE ART OF PERSUASION   193

WRITINGS ON GRACE   205
   Letter on the Possibility of the Commandments
   Treatise concerning Predestination

Explanatory Notes   227

Thematic Index   249

INTRODUCTION

THE *Pensées* as we have them were never meant to be read. They were miscellaneous private jottings concerning God, religion, and many sorts of human behaviour, analysed in support of Pascal's religious views. After Pascal's death, they were selected, arranged, edited, modified in the interest of intensifying their power of religious edification, compiled into a structured work with a long preface and thirty-two chapters, and published in 1670 by his family, friends, and admirers under the then modish title of *Pensées de M. Pascal sur la religion, et sur quelques autres sujets.*

Some of the fragments from which the original editors worked had been noted down in the context of writing a projected apologetic for the Christian religion. If it had ever been written, it might at one time have been based on miracles, and then a little later probably on the fulfilment by Jesus of the Old Testament prophecies instead. Some fragments, not many of which are here translated, go into great detail about the figures and announcements in the Old Testament of the Messiah to come. Others, omitted altogether both in 1670 and here, were notes for the flysheets known as the *Lettres provinciales*, attacking first the anti-Jansenist Paris theology faculty, then casuists from all orders, but mostly Jesuits, then the Jesuits as a body, and finally by name the Jesuit polemicist and royal confessor, François Annat (1590–1670).

As they were left, none of the individual fragments was intended for publication. They vary from the half-dozen in extended prose of extraordinary brilliance and psychological penetration to cryptic notes intelligible only to Pascal himself. Even he may not necessarily have remembered the ideas which prompted the jotting down of some key word or phrase. The fragments naturally contain quite incompatible attitudes and arguments with which Pascal was toying in his mind, sometimes trying them out by writing down headings, or attempting a short development, no doubt with a view to possible further elaboration. He was clearly interested in the possibility of using different genres for a longer work, as well as different orders in which material could be treated, but he stopped short before undertaking the process of selecting what material might be used, and which genre, and either eliminating or incorporating the other possibilities.

The best known of the longer fragments, numbered 680 and often known as 'the wager', was written on four sides of a single folded sheet of paper and contains paragraphs crammed into the text, others written vertically up the margins, and even upsidedown at the top of the page. There is no certainty that the added passages were ever intended to belong together, and some of them are at best either tangential to the original argument, which must have been that written in normal horizontal fashion, or they contradict it, and some are incompatible with others. No matter how the constitutive pieces are arranged, the four sides of manuscript cannot be made to yield a single coherent linear text, even if we take into account that what they contained was at least partly a dialogue in which a Christian believer confronts a doubter about immortality.

We are left with a jumble of notes whose envisaged form clearly changed before the projected book was abandoned. We do not know in what order Pascal wrote them, although it has been speculatively conjectured that each of the *liasses* or bundles into which Pascal arranged the fragments was compiled in such a way as to leave the earliest fragment it contains on the bottom, so that the last fragment to have been composed was placed on top and now comes first. If that were the case, then the order in which the fragments of any given *liasse* appear is the reverse of the order of composition. The real fascination of the text as Pascal left it, however, lies not in the impossible intellectual conundrum of reconstituting the order in which the fragments were composed, but in the frequency with which Pascal's imagination returns to certain recurring cardinal points, mostly concerning the religious difficulties occasioned by his theological views, and what must have been the progressively deepening analysis of human motivation and behaviour which supports them.

If, as has been repeatedly suggested, the text as left by Pascal does have a structure, no demonstration of what it was among the dozen or so which have been closely argued over the last fifty years has yet commanded anything approaching general consent. We know too little about the dates at which many of the various fragments were written to get beyond an educated guess at the way in which Pascal's mind moved. There are indications from the biography, but they are uncertain. It now seems clear that the project to write an apologetic was not abandoned for reasons of health, as is still often assumed, and even that, on Pascal's own premisses, the intended apologetic could have served no purpose, but we have no clear indication from his pen of why he gave up.

Pascal makes intense imaginative efforts and achieves disturbingly perceptive psychological penetration in his attempts to resolve his dilemmas. He may be thought in the end not to have succeeded, and even to have been aware that this was the case, but the interest of his text resides in the power which he brings to defining the dilemmas and in the extraordinary intellectual insights into the human condition he brings to their resolution. He was, after all, dealing with what was for him the ultimate question: how do we explain to which of the two alternative but eternally unalterable fates each rational human soul is destined after death? Pascal believed that without Christian belief and practice the individual's fate was certainly eternal damnation, but, if salvation was God's gratuitous gift to a minority of chosen human souls, how could any moral act, and in particular any freely chosen commitment of belief or behaviour, affect the individual's eternal destiny? The alternatives were only hell or heaven, the never-ending and never-altering experience of either ecstasy or torment.

It is essential not to regard Pascal's fragments as if they constituted a sequential text which can meaningfully be read from beginning to end. Any reader attempting to find a meaning in the fragments simply by reading through them will almost certainly be foiled by Pascal's arrangement of nearly half the fragments into the *liasses* based at best on only the loosest internal unity of subject-matter. Indeed, the reader approaching Pascal for the first time may well find it easier to identify the individual problems to which the fragments explore possible avenues of resolution by starting with the *Discussion with Monsieur de Sacy*

or the short *Art of Persuasion* before going on to the passages
from the *Writings on Grace*, which are included here primarily to
show the way in which Pascal himself envisaged the intractable
theological problems behind the abandoned efforts to write the
apologetic. Even if a reader takes the *Pensées* on their own, the
first two *liasses* are not the best place to begin. They are largely
concerned with the orders in which Pascal at different moments
considered disposing his material. To achieve an understanding
of Pascal's text it is likely to be much quicker to use the thematic
index, which is designed to help the reader identify the subjects
to which Pascal most frequently returned and to understand the
sense of urgency communicated by the *Pensées*. The absence of
any sequential text makes it inappropriate to talk of repetitious-
ness where there are only recurring centres of concern.

In the present translation of the *Pensées*, some fragments of
nearly all varieties have been included, as has the entire contents
of most of the titled *liasses*, together with the principal fragments from the unclassified series. Pascal never wrote a book,
and himself published nothing included in this volume. His own
publications, apart from the *Lettres provinciales*, were limited to
scientific and mathematical papers. As far as seemed reasonable,
necessary background information is given in the explanatory
notes, but for readers unfamiliar with the political and theological history of seventeenth-century France, and with its secular
and ecclesiastical power relationships, some introduction may
well be indispensable. An understanding of the *Pensées* certainly
requires some acquaintance with the context of their gestation in
the circumstances of Pascal's physical, intellectual, and spiritual
development. The next section of this introduction is, therefore,
devoted to those aspects of Pascal's personal history and background essential to an understanding of the texts, themselves
considered in the final section.

The biographical and spiritual background

Sickly, nervously intense, treated when still a child almost as if
he had been an adult, educated entirely at home, and precocious
enough to have mixed in his teens in his father's scientific circles, Pascal had fragile health which was already deteriorating

when, in 1646, the two brothers Deschamps came to look after Pascal's father in his Rouen house during convalescence from a broken thigh. They were members of a charitable group drawn mostly from the minor gentry whose leader had been a penitent of the influential abbé de Saint-Cyran (1581–1643), himself regarded by Richelieu as potentially subversive, had been imprisoned from 1638 until after Richelieu's death in December 1642, and had died in 1643. Starting from the Neoplatonist religious ideas of the early French Oratorians, especially their first general Bérulle (1575–1629), and his successor, Condren (1588–1641), Saint-Cyran had independently evolved his own rigorist spirituality. Condren had insisted on the 'nothingness' of human nature, and the need for it not to be healed but replaced by the life of grace, and Saint-Cyran had moved on to a guilt-obsessed spirituality which attracted to him some highly connected penitents. He was also in charge of two fashionable convents, one of which was the celebrated Port-Royal.

Saint-Cyran had earlier shared with Cornelius Jansen (1585–1638)—a professor of scripture consecrated in October 1636 bishop of Ypres—a vision of renewing the Church on the model of its state in the fifth century. Jansen's intentions were modified by his discovery in 1621 of the importance of the theology of Adam's state before original sin, and in 1628 he began work on his 1640 *Augustinus*, which interpreted Augustine's theology in a way which justified Saint-Cyran's spirituality. Richelieu found a pretext for imprisoning Saint-Cyran in his attack on Louis XIII's prayer to the Virgin for the protection of France, published on 10 February 1638, and Jansen died before the publication of his great work. Saint-Cyran, although almost blind in prison, prepared a digest of it, and Antoine Arnauld (1612–94), whose family was intimately connected with the Port-Royal monastery, became on Saint-Cyran's death the obvious and willing champion of both Saint-Cyran's spirituality and Jansen's theology.

The group to which Pascal was strongly drawn through the Deschamps brothers in 1646 was already associated with Saint-Cyran's spirituality, with Jansen's theology, which had not yet been condemned, and with Arnauld and Port-Royal, the repositories of Saint-Cyran's spiritual legacy. It has been shown that it was from Saint-Cyran's *Le Cœur nouveau* that Pascal derived his reliance on the heart as the organ of a spiritual knowledge which was also virtuous, so circumventing the firm scholastic distinction between acts of the will, directed towards the good, and acts of the intellect, directed towards the true. The two ways of knowing two sorts of truth in Pascal's *Art of Persuasion* must also derive from Saint-Cyran, perhaps through the 'Liber prooemalis' of the second volume of the *Augustinus*, based on a text which Saint-Cyran had sent Jansen in 1623.

Saint-Cyran was probably also to be the proximate source for the interpretation of the term *amour-propre* as absolutely opposed to the love of God, and incapable of coexisting with justifying grace in the soul. Augustine had used the Latin *amor sui* in this way, but only rhetorically, in *The City of God*, and Jansen had followed him, interpreting literally what Augustine had said metaphorically. A whole series of French authors, including Senault (1601–72), Nicole (1625–95), and La Rochefoucauld (1613–80), as well as Pascal, was to exploit the theologically pejorative overtones acquired by the word *amour-propre* in the mid-seventeenth century.

In 1647 Pascal returned with his sister Jacqueline to Paris. He had for a period been paralysed from the waist, was irritable and impatient, and could take only very warm liquid nourishment, administered drop by drop. His doctors tried to diminish the damaging nervous intensity, but he continued with his scientific experiments, and was called on by Descartes, whose conclusions he opposed but whose ideas he used, although he did not acknowledge their provenance. He began to frequent Port-Royal, rather aggressively taking the monastery's side in the bitter debate developing about Jansen's theology, as defended by Arnauld. The touch of arrogance in his partisanship was quickly noticed by the senior *solitaires*, the males who lived solitary lives of prayer and study, first in the enclave of the Paris convent, occasionally coaching children of friends of the monastery, and from 1638 expelled to Port-Royal-des-Champs, a dependency of the Paris house about ten kilometres south-west of Versailles. Their activities as teachers grew into the *écoles de Port-Royal*, but the 'schools' were what would today be known as classes, not separate educational establishments.

Pascal's father took Jacqueline and Pascal himself to Clermont-

Ferrand to escape the 1649 Fronde civil war in which the *parlement* opposed the court essentially over taxation, and returned to Paris in 1650, to die less than a year later on 24 September 1651. Jacqueline's desire to become a nun at Port-Royal had been opposed by her father, and was now opposed by Pascal himself, who had previously supported her, probably on account of the size of the dowry Jacqueline wanted. The elder sister, Gilberte, had come to Paris in December 1651 to help settle her father's estate, and arranged for Jacqueline to slip away to the convent before dawn on 4 January 1652. Pascal was himself later generous in the matter of the dowry and attended Jacqueline's profession as a nun on 5 June 1653, but seems for a period to have been short of money.

His religious enthusiasm may also have waned. Biographers have speculated that he may have been emotionally attached to the young Mlle de Roannez, daughter of the devout and intransigent duc de Roannez (1627–96), Pascal's intimate friend and governor of Poitou. Pascal spent some time in the company of the chevalier de Méré (1610–84), a self-styled arbiter of manners and occasional author, and of Damien Mitton (*c*.1618–90), financier, financial administrator, and gambler, both of whom may have stimulated Pascal's interest in probability theory, about which Pascal corresponded with the mathematician Pierre de Fermat (1601–65). Mitton, like Pascal, was an occasional guest of Roannez. Pascal spent the autumn of 1653 in Poitou with Roannez and Méré, and during the following year his intellectual life was at its most intense, although Jacqueline tells us that he was overcome by the shallowness of his pursuits. He moved his lodgings on 1 October, and on 23 November underwent the famous spiritual experience noted in the *Memorial* (p. 178), which for the rest of his life he kept on his person, sewn into his jacket. It was a not unusual way of treating treasured written documents.

The experience of 23 November no doubt released a spiritual tension which had been building up over months or years. By early December Pascal had put himself into the hands of the most distinguished spiritual director of Port-Royal's *solitaires*, Antoine Singlin (1607–64), and in January 1655, after confiding in Roannez, Pascal went to make a fortnight's retreat at

Port-Royal-des-Champs, where the community, including Jacqueline, had been since 15 January 1653. It must have been during his fortnight's stay, partly with the *solitaires* on the hill known as Les Granges overlooking the monastery, that the meetings with Sacy (1613–84) took place which are recorded in the *Discussion with Monsieur de Sacy*, drawn up much later by Sacy's secretary and first published in 1728 (pp. 182–92). Pascal visited the Paris house of the monastery before returning home. Jacqueline found Pascal a shade too pleased with himself for a true penitent. Later that year Roannez renounced for religious reasons the marriage his family had hoped he would make.

The bull *Cum occasione* condemning five Jansenist propositions had been signed in Rome on 31 May 1653, and it was followed by the further decree of 23 April 1654 implying that Jansen had in fact held them. Mazarin, the first minister of the still adolescent Louis XIV (1638–1715), had needed Rome's acquiescence in what he regarded as the politically necessary resignation of Retz from the See of Paris, and was not going to jeopardize Rome's moderate goodwill by opposing the necessary formal reception of the bull. He had letters patent accepting it signed on 4 July 1653, and a decree or *mandement* was drawn up, slipping in the words 'extracted from Jansen's book', which Rome had carefully avoided putting into the bull. Procedural delays and Mazarin's policies prevented the imposition of a revised *mandement* and attached 'formulary' or declaration from being imposed until the presiding council of the assembly of the clergy was called to the Louvre on 13 December 1660, apparently a simple formality. However, Louis XIV made an announcement, and Mazarin explained the decision in a discourse which lasted an hour and a quarter. The assembly agreed on 1 February 1661 to impose the formulary, and the Conseil d'État ratified the measure on 13 April.

Meanwhile, on 1 February 1655, one of Port-Royal's grander sympathizers, Roger du Plessis, marquis de Liancourt, duc de la Rocheguyon (1599–1674), was refused absolution at Saint-Sulpice on the instructions of the parish priest, Jean-Jacques Olier (1608–57). On 24 February Arnauld published his *Lettre d'un Docteur de Sorbonne à une personne de condition*. A pamphlet war ensued, during which Arnauld wrote his *Seconde lettre à un duc et pair*, dated 10 July, holding that the pope had had no right to declare that the condemned propositions were in the *Augustinus*, and that Saint Peter, when he denied Jesus, sinned because he was denied the grace not to. On 4 November the theology faculty appointed a commission to examine Arnauld's second letter. The report, presented on 1 and 2 December, led tortuously and in spite of protests and efforts at conciliation to the formal and successful attempt to strip Arnauld of his doctorate in votes on what was called the matter of fact, whether or not the five propositions were in the *Augustinus*, on 14 January, and on the proposition on grace, the 'question de droit', on 29 January. The condemnation, consistent with that of Jansen by Rome, had been all but openly enforced by the administration.

Pascal, enlisted into Arnauld's defence, wrote the eighteen *Lettres provinciales*, of which the first is dated 23 January 1656, and the second the 29th, although it was not printed until 1 February, after the second condemnation, and not circulated until the 5th. At first brilliantly ironic, the *Lettres* become incandescent with outrage at what Pascal takes to be Jesuit moral teaching, although in fact what he attacks are the handbooks for forming confessors in the interests of normalizing confessional practice, and he objects as much to the 'extravagance' of Jesuit baroque values and style as to the moral teaching which, he suggests, is the cause of their teaching on grace. Pascal's own unfinished *Writings on Grace* in the state in which they were left must, as Jean Mesnard convincingly argues in the third volume (1991) of his critical edition of the *Œuvres complètes*, date from the latter part of 1655, extending into the early weeks of 1656. They may have been drafted earlier. The probable date of *De l'esprit géométrique* (*The Mathematical Mind*), a title in which 'géométrique' refers not just to geometry but to mathematics as a whole, and which implies the distinction between the mathematical mind and the intuitive mind (see Fragments 669 and 670), is also the second half of 1655. The essay also includes *The Art of Persuasion*.

After the fifth letter, Marguerite Périer, daughter of Pascal's elder sister Gilberte and a boarder at Port-Royal, was cured on 24 March 1656 of an ulcer, or perhaps a tumour of the lachrymal duct, after the application to the sore of a borrowed relic of the crown of thorns by what was taken to be divine intervention. There is medical evidence from eight weeks before the cure, and from seven days after it. Port-Royal knew many such cures, but this one was declared by the diocesan authorities to be miraculous on 22 October. It is virtually certain that at least the form of a Christian apologetic based at first on miracles, and for which the *Pensées* contains the notes, was conceived in the wake of Marguerite's cure.

During the production of the *Lettres provinciales*, in whose composition Pascal was helped by a small team of collaborators, including Arnauld and Nicole, Pascal led the life almost of a fugitive. He spent some time at an inn, stayed with Roannez, who had come back from Poitou in May 1656, and from time to time stayed at Port-Royal-des-Champs. A fragment of a nineteenth letter exists, abandoned probably when it seemed clear in May 1657 that the 1653 decree imposing signature of the formulary would be registered, but a reply to the *Lettres provinciales* by the Jesuit Georges Pirot (1599–1659) which appeared in December 1657 was immediately attacked by a series of *Écrits des curés de Paris*. Pascal certainly had some hand in the first two, and he is said to have regarded the fifth as the best thing he had written.

It was probably late in 1657 that Pascal decided on a much wider basis for his apologetic than that provided by the probative power of miracles or the implementation of prophecies. The most interesting of the fragments as we have them are certainly those analysing the human situation in the world, the certainty of death, the psychology of human behaviour, and the significance which only the Christian revelation can bestow on the meaning of human life. All important such fragments are translated here. The classification of so many of the fragments—and no doubt the composition of further notes or other texts—seems likely to have been undertaken in loose connection with a conference said ten years later to have been given by Pascal at Port-Royal in 1658. If it was given, it was more probably in May than in October. We cannot be absolutely certain even that the conference took place at all. It is just possible that it was a literary fiction.

Jean Filleau de la Chaise (*c*.1630–93), Roannez's secretary, wrote the only account of the conference a decade later, in 1668, for what was intended to be a preface for the 1670 edition of the *Pensées*, saying that he had himself had an account 'from someone who was there', but the document was rejected by the editorial committee. According to Pascal's nephew, Étienne Périer, dependent on Filleau de la Chaise and closely following him, the conference lasted two or three hours, but was given without premeditation or preparation. Pascal could, of course, have written down notes of what he had said after giving the conference, but there is no guarantee that the letters 'A.P.R.' in the Fragments 155, 182, and 274 mean, as has often been assumed, 'A Port-Royal'. It seems, however, likely on any hypothesis that the bulk of the fragments was written, but not at first put into *liasses* or other files, in 1657 and probably the earlier part of 1658.

In 1658 Pascal, who had already invented a proof for the binomial theorem, worked on the properties of the cycloid and produced textbooks on grammar and geometry for the 'little schools'. Roannez offered a prize to any mathematician who could solve six problems connected with the mathematics of the cycloid which Pascal had already solved, but he did not know that Roberval (1602–75) had already also solved four of them, and the affair collapsed in bitterness and recriminations. Pascal's religious fervour was meanwhile undiminished. He wrote letters of encouragement to Roannez's younger sister, who defied her mother's opposition to become a nun at Port-Royal in 1657. She later left the monastery, but kept her vow of chastity until relieved of it in 1667 to marry. When in 1659 the socially climbing Périer family were envisaging an advantageous marriage for Jacqueline, their daughter still boarding at Port-Royal, the nuns were strongly opposed, and Pascal wrote denouncing marriage as 'the most dangerous and the lowest of Christian conditions'.

The Paris *parlement* was resisting Rome and Mazarin in the matter of the formulary, a balanced state of affairs which suited almost everyone. Mazarin was himself neither forfeiting Rome's goodwill nor incurring any danger from the *parlement*; Rome was maintaining its authority but was not going to risk pushing France into schism; the *parlement* was brandishing its rights in a power struggle against both Rome and the king which it was bound to lose; and not much political damage was being done in

France by allowing the clergy to believe what it pleased about the operation of grace in the soul, and about what Augustine believed about it.

From February 1659 until June 1660 Pascal was again ill. Gilberte Périer, sometimes verifiably wrong, tries to present her brother in an edifying light, and insistently finds excuses in his health for the abandonment of the apologetic. But her view has been vigorously and convincingly challenged. It seems likely that Pascal himself realized that his project was self-defeating. An apologetic, while it might convince and even lead to persuasion, which implied in addition to intellectual conviction the observance of spiritual norms and the adoption of devout practices, could in Pascal's theology contribute nothing to the salvation of anyone's soul.

Pascal was certainly not prevented by his health from continued intellectual effort. By May 1660 he was taking the waters at Clermont, and a report on his health in a letter to Huyghens (1629–95) of 28 July says how much better he was. On 10 August Pascal wrote to Fermat from Clermont that he needed a stick for walking and still could not ride, but was engaged on work unconnected with mathematics. He was uncertain about travelling by water to stay in Poitou until Christmas. By October he was back in Paris, and in November wrote and orally delivered the three *Discours sur la condition des grands* for Luynes's son, the young duc de Chevreuse (1646–1712). In the following month he wrote to the socially distinguished, influential, intellectually ambitious, notoriously hypochondriac, and now devout Mme de Sablé (1599–1678) about a book she had sent him written by her Calvinist doctor, Antoine Menjot (1615–94), and in December he visited Huyghens with Roannez to discuss physics.

Then in 1661 the signature of the formulary was imposed. Pascal persuaded his sister Jacqueline to sign with the rest of the nuns on 22 June, and it was partly overcome with remorse that she died on 4 October. On 31 October a new formulary was imposed, apparently now not allowing the saving distinction between *fait* and *droit*. Pascal, the lawyer Domat (1625–96), and Roannez refused to sign, although Arnauld and Nicole tried to persuade Pascal to sign, as they themselves did. Pascal wrote an

Écrit sur la signature of which we have only an abbreviated version, and withdrew from further controversy.

His doctrinal position had hardened, but the apologetic remained unwritten, and it is perfectly possible that in late 1661 Pascal was uncertain about how far he was prepared to allow his theological commitment to go in the face of the religious realities he had to envisage, including the unceasing pain of the damned on account of no personal choice of their own. Pascal was certainly a Jansenist only in the loose sense in which that word is applied to the spirituality of Saint-Cyran, but he was not publicly committed to the theology of Jansen, Arnauld, or even of his own unpublished *Writings on Grace*, and he was certainly not guilty of heresy, an ecclesiastical *crimen* which requires the public dissemination or defence of heterodox doctrine.

On 18 March 1662 Pascal and Roannez inaugurated the first regular omnibus service in Paris, with a first line running from the Porte Saint-Antoine to the Luxembourg. Others were soon added. Pascal took to visiting the poor, and left half his income from the omnibus service to them. The Périers had been living in Paris again since 1661, and, when Pascal fell ill again in the spring of 1662, Gilberte called regularly to look after him. He had begun to live very simply, without horses or much furniture. However, the daughter of the couple who looked after him caught smallpox, and Gilberte, frightened of carrying the infection to her own children, had Pascal brought to her own house on 29 June. He was to die there seven weeks later.

Pascal's texts

In his preface to the *Pensées* published in 1670, Étienne Périer, Gilberte's son, speaks of Pascal's intention to write simply a 'work' on religion. However, his account of the Port-Royal conference, derived from Filleau de la Chaise, makes clear his view that Pascal intended to write an apologetic. He talks of 'proofs', 'persuasion', 'marks of certainty and evidence', suggesting that Pascal's Port-Royal conference indicated an intention to start the work with a depiction of the human condition, to be followed by a quest for the truth that would explain it. After considering the answers of the philosophers and of other religions, Pascal would have come to the Old Testament, which presented irresistible truth, but which also merely prefigured the coming of Jesus Christ. He would then have proved the truth of the Chrisitian revelation in the gospels, to which apostles, martyrs, and saints subsequently bore witness.

Périer goes on to say that Pascal was insufficiently able to concentrate during the last four years of his life to write his projected work on religion, but that during those last four years he composed the 'fragments' to be found in the *Pensées*. We know that the fragments must have been begun sometime after the experience recorded in the *Memorial*, and it is extremely unlikely that they were for the most part written other than between the miracle of March 1656 and the period of severe incapacity beginning in February 1659. Isolated non-classified fragments must have been written later, 622 after the restoration of Charles II on 29 May 1660, and 650 on the paper used by Pascal in Auvergne in 1660. It is reasonable to assume from what we know from elsewhere that the preface exaggerates the disabilities suffered by Pascal between the summer of 1660 and the spring of 1662.

It looks likely that, by the time the fragments began to be written down, Pascal had already brought the *Writings on Grace* to the state in which we have them, that the discussions on which the *Discussion with Monsieur de Sacy* is based had already taken place, and that the *Art of Persuasion* had also been written. The presumption is that the project to write a work of religious apologetic was conceived after Pascal had already adopted, or was at least seriously considering, a theory of grace according to which religious belief was of no avail in the furtherance of salvation, dependent not only on belief, but also on the gift of the virtue of faith inspired by grace and bestowed arbitrarily by God. The idea for an apologetic may therefore even have postdated the elaboration of a theory of grace which would render its composition nugatory, although not that of some other work on religion, perhaps dealing with the congruence of the Christian revelation with the human condition.

If that were to have been the case, the fragments, which carefully indicate the need of persuading rather than convincing, of breaking the power of instinct, passion, and sensual desire in order to believe, must be interpreted largely as an attempt by Pascal to come to terms with the relationship between credal belief, religious submission, and the order of grace depending entirely on a gratuitous and arbitrary divine initiative. The theory of grace outlined in the *Writings on Grace*, if accepted, totally subverts the usefulness of the apologetic which Périer thought Pascal intended to write, and offers at least a possible reason for its eventual abandonment, at least in its apologetic form, when Pascal found that the theory of grace to which he appears to have become increasingly committed up to the refusal to sign the second formulary in 1661 was incompatible with the apologetic he had seen the need to write in 1656.

The other texts in this volume deal with particular issues raised by the project of which the *Pensées* constitute the residual realization. Since, however, the earliest text of all is almost certainly the dated *Memorial* (742), the intensity of the experience it records should no doubt be noted as a preliminary. The intensity is extraordinary without being abnormal, and it is better to avoid the word 'mystical'. In the strict sense, the document testifies to an experience generally known in mystical theology as 'consolation without [identifiable] cause', and, together with its explicit repudiation of the God of the philosophers in favour of the God of the Jews, it is really only the language which gives the experience noted in the *Memorial* its specifically religious significance. The result of the experience is not a conviction, but a submission.

The intensity is conveyed by the lack of syntax, the simple juxtaposition of words and phrases, the biblical and liturgical allusions, and quotations in both Latin and French. In his desire to give the moment as great a formal significance as possible by naming the date, the day of the week, the saint's day, and the list of martyrs in the Roman (and not the Paris) breviary, Pascal betrays his unfamiliarity with monastic liturgical practice. The martyrology read at prime lists the martyrs for the following day, so that on the feast of Saint Clement the names in the martyrology would have been those for the 24 November, not the 23rd. Pascal was not at this date used to the intricacies of liturgical rubrics.

The status of the first *liasse* preceded by the table of twenty-eight titles has been disputed. The most authoritative editor of the *Pensées* to date, Philippe Sellier, and Jean Mesnard, editor of the *Œuvres complètes*, both believe that the table is the first fragment of the first *liasse*, which, in their view, is a condensed table of contents for the apologetic volume as projected in 1658. That view must command serious consideration, although it is far from commanding general acceptance. The most authoritative manuscript, the 'seconde copie' or 'C2' (see the Note on the Text), puts a dash under the table, making it into a *liasse* of its own, and it may not indicate more than the headings under which Pascal was filing his fragments for reasons at which we can only guess, rather than the prospective set of chapter titles it has been taken for. The *liasse* 'Commencement' reads as if it might in 1658 have been intended to furnish the contents of the first chapter.

When he was close to death, Pascal is said to have regretted only that he had not written his work about religion. We do not know whether any book he was still contemplating would have been an apologetic, and, because Pascal never undertook the final processes of selection, rejection, and further classification which would have had to precede the final composition of any book on religion, apologetic or not, we cannot be certain at any date exactly what projects Pascal mentally abandoned or modified, or at any particular date what book he might have ended up by writing, or what use he would have made of the fragments. The order of the first *liasse* is not imposed by strict logic, but simply collects many of the major themes which appear in the classified fragments, and from those fragments not classified but on scraps of paper probably cut from the original sheets at the same time as those which were. The process of literary composition makes it impossible to say even that at any given moment Pascal would have followed any order thought to be discoverable in the first *liasse*.

The status of the *liasse* 'Ordre' presents less difficulty. Its first fragment announces a major theme, the wretchedness of the human condition without Christianity. All human beings everywhere show their need for the coming of the Messiah and all that it entails. This fragment has been the object of clearly unsustainable interpretations, even by those who have picked up the obvious liturgical reference, the 'always and everywhere' of the thanks which are 'fittingly and rightly' given to God at the beginning of the most solemn part of the Roman mass. Pascal's point, which in the Latin liturgy comes later, is that those who offer thanks are also needy. The next fragment includes considerations involving both dialogue and letter form, which had been merged together as dialogues in letter form in the *Lettres provinciales*.

The following fragment, 39, suggests what appears to be an alternative order and raises the principal issue of the whole text. Even if an unbeliever were convinced by proofs, it would do no good. Pascal urgently, but with more intensity than logic, suggests here, as in Fragment 45, that the submission brought about by true conversion, the throwing-off of the power of the reflex reactions of 'the machine' implied by persuasion, might resolve the problem, although, according to his own theory of grace, it could not. If by our own efforts we could break the power of the machine, or modify the machine's operation, we would be able to affect the order of grace, and nature would have the power to achieve something in the supernatural order. Pascal is similarly concerned with the problem in Fragment 41, and, of course, in Fragment 680, touching in his own coded terms on the problem of God's arbitrary choice of whom to save in Fragment 43. Fragment 44 then opens up the theme of *divertissement*, a word for which the modern English equivalents, 'diversion' and 'distraction', have both become debased in everyday usage. Much in the *Pensées* deplores the individual's use of diversion to distract from awareness of the horrors of the human predicament.

The difficulty is that, however ridiculous it might be to affect or achieve distraction in the face of imminent condemnation, there is, in Pascal's own terms, absolutely nothing the individual can do about his eternal condemnation, now or ever. The final fragment of the *liasse*, 46, suggests a plausible order only for an apologetic in which human belief, submission, desire, or behaviour could achieve something in the order of grace, or in some way affect God's predestinatory decree, which, for Pascal by this date, it cannot. It is at this point that the reader of the *Pensées* not conversant with what Pascal takes to be Augustine's views on the operation of grace needs to become acquainted with them to see the enormity of the task Pascal is envisaging, and the catastrophe of the impossibility of its successful completion. It is also important to learn from the *Art of Persuasion* the distinction already pervading Pascal's mind between conviction and proof on the one hand, and, on the other, persuasion and submission.

Against the background of the theory of grace, the view expressed in Fragment 41 that 'proof is often the instrument' of faith is hard to distinguish from wishful thinking. There can, in Pascal's interpretation of Augustine, be no instrument in reason or proof in what concerns the bestowal of the grace required even for faith, and still less for justification. Most modern theologians see some tension between the rhetorical stylistic register so often used by Augustine, invariably concerned with such large issues as the salvation of the human race, and the quite literal meaning given to his terms when Pascal, in common with most post-medieval theologians, applies them literally to the psychology of the interaction of grace and the individual human will.

The difficulty is that submission, even taken to the lengths of reducing the reflexes of the machine to the purely animal level devoid of pride mentioned in Fragment 680—the famous 'cela vous abêtira'—still achieves nothing at all in the order of grace. The break between Pascal's sympathetic understanding of the plight of the human race and his theory of grace is unhappily absolute, and towards the end of his life he seems to have hardened in his theological conviction that human natural capacity was incapable of contributing anything at all in the supernatural order. His theology of grace differs from Calvin's principally by anchoring unavoidable guilt firmly in Adam's original, and for his progeny disastrous, free choice.

Pascal's tendency to put the pastoral rhetoric of Augustine's writings on the level of considered theological argument suggests that his strictly theological expertise was less than has often been suggested. He had, of course, never studied formal theology, and actually knew little of the dilemmas which circumscribed scholastic modes of thinking. It has also been shown clearly enough that Pascal's notion of necessarily irresistible efficacious grace cannot properly be derived from Augustine's 'adiutorium quo (grace by which)', as distinct from the 'adiutorium sine quo non (grace without which not)', in Augustine's *De correptione et gratia*, probably of AD 426. What Pascal was fighting for was more a spirituality than a theology.

Jansen had died submitting the *Augustinus* to the teaching authority of the Church in advance, and advocating only conformity to that authority. Nicole's theory of general grace avoided Pascal's impasse, and after Pascal's death only Arnauld was left to defend the position into which he had defiantly dug himself in the second letter of 1655. The modern solution to the problem allows that nature itself was redeemed, so that Adam fell into a state of fallen but also retroactively redeemed nature, and our natural powers can stretch out towards supernatural fulfilment without the heretical implications entailed by the view that pure nature can achieve or aspire to any fulfilment in the supernatural order, like justification and salvation. By virtue of the redemption, human beings can even act meritoriously. Human salvation on this view still does not depend on purely natural effort, but on individual choices made on the basis of the natural aspirations determined not only by the fall, but also by the redemption.

That solution, if at all possible, was still at least difficult to reach in the seventeenth century, because it meant allowing grace to 'pagans', who must also have had redeemed natures and what theologians had to regard as supernatural aspirations, which God could not have left incapable of fulfilment. It is still disputed by some theologians at the end of the twentieth century exactly what is the content of the belief absolutely required for salvation, and therefore exactly what constitutes 'paganism' in the sense of unbelief. No one any longer doubts that there are virtuous unbelievers. Even before the seventeenth century, the belief essential for salvation, often thought to be belief in a creator and in a remunerator after death, was sometimes regarded even in reactionary Paris as implied in views held by those who had never been evangelized.

It is, however, even at the date of Pascal's death, difficult to envisage the recognition as orthodox of any formal theology which allowed that nature itself was endowed by the redemption with an aspiration to supernatural fulfilment. François de Sales

(1567–1622) certainly implied it, and his doctrine was specifically endorsed when he was canonized in 1665, but he was much better known for his pastoral work, his spiritual direction and writings, and his role in the foundation of the Visitation Order, than for his frank theological espousal of the Molinist doctrine that Pascal considered heretical because it effectively allowed to individual human beings the autonomous power of self-determination.

Fragments like 196 and 222, concerned with the order of presentation of the argument of the projected book, are scattered throughout the *liasses* and the other fragments, so increasing the sense that the interest of the text can more easily be perceived by tracing its individual threads than by regarding it, as any printed edition must invite the reader to regard it, as a woven tapestry. Sometimes the encoding is easily penetrated. Like the allusion to flies in Fragment 56, all references to Cleopatra recall the dependent contingency of human existence and of what appears momentous on what is apparently insignificant. Many of the fragments, on the other hand—here generally omitted after the first score of *liasses*—demonstrate the heterogeneity of forms and styles used by Pascal, or are incomprehensible, while many others depend on conventions with which today's readers are not necessarily familiar. The ubiquitous and anomalous *Jésus-Christ*, for instance, was the only form of the name available to a Catholic writer. The form is so similar to that used today, joining a forename to a family name, that we tend to overlook that 'Jesus "the Christ [the anointed one]"' makes a theological statement, and is not simply a name. The simple name *Jésus*, which Pascal would no doubt have preferred, had been appropriated by the Protestants, and *le Christ*, in French requiring the article, obscures the reality of Jesus' humanity, on which the redemption depends as much as on his divinity.

The notes point out where Pascal still assumes a propitiatory theory of the redemption in which Jesus placates or pays a price to the Father, atoning by suffering for the sin of Adam, a view still common in the tradition of 'Augustinian' theology in seventeenth-century France, but differing to the point of incompatibility with the theory of Augustine himself, who almost invariably uses the ransom metaphor, especially in the greatest of all his formal theological works, the *De Trinitate*. The devil is tricked by Jesus into asserting over him the rights he possesses only over every other member of the human race, and emerges 'non ditatus sed ligatus (not enriched but enslaved)'. Jesus' sacrifice for Augustine was essentially rooted in the union of the divine and human wills in the single person of the Logos. It is for the power of his moral and spiritual insights rather than for his formal theology that Pascal invites our admiration.

The *liasse* 'Vanity' contains some remarkable examples of what after all is a commonplace theme of moralizers, and well illustrates some of the difficulties of the text. A good index to Montaigne's *The Essays* reveals the subject of the allusions of Fragments 49 and 52, but Pascal's editors have so far failed to discover what is behind Fragment 53. Montaigne (1533–92) published *Les Essais* in 1580 with a much augmented edition in 1588, to which he again added much in the margins of a working copy published posthumously with the additions in 1595. The title does not mean essays as we understand the word, but something more like 'soundings', and it contains chapters which are almost an invitation to a dialogue with his reader, not essays expounding some topic or moralizing on a theme. Written wholly during the religious wars, *The Essays*, as they are invariably translated, remain committedly Catholic but conservative and defensive, with a relativist core which has been mistaken for scepticism.

By far the longest chapter in Montaigne, that devoted to a merely ostensible defence of Raymond Sebond's *Theologia naturalis*, plays heavily on human incapacity, although Montaigne is almost stoic in his reverence for rational norms of behaviour. Pascal draws heavily on him throughout the *Pensées*, particularly for examples of human fallibility and inadequacy. The *Discussion with Monsieur de Sacy* does not do justice to Montaigne's spirituality, but it does show Pascal's reasons for admiring him. Like Montaigne, Pascal could not easily reconcile the human failure to live according to rational norms with the certainty that human dignity lay primarily in human intelligence. Pascal, like Montaigne, believed that the intellect was the faculty which distinguished humanity from the animals, but, more than Montaigne, Pascal was also concerned to humble rational pride in the interests of inducing submission to God, and Pascal needed

to be even more aware than Montaigne of the reasons for preserving the legitimacy of a belief prompted by grace rather than
by reasoning.

It is in reaction to Montaigne's neo-stoicism, and to the exu-
berant optimism of French baroque during the period following
the end of the religious wars, the period of Descartes, the elder
Corneille, d'Urfé, and François de Sales, that Pascal's preoccupation with human wretchedness has to be understood. He undoubtedly responded to a strong undercurrent of unease
emanating from Bérulle's Oratory and flowing through the spirituality of Saint-Cyran. The theology of Jansen came to buttress
that spirituality, and Arnauld had little difficulty in combining
the two, but few of the Port-Royal supporters really understood
the intricacies of Jansen's theology, and the disputes about the
operation of grace in the soul ceased to be a central religious
concern certainly about the time of Pascal's death, if not earlier.
There was a massive if forbidden exile of Huguenots from France
on the occasion of the revocation of the Edict of Nantes which
had 'tolerated' Protestantism until 1685, but by that date there
were few upholders of strict Calvinist predestinationist theology
even in Geneva.

Pascal's greatness lies elsewhere, in his penetrating analysis of
human incapacity, contingency, fragility, and wretchedness, and
in his despairing efforts to retrieve belief in human dignity, to
re-establish spiritual contact with the hidden God of Fragments
260 and 275, and to explain the contradictions of human existence, the polarities of light and darkness, knowledge and ignorance, greatness and wretchedness, doubt and certainty, anxiety
and boredom, and fear and confidence. His thought patterns
almost automatically resolved paradoxes into dilemmas and
polarized contrasts into contradictions. Wherever possible, as on
grace, Pascal would seek to present his chosen preference as the
middle way between extremes. On the whole he failed: Augustine's theory of grace as Pascal understood it left the individual
human being just as helpless as did Calvin's. But it is the urgency with which he saw the problem, the terror with which the
very speciousness of some of his arguments communicated the
realities of our predicament, and the insistence with which
he tried to find ways of averting the consequences of what he

believed to be the metaphysical and religious situation of everyone that give power to his thought and edge to the magnificently
balanced cadences of his prose style.

There are moments of intellectual weakness, when Pascal
substitutes simple word-play for argument, as in Fragment 146.
There are simple passing thoughts, like Fragments 71–7, possibly jotted down for later development in a way Pascal has not
indicated. His own memory was prodigious, and some of the
fragments had a significance for him which he has not communicated to any hypothetical reader, whom he did not anyway
envisage. Sometimes he was struck by something he had read,
not only in Montaigne but, perhaps more than has been thought,
in Nicole's then still unpublished texts. There is some striving
for aphoristic effect, and there is an almost astonishing spectrum
of variation between the cryptic single-word *aide-mémoire* to
himself and such elegantly thought-out and beautifully penned
elaborations of thoughts not in themselves very original as we
find in Fragment 230.

Of the more extended passages taken from outside the *Pensées*,
the first, the *Discussion with Monsieur de Sacy*, is not by Pascal at
all, although it must have been based on detailed notes supplied
by him, and was published over his name. When Pascal made
his retreat at Port-Royal-des-Champs from 7 to 28 January 1655,
his director was Isaac Le Maître de Sacy (1613–84), Arnauld's
nephew and a Port-Royal *solitaire*, later to become the effective
superior of Port-Royal. Sacy asked Pascal about his reading of
philosophers, and later invited him to write an account of what
he had said, probably in the pedagogical context of material
which might somehow be used for the 'petites écoles'.

Epictetus (*c*.55–135 AD) was translated a number of times
during the revival of interest in stoicism in late sixteenth-
century France, and his celebrated *Manual* had been adapted
to Christian usage in a number of works by Guillaume du Vair
(1556–1621), himself a certain source for Descartes. Pascal
acknowledges Epictetus' rightness about human duty towards
God, but reproaches him for his reliance on natural endeavour,
his pride. Montaigne, on the other hand, fully understands
human weakness, but Pascal reproaches him with under-
estimating human reason on its own, without Christian faith,

thereby naturally showing how high a price Pascal himself put on reason as the distinguishing feature of human beings, as behind the word-play of 146.

The comparison between Epictetus and Montaigne culminates in Sections 33 and 34 with the contrast of Fragment 240 between 'laziness' (*lâcheté/paresse*), meaning unconcern for salvation, and 'pride/vanity' (*orgueil/vanité*), meaning observance of the outward forms of virtue without the grace required to give them religious validity. Both in the *Discussion* and in the fragment Pascal, like both Augustine and Jansen before him, is playing on the ambiguity between the theological states of grace and its absence, on the one hand, and the psychological plane of motivation, on the other. Psychological indolence may be reprehensible, but it does not condemn to hell, as does *paresse* when it refers to a theological state. Section 34 of the *Discussion* is very nearly a complete sketch for an apologetic based on the Christian revelation as an explanation of simultaneous human greatness and wretchedness.

The *Art of Persuasion* has to do with the nature of intellectual demonstration, and is clearly important in the context of an attempt to write a Christian apologetic based on an analysis of human experience with which only the Christian revelation as Pascal understands it is thought to be congruent. Pascal is starting from a spirituality which heavily emphasizes human wretchedness and the arbitrary divine decision to bestow the graces of justification and perseverance on only a few. The rest of humanity will suffer infinitely, because unendingly, on account of guilt inherited from Adam's sin. Pascal's analysis of human nature must support that spirituality, while making it correlative both to the Christian God of love and to recognizable human experience.

Pascal's reflection on persuasion has to consider not only the content of what people have to be persuaded of, but also the psychological mode by which persuasion occurs. The exclusion of divine truth from the workings of human persuasion is traditional, and made necessary by the fact that, for credal belief to be effective in the order of salvation, intellectual conviction must be accompanied by, and indeed be dependent on, the action of grace in the soul, which must be capable of taking place even in those not able to follow the arguments. So Pascal transposes the traditional division of the sciences in sixteenth-century authors from those based on memory and those based on experiment or reasoning into a division between those involving submission and the others. If 'only God can put religious truths into the soul', it may be difficult to see how human persuasion, even leading to submission, can help in the supernatural order, but at least Pascal can set out to humiliate 'that proud power of reasoning' which can be an obstacle to belief.

Pascal surreptitiously oscillates between references to the will, which seeks only that which delights, and to the heart, to which scripture, unlike the scholastic theologians, gives the power of religious cognition. Like Descartes, Pascal was unable to overcome the scholastic anthropology whose psychology of the faculties of the soul was unable to account for acts which were at the same time cognitive and volitive. After its exceedingly important opening, the short treatise is largely devoted to the psychology of persuasion, and its dependence on the delight of the will as well as on the strength of the proof. On the basis of the psychology, Pascal elaborates a whole new rhetoric of argument, codifying and innovating in a way which makes clear the progress of educational reform in the seventeenth century. Like Descartes, he is preoccupied with 'method', the word which was beginning to replace the fashionable 'art of . . .' and which Pascal uses, although it may well have been Arnauld who gave the title *The Art of Persuasion* to the last section of *The Mathematical Mind*.

The three sections of the *Writings on Grace*, here translated from the text reconstituted by Jean Mesnard for his edition of the *Œuvres complètes*, are included to provide a guide to Pascal's theological thinking in his own words, either composed or at least revised late in 1655 and in 1656. Much about the autonomy and purpose of these texts remains obscure, but Pascal appears to have adopted the form of a fictional letter, probably intended for the duc de Roannez and written before the end of 1655, and then to have continued in the early months of 1656, probably after the early *Lettres provinciales* dealing with the intricate questions of the theology of grace.

The difficulty was the aristocratic heresy of Pelagius, which started as an exaggerated anti-Arianism supported by an elevated view of the human nature assumed by Christ and essentially denying the inherited guilt of original sin. In the ancient church, 'Pelagianism' was a more or less intense and explicit agglomeration of loosely associated attitudes, for serious theological reasons attributing higher powers to human nature than Augustine was prepared to concede. The term 'semi-Pelagian', first attested in the last decade of the sixteenth century and first used in documents of the magisterium in the seventeenth, signified as heretical any doctrine which attributed to human nature any power at all in the supernatural order. Justification, perseverance, and salvation could not be merited, and without supernatural aid human beings could not, in virtue of their natural powers, even accept proferred grace.

Part of the argument turned on whether 'pure' human nature had ever existed, perhaps in Adam before his sin, or whether it was even conceivable. Many sixteenth-century scholastics spoke as if the supernatural finality of human nature, which clearly implied an aspiration and an exigence, was added to pure nature like a tier to a wedding cake. That, as Jansen saw, is a theological and philosophical impossibility, but it was simple and clear, and it avoided the view which had long since been condemned, that God could not have created rational creatures without endowing them with an aspiration to supernatural fulfilment.

If Adam had been created with pure nature and lost at the fall only an added supernatural destiny, humanity could not have aspired to or been fulfilled by any supernatural gratification such as that entailed by salvation. Jansen argued that pure human nature was an unrealized and impossible hypothesis, that even before the fall Adam needed the extra gifts of 'elevated' nature to aspire to supernatural beatitude, and that after his sin fallen human nature was certainly incapable of any religiously valid virtuous act without special divine aid. Arnauld in 1655 merely said that Peter could not avoid the sin of denying Christ, because he was not given the necessary grace.

The decree of the sixth session of the Council of Trent was promulgated on 13 January 1547. Pascal refers in the tenth paragraph of the 'Letter' to the decree's eleventh and thirteenth chapters. The eleventh chapter deals with the necessity and

possibility of observing the commandments. The eighteenth
canon, which is attached to it, condemns the proposition that
the commandments are impossible even to the justified, and the
twenty-fifth that even in good works the just person sins at least
venially. The sixteenth and twenty-second canons, loosely attached to the thirteenth chapter, lay down that not even the just
can be certain of the gift of persevering.

It is difficult not to think that Pascal is distorting the plain
meaning of the Latin and forcing the meaning of the canons.
Since virtue is normally regarded as a *habitus*, the decree does
not support Pascal's conclusion that perseverance is the result
only of a continually renewed special grace. The council intended to define both that grace was needed to keep the commandments, and that the just did have the power not to sin,
but it did not reconcile the two definitions, leaving that to the
theologians, who were bitterly to dispute it. There was a serious sixteenth-century quarrel between the Dominicans and the
Jesuits, and the matter was convoked to Rome, where, after an
inconclusive series of congregations at the turn of the century,
silence was enjoined on both sides. There had also been internal
disputes among the Jesuits, who tried to use the decree imposing silence to prevent the publication in 1640 of the *Augustinus*,
which defended a view of grace incompatible with any autonomous human power of self-determination.

In the treatise Pascal polarizes the positions of his opponents
so as to present his own view as a middle path. The view he puts
forward as that of the followers of Saint Augustine was not held
by Augustine himself, and it would have been heretical to maintain publicly that Christ had not redeemed the whole of the
human race. To hold that Christ redeemed only some members
of the race also implies that the redemption was propitiatory. If
it had been based simply on the assumption of human nature
and the ensuing union of human and divine wills in Christ—the
alternative to the propitiatory hypothesis—it would necessarily
have extended to the whole human race. Pascal, by making
concupiscence the punishment of sin, also gives a veneer of
reasonableness to the guilt of all Adam's descendants, in whose
generation concupiscence, at least associated with sin if not actually always entailing it, necessarily plays a part. The theology

outlined by Pascal still leaves Christians unable in any way to affect or contribute towards their salvation, religiously abandoned to exactly the same fate as in the theology of Calvin, as Pascal understood it.

We can only speculate if and when Pascal realized that his theology of grace was incompatible with the presumable purpose of an apologetic—to lead doubters towards their salvation. It is reasonable to assume that Pascal, starting from an attempt to convince, came quickly to realize that he needed a tool weightier than logic if he was to persuade rather than merely to prove. It is even possible that Pascal modified his views on grace. All we know is that he neither finished the *Writings on Grace* nor published any part of them. The views he regarded as those of the followers of Saint Augustine were clearly heterodox; and Pascal was never in his public utterances or actions a heretic. At least until he deviated from Arnauld's line by refusing to sign the second formulary, he could easily have published anything he chose.

Pascal withdrew from controversy when the second formulary was imposed, but others, too, refused to sign, and the French ecclesiastical authorities certainly exceeded their legitimate powers, as Pascal realized, by insisting on the signature of a statement that the condemned propositions were actually in the *Augustinus*. Only the first of them verbally was. The chief interest of the *Writings on Grace* in the present context lies, however, not so much in unravelling in detail how Pascal's doctrinal commitment to the Church's teaching authority may have differed from his attitude to the jurisdictional authority of the French episcopacy and secular courts in imposing the second formulary, as for their incompatibility with the presumptive purpose of writing an apologetic in the first place.

It is arguable that the literary interest of the *Lettres provinciales* equals or exceeds that of the *Pensées*, for which, however, Pascal seems destined chiefly to be remembered. They can only have emerged from the tortured confrontation with the possibility that some human beings were destined irrevocably from birth for eternal damnation, and from the anguished need to try to persuade them to submit themselves to orthodox belief and religious submission, however useless in the supernatural order

Pascal was forced to think that endeavour. After the splendid Fragment 230 devoted to the double infinity between which humanity is sandwiched, surely one of the most awe-inducing pieces of prose to have emerged from seventeenth-century France, the two most striking fragments are probably 142, with its discovery of the heart as a means of bypassing the need to choose between knowledge and volition, and 680, with its final, because upside-down at the top of the page, desperate need to place faith in the heart, so that it remains a moral virtue without excluding a basis in rationality. Once the reflexes of the machine are tamed, God can endow the human heart with religiously valid faith, but, in the final paragraphs written on the sheet, Pascal despairingly tries to retain the connection between faith and what remained for him, however strongly he resented the pride it also bred, the highest power that dignified human nature above the animals: human reason.

It is the penetrating analysis of the signs of human wretchedness which makes the *Pensées* the masterpiece it is. Pascal does not denounce great crime or seek out depths of cruelty. He merely points to human puniness, the spiritual weakness which forces us to seek distraction at all costs rather than confront our fate, the inadequacy of the human intellect as the instrument on which we must rely to find our bearings in the world. Some of the comments on patterns of human behaviour are strikingly acute; others work by ironically pointing to the absurdity of human dignity and the triviality of our ordinary concerns; yet others by the contrast between how we think of ourselves and the cosmic unconcern for our existence. Only Christianity, Pascal wants to argue, can give sense or dignity to the tawdriness of human life, and to the idiocies which govern human social behaviour. He is torn on the subject of rationality, the source at once of human dignity and of the pride which blinds us.

Pascal must keep in mind the validity of the faith of those too ill-educated to follow the arguments, yet accept that credal belief is the legitimate subject of argument. Other themes suggest his concern that the attractions of sensual gratification, pride, or dignity may preclude conviction. He is at his most psychologically perceptive when suggesting the need for humility, for breaking the power of custom, esteem, and self-interest, everything he sums up as 'the machine' in order to free the mind to accept what is true, even if the truth is uncomfortable. There is what appears to be a further focus. Can the gratuity of the supernatural order be preserved simply by recourse to the need for perseverance, a special grace, of which no one can be certain, but the need for which leaves hope for all as well as providing a spur for behaving in accordance with forms of Christian virtue?

Pascal's analysis of the ecological fragility of the human race is elegantly expounded in prose constructed as if it were music, with ever bigger antitheses sometimes chiasmically encompassing smaller and smaller ones in balanced phrases with cadenced endings. The fragments are no doubt seldom as polished and brilliant as some parts of the *Lettres provinciales*. Only very few of them were sufficiently developed to have been incorporated as they stand into any published work. Pascal is at his sustained literary best in the *Lettres provinciales*, where he also draws on a whole range of styles, from the brilliantly ironic to the indignantly outraged. What the *Pensées* show with overwhelming vigour is the power to penetrate to the realities of human existence, whether humanity is considered as a race, as a series of societies, or as individuals.

As a Christian Pascal has to combine belief in a loving and lovable God with a revelation which he acknowledged to contain the truth that the majority of the human race is created by that God as a *massa damnata*—that is, in circumstances which admit only of eternal damnation. He cast around with immense ingenuity for signs in individual behaviour of personal guilt, toyed at least with the justice of the transmission of Adam's guilt to each human soul, tried to erect a truly Christian spirituality, which he thought Augustinian, on a starkly arbitrary divine selection, and investigated whether conviction, or persuasion, or devout behaviour might assist the waverer, while reserving to God the only essential gift, which was perseverence.

The modern reader easily misses the religious clamp of the constraints on Pascal's vision, and therefore also the huge imaginative power which underlies the *Pensées*. The very inconsistencies of approach which the fragments contain testify to the urgency of Pascal's quest for satisfactory resolutions, but also to the difficulty, or even the impossibility, of achieving them within the parameters which Pascal considered unalterable. Those parameters were constituted by divine revelation as he understood it, and human experience as his society underwent it. His essential need was to reconcile the two. The Pascal of the *Pensées* is not a great theologian or a great philosopher. It is as a *moraliste* that he is unsurpassable, not a teacher of morals, but an observer of the poignancies and absurdities of the human predicament as he envisaged it and which, however his religious beliefs may have lost all or some of their hold, still so often ring true.

NOTE ON THE TEXT

NONE of the French texts translated here was published during Pascal's lifetime and, apart from those few of the fragments not in a secretarial hand used for the 1711 *Recueil original* and one version of the *Mémorial*, none now exists in Pascal's handwriting, or was first printed directly from a text in his hand. All the texts, however, reflect the intense reverence paid to everything Pascal left in writing. Every scrap of paper was preserved with meticulous care by Pascal's family and, if it seemed to have religious significance, was copied, recopied, and widely circulated in manuscript. The respect for everything Pascal left extended in the 1660s to the leading figures associated with the defence both of Jansen's theology and of the spirituality connected with it, for which the monastery of Port-Royal, both the Paris house and the much larger Port-Royal-des-Champs, served both as a symbol and a repository.

The *Pensées*, a pile of papers concerning religion, were originally written on mostly large sheets of paper, some of which were subsequently cut into individual passages, of which again only some were then divided into twenty-seven bundles with titles attached. The passages forming each bundle or *liasse*, 414 in all, or just under half the total, were then attached together by thread running through holes pierced in the top left corner and knotted after the title had been given to the group. A list of *liasse* titles certainly attributable to Pascal contains twenty-eight headings. No fragments are filed under one of the titles, so that it is likely that Pascal subsequently ran together papers from two projected groups. There remained thirty-three untitled batches, containing some 450 fragments in thirty-three unclassified bundles, now known as 'series' to distinguish them from the titled *liasses*. After Pascal's death a copy of the fragments was made 'as they were, in the same confusion as that in which they had been found', says Pascal's nephew, Étienne Périer, in his preface to the 1670 edition. That copy itself has been lost, but two copies of it have survived.

The fragments themselves from which the lost copy was made

were later stuck on to large sheets of paper, bound, and deposited in 1711 as the *Recueil original* in the Bibliothèque de Saint-Germain-des-Prés. It is now in the Bibliothèque Nationale (fonds français 9202). The first of the two derivative copies of the original lost copy made on Pascal's death is known as C1 and is now also in the Bibliothèque Nationale (fonds français 9203). It contains each of Pascal's dossiers in a separate notebook, with notes, remarks, comments, conjectures, and amendments by Arnauld and Nicole, never working on the same notebook, as also by others and by Étienne Périer, Gilberte's son. Arnauld and Nicole appear to have shared the task of helping to prepare an edition, and the notebooks were no doubt not always kept together in the same place. C1 was used as the basic text by Louis Lafuma (1951 and 1963), and for a 1966 English translation, on the erroneous assumption that it was itself the 'mastercopy'. It is, in fact, difficult to disentangle in it the text of Pascal from the accretion of comments and suggestions.

In 1976, however, Philippe Sellier edited the second copy made from the original, C2, also now in the Bibliothèque Nationale (fonds français 12449), whose greater closeness to the original state in which Pascal left the fragments he convincingly demonstrated. He also strongly argues the importance of the placing in C2 of the first *liasse*. C2 has notes only in the hand of Étienne Périer, and does not separate the *liasses* into notebooks, but runs an individual *liasse* into a new notebook whenever an old one has been finished. This translation follows the order of C2, adding only the *Memorial*, of which Pascal kept a copy sewn into his jacket, and uses the numbering of the Sellier edition. The status of textual fragments not contained in C2 is conjectural. Nevertheless, on account of their importance, Fragments 739 and 740, from the 1678 edition based on C1, have been translated here, as has Fragment 743, from the now lost 'Manuscrit Périer', containing undoubtedly authentic texts left aside by the initial copyist, but collected by Pascal's nephew, the abbé Louis Périer, probably about 1680. A copy of the manuscript, partly printed in 1728, still exists. Any *pensée* numbered from 1 to 414 in this translation comes from the classified *liasses*.

The other texts translated here have all appeared in the third volume (1991) of the critical edition of Pascal's *Œuvres complètes* by Jean Mesnard, although also elsewhere, but without the critical justification. The *Discussion with Monsieur de Sacy on Epictetus and Montaigne*, first published in 1728 by Père Desmolets, was originally taken from the *Mémoires* of Nicolas Fontaine (1625–1709), who had been the chronicler of Port-Royal and the secretary of Isaac Le Maître de Sacy (1613–84), with whom he was sent to prison for his association with Arnauld and Port-Royal in 1666. Fontaine was writing in the last years of the century, certainly using polished notes by Pascal, now lost, of what might have been more than a single conversation with Le Maître de Sacy in January 1655, as well perhaps as notes taken from Le Maître de Sacy himself.

The text of *The Art of Persuasion*, here translated in its entirety, became detached from *De l'esprit géométrique*, of which it was once part, and no autograph exists. The first and faulty published version is again that of Père Desmolets in 1728. The translation, like that of the *Discussion with Monsieur de Sacy*, has used the section numbers from the critical edition by Jean Mesnard, which are likely to become standard. Except in punctuation, the critical edition of the translated portions does not change the previously available text.

The two drafts of letters are in fact sketches in letter form for one or more treatises, first published in 1914, and are part of what are now known as the *Écrits sur la grâce* (*Writings on Grace*). Jean Mesnard has painstakingly analysed the textual tradition for his critical edition, finding in the end a total of fifteen documents, divided into three groups, intended respectively to constitute a 'letter', a 'discourse', and a 'treatise'. The extracts translated again use M. Mesnard's section numberings. The text itself, less expertly divided, has been available in other editions for some time. The extracts here translated have been chosen to illustrate Pascal's theological thinking, and were probably composed late in 1655 and early in 1656.

In the text the titles of the *liasses* are given in capitals. The numbers of the fragments are those given by Philippe Sellier to the fragments in his 1976 edition of C2. Passages crossed out by Pascal, then copied and crossed out by the copyist, are given between angled brackets. Titles of individual fragments are given in italics. The short horizontal lines within the fragments are reproduced from Pascal's text. Since Pascal used chiefly the Vulgate Latin, which is based on a canon of which some books are not in the Authorized Version and whose text Pascal did not always correctly quote, and since he also used at least three other translations (Louvain 1550; Robert Estienne 1545; and the Polyglot 1586) based on Hebrew or Aramaic originals, all translations from Scripture have been taken from the English Jerusalem Bible (1966). Pascal frequently quotes Montaigne, always from the 1652 edition of *Les Essais* (incorrectly, but universally translated as *The Essays*), to which his page numbers refer. The first nineteen *liasses*, as is clear from the numbering of the fragments, have been translated in their entirety to show the spectrum of variation from polished literary texts to cryptic notes unintelligible to anyone but their author, minutes from Pascal to himself about how to proceed, and snippets trying out different genres, particularly dialogue and letter forms.

SELECT BIBLIOGRAPHY

Texts

Œuvres complètes, ed. Jean Mesnard, 4 vols. to date (Paris, 1964, 1970, 1991, 1992). Excellent critical edition. The texts of the *Lettres provinciales* and of the *Pensées* have not yet appeared.

Les Pensées, ed. Philippe Sellier (Paris, 1976). In Classiques Garnier collection, Paris 1991, with helpful introduction. Follows 'seconde copie', the most authoritative of the three manuscripts.

Les Provinciales, ed. L. Cognet (Classiques Garnier; Paris, 1965). Excellent introduction and notes.

Opuscules et lettres, ed. Louis Lafuma (Paris, 1955). All the minor texts have now appeared in the *Œuvres complètes*, but this inexpensive edition is still excellent and useful.

Pensées de M. Pascal sur la religion et sur quelques autres sujets (Paris, 1670). The original Port-Royal edition is now available in a 1971 facsimile.

Les Pensées de Pascal, ed. Francis Kaplan (Paris, 1982). Modern attempt to reconstitute the apologetic. Important preface.

No other editions are recommended, but the 1963 'Intégrale' edition, no longer to be used for the '*Writings on Grace*', is still useful.

Works on Pascal and the Pensées

Works in English include:

Broome, J. H., *Pascal* (London, 1965). Still offers the best all-round book-length non-theological introduction in English.

Miel, Jan, *Pascal and Theology* (Baltimore, 1969). The only monograph in English with an adequate theological background.

Davidson, Hugh McCullough, *The Origins of Certainty: Means and Meaning in Pascal's Pensées* (Chicago, 1979).

—— *Blaise Pascal* (Paris, 1983).

Nelson, Robert J., *Pascal, Adversary and Advocate* (Cambridge, Mass., 1981). Concentrates on Pascal's use of language.

Coleman, Francis X. J., *Neither Angel nor Beast: The Life and Work of Blaise Pascal* (New York, 1986). Readable, but out of date when published.

Norman, Buford, *Portraits of Thought* (Ohio, 1988).

Hammond, Nicholas, *Playing with Truth: Language and the Human Condition in Pascal's 'Pensées'* (Oxford, 1994).

The most important works on Pascal are in French. They include:

Brunet, Georges, *Le Pari de Pascal* (Paris, 1956). A fascinating and rigorous analysis of the wager fragment.

Sellier, Philippe, *Pascal et saint Augustin* (Paris, 1970). Excellent on the theology of Pascal.

Mesnard, Jean, *Pascal* (Paris, 1967).

—— *Les Pensées de Pascal* (Paris, 1976).

Lønning, Per, *Cet effrayant pari: Une 'pensée' pascalienne et ses critiques* (Paris, 1980). Best published criticism of the four preceding works in book form.

Words more specifically relevant to the *Lettres provinciales* have not been included.

Background to Pascal

Levi, A. H. T., *Guide to French Literature*, 2 vols. (Detroit, 1992, and 1994). The lengthy entries on Pascal, Jansen(ism), Nicole, Port-Royal, and Saint-Cyran are intended to provide different sorts of literary, theological, and philosophical background material, some of it technical. All quotations given in French and also in translation.

A CHRONOLOGY OF
BLAISE PASCAL

1620   Birth of Gilberte (1620–87), eldest child of Pascal's parents to survive infancy. The parents, Étienne Pascal (1588–1651) and Antoinette Begon (1596–1626), had married in 1616 or 1617. After Étienne Pascal had studied law, the post of tax assessor was bought for him, then that of second judge of the tax court at Montferrand (Président à la Cour des Aides).

1623   Birth of Blaise Pascal, author of the *Pensées*, at Clermont-Ferrand.

1625   Birth of Jacqueline Pascal, who is to become Sœur Sainte-Euphémie at Port-Royal.

1626   Death of Pascal's mother.

1631   Move of Pascal family to Paris. Blaise, after sickly infancy, is educated at home, and early introduced to scientific and literary circles. After the death of their mother, the children are cared for by a governess, Louise Delfault.

1635–8   Financial crisis bound up with Étienne's Pascal's investment in municipal bonds. Étienne in hiding after imprisonment of leaders of bond-holders' protest by the chancellor, Séguier.

1639   Rehabilitation of Étienne arranged by Richelieu's niece, the duchesse d'Aiguillon.

1640   Étienne Pascal posted to Rouen. Publication of Jansen's *Augustinus*.

1641   Marriage of Gilberte Pascal to Florin Périer.

1643   Death of Jean Duvergier, abbé de Saint-Cyran.

1645   Dedication of the calculating machine to the chancellor, Pierre Séguier, in exchange for what amounted to a patent.

1646   Étienne Pascal breaks a thigh by falling on ice, and is converted, as gradually is his family, to the spirituality of Saint-Cyran by two brothers belonging to a group dedicated to caring for the sick.

1647   Pascal has severe headaches and can take only warm liquid nourishment. Designs experiments to demonstrate atmospheric pressure. Descartes calls on him in September. In October Pascal publishes the *Expériences nouvelles touchant le vide*. Attacks work of Père Saint-Ange on faith and reason. Begins to attend Singlin's sermons at Port-Royal.

1648   Pascal publishes a further paper on the vacuum, *Récit de la grande expérience*.

1649–50   May: Pascal and Jacqueline are taken to Clermont to escape the Fronde uprising in Paris. Return November 1650.

1651   Death of Étienne Pascal. Jacqueline enters Port-Royal. Pascal writes *Préface sur le traité du vide*.

1651–4   Works on mathematics, and mixes socially. Close friendship with duc de Roannez and with Méré.

1653   Papal bull *Cum occasione* of Innocent X condemns five Jansenist propositions.

1654   Undergoes spiritual experience recorded in *Mémorial*, 23 November.

1655   January: Makes retreat at Port-Royal-des-Champs. Discussions with Le Maître de Sacy. Arnauld's two theological letters which resulted in stripping of his doctorate and imposition by Sorbonne of anti-Jansenist oath. *Écrits sur la grâce*, 1655–6.

1656   Pascal's *Lettres provinciales* started. Gilberte Périer's daughter Marguerite miraculously cured at Port-Royal.

1657   Last of *Lettres provinciales*. Project of an apologetic conceived.

1658   Conference at Port-Royal probably held in May or October. Work on the cycloid.

1659   Renewed illness, February 1659 to June 1660.

1660   *Discours sur la condition des grands* written for son of duc de Luynes.

1661   Imposition of signature of first anti-Jansenist formulary. Jacqueline signs on 22 June and dies, partly of remorse, on 4 October. Pascal himself refuses to sign second formulary, signed by Arnauld and Nicole, and withdraws from controversy.

1662   Inauguration with Roannez of first omnibus service in Paris on 18 March. Pascal falls ill in the spring, is taken to Gilberte's house on 29 June, and dies there on 19 August.

1670   Port-Royal edition of *Pensées*, selected and adapted for edification.

PENSÉES
and Other Writings

PENSÉES

[TABLE OF *LIASSE* TITLES]*

Order	A.P.R.
Vanity	Beginning
	Submission and use of reason
Wretchedness	Excellence
Boredom	Transition
<Sound opinions of the people>	Nature is corrupt*
Causes and effects	Falseness of other religions
Greatness	To make religion attractive
Contradictions	Foundation
Diversion	Figurative law
Philosophers	Rabbinism
The sovereign good	Perpetuity
	Proofs of Moses
	Proofs of Jesus Christ
	Prophecies
	Figures
	Christian morality
	Conclusion

TABLE OF *LIASSE* TITLES*

2 To be insensitive to the point of looking down on things which concern us and to become insensitive to the matter which concerns us most.

3 The Maccabees from the time they no longer had prophets. The Massorah since Jesus Christ.*

4 But it was not enough that the prophecies* existed, they had to be distributed in every place and maintained in every age.

   And in order for the coming not to be taken to be the result of chance it had to have been predicted.

   It is much more glorious for the Messiah that they should be the observers and even the instruments of his glory, apart from the fact that God had chosen them.

5 *Fascinatio nugacitatis.** [The fascination of evil (Wisd. 4: 12).]
   So that passion can do no harm let us act as if we had only a week to live.

6 *Order.* I should be much more frightened of being wrong and finding out that the Christian religion was true than of being wrong in believing it to be true.

7 The two Testaments look to Jesus Christ, the Old as its expectation and the New as its model, and both have him as their centre.

8 Why did Jesus Christ not come in a visible way instead of drawing his proof from previous prophecies?

———

Why did he have himself predicted by figures?

9 *Perpetuity.* Consider that from the beginning of the world the expectation or adoration of the Messiah has been uninterrupted, that there have been men who have said that God had revealed to them that a Redeemer was to be born who would save his people. That Abraham then came to say that he had had a revelation that he would be born of him through a son that he would have, that Jacob declared that of his twelve children he

would be born of Judah, that Moses and the prophets then came to declare the time and manner of his coming, that they said the law they had would last only while awaiting that of the Messiah, that until then it would be permanent but that the other would last eternally. That in this way their law or that of the Messiah of which it was the forerunner would be on earth for ever, that in fact it always has lasted, that finally Jesus Christ came in all the prophesied circumstances. That is to be wondered at.

10 If it was so clearly prophesied to the Jews, why did they not believe it, or why were they not destroyed for having resisted something so clear?

My answer is this. First of all, it was prophesied both that they would not believe so obvious a thing and that they would not be destroyed. And nothing is more glorious for the Messiah, for it was not enough that there should be prophets, they had to be kept above suspicion. But, etc.

11 *Figures*. God, wishing to create a holy people whom he would separate from all the other nations, whom he would deliver from its enemies, whom he would establish in a peaceful place, promised to do this and foretold through his prophets the time and manner of his coming. And meanwhile, to strengthen the hope of his chosen people throughout the ages, he allowed them to see the image, never leaving them without assurances of his power and of his desire for their salvation. For in the creation of mankind Adam was the witness and repository of the promise of a Saviour who was to be born of a woman, when mankind was still so close to the Creation that individuals could not have forgotten their own creation and their fall. When those who had seen Adam were no longer in the world, God sent Noah and saved him, and drowned the whole earth in a miracle which sufficiently underlined both his power to save the world and his desire to do it, and to have the one he had promised born of the seed of a woman.

This miracle was enough to strengthen the hope of [mankind].

The memory of the flood was still so fresh among mankind when Noah was still alive that God made his promises to

Abraham. And when Shem was still alive, God sent Moses, etc.*

12 The true nature of man, his true good, true virtue, and true religion, cannot be known separately.*

13 Instead of complaining that God has kept himself hidden, you will give him thanks that he has made himself so visible. And you will give him further thanks that he has not revealed himself to the wise people full of pride, unworthy of knowing so holy a God.

———

Two sorts of people have such knowledge: those who have a humble heart and who embrace lowliness, whatever their degree of mental power, or those who have sufficient understanding to see the truth, whatever resistance they might have.*

14 When we want to think of God, is there nothing which turns us aside, tempts us to think of other things? All that is bad, and it is born with us.

15 It is unfair that anyone should be devoted to me, although it can happen with pleasure, and freely. I should mislead those in whom I quickened this feeling, because I am no one's ultimate end, and cannot satisfy them. Am I not near death? So the object of their attachment will die. Therefore just as I should be guilty if I caused a falsehood to be believed, however gently persuasive I had been and however pleasurably it had been believed, giving me pleasure too, in the same way I am guilty if I make myself loved and if I attract people to become devoted to me. I have an obligation to warn those who would be willing to agree to the lie that they ought not to believe it, whatever advantage it may hold for me, because they must devote their lives and their efforts to pleasing God, or searching for him.

16 True nature having been lost, everything becomes natural.
In the same way, the true good having been lost, everything becomes their true good.

17 The philosophers did not prescribe feelings commensurate with the two states.

They inspired movements of pure greatness and that is not man's state.

They inspired movements of pure baseness and that is not man's state.

Movements of abjectness are necessary, arising not from nature but from repentance, not in order to stay in it, but as a step to greatness. We need moments of greatness, arising not from merit but from grace, having passed through the state of abjectness.

18 If man is not made for God, why is he only happy with God?
If man is made for God, why is he so hostile to God?

19 Man does not know on which level to put himself. He is obviously lost and has fallen from his true place without being able to find it again. He looks for it everywhere restlessly and unsuccessfully in impenetrable darkness.*

20 We want truth and find only uncertainty in ourselves.

We search for happiness and find only wretchedness and death.

We are unable not to want truth and happiness, and are incapable of either certainty or happiness.

This desire has been left in us as much to punish us as to make us realize where we have fallen from.

21   Proofs of religion.
Morality. /Doctrine. /Miracles. /Prophecies. /Figures.

22   Wretchedness.
Solomon* and Job knew best and spoke best of man's wretchedness, one the happiest and the other the unhappiest of men, one knowing the vanity of pleasure through experience, the other the reality of affliction.

23 All these contradictions which used most to keep me away from the knowledge of any religion are what have led me soonest to the true religion.

24 I blame equally those who decide to praise man, those who blame him, and those who want to be diverted. I can only approve those who search in anguish.

25 *Instinct, reason.* We have an inability to prove anything, which is impregnable to all dogmatism.

We have an idea of truth impregnable to all Pyrrhonism.

26 The stoics* say: 'Go back into yourselves. There you will find peace.' And it is not true.

Others say: 'Go out, look for happiness in some distraction.' And that is not true. Illness is the result.

Happiness is neither outside us nor within us. It is in God, and both outside and within us.

27 A *Letter* on the folly of human knowledge and of philosophy. This *Letter* before that on *Diversion*.

Felix qui potuit. [Happy the man who could (know the reasons for things) (Virgil, *Georgics*, 2. 490, quoted in Montaigne, *The Essays*, III. 10).]

Felix nihil admirari. [Happy he who is surprised at nothing (Horace, *Epistles*, 1. 6. 1).]

Two hundred and eighty kinds of sovereign good in Montaigne* (*The Essays*, ii. 12).

28 False position of the philosophers who did not discuss the immortality of the soul.

False position of their dilemma in Montaigne.*

29 This interior war between reason and the passions meant that those who wanted peace divided into two sects. Some wanted to renounce the passions and become gods, the others wanted to renounce reason and become brute beasts. Des Barreaux. But neither group succeeded, and reason is still there accusing the baseness and injustice of the passions and disturbing the peace of those who give way to them, and the passions are still alive in those who want to reject them.*

30 *Man's greatness.* We have such a high idea of man's soul that we cannot bear to think that this idea is wrong and therefore to be without this esteem for it. The whole of man's happiness lies in this esteem.

31 Men are so necessarily mad that it would be another twist of madness not to be mad.

32 Those who wish to know fully man's vanity need only consider the causes and effects of love. The cause is a *je ne sais quoi*. Corneille.* And the effects are devastating. This *Je ne sais quoi*, such an insignificant thing that it cannot be recognized, disturbs the whole earth, princes, armies, the entire world.

If Cleopatra's nose had been shorter, the whole face of the earth would have changed.

33 *Wretchedness*. The only thing that consoles us for our miseries is distraction, yet that is the greatest of our wretchednesses. Because that is what mainly prevents us from thinking about ourselves and leads us imperceptibly to damnation. Without it we should be bored, and boredom would force us to search for a firmer way out, but distraction entertains us and leads us imperceptibly to death.*

34 *Agitation*. When a soldier or a labourer etc. complains about his hard work, give him nothing to do.

35 *Nature is corrupt*. Without Jesus Christ man is necessarily in a state of vice and wretchedness.

With Jesus Christ man is free from vice and wretchedness. In him lies all our virtue and all our happiness.

Separated from him there is only vice, wretchedness, error, darkness, death, despair.

36 Not only is it through Jesus Christ alone that we know God but it is only through Jesus Christ that we know ourselves.* We know life and death only through Jesus Christ. Without Jesus Christ we do not know what our life, nor our death, nor God, nor ourselves really are.

In the same way without the Scriptures, which have Jesus Christ as their sole object, we know nothing and see only darkness and confusion in the nature of God and in nature itself.

II. ORDER

37 Psalms sung over the whole earth. (cf. Ps. 98: 4.)
Who bears witness to Muhammad? Himself.

Jesus Christ wants his witness to be nothing.

The quality of witnesses means that they must always and everywhere be wretched. He is alone.

38 *Order by dialogues.* 'What should I do? I see everywhere nothing but darkness. Shall I believe that I am nothing? Shall I believe that I am god?'*

———

'All things change and follow on one another.'

'You are wrong, there is . . .'

———

'So, do you not say, yourself, that the sky and the birds prove God?' No. 'And does your religion not say so?' No. For while that is true in a sense for some souls to whom God gave this enlightenment, it is nevertheless false in respect of the majority.

———

Letter to encourage man to seek God.

And then to seek him amongst the philosophers, Pyrrhonists,* and dogmatists, who will trouble the man who studies them.

39 *Order.* A letter of exhortation to a friend to encourage him to seek. And he will answer: 'But what use will it be to me to seek? There seems to be nothing.' And as answer to him: 'Do not despair.' And he would answer that he would be happy to find some enlightenment, but that according to this religion itself, even if he did believe it would be of no use to him and he is therefore quite happy not to seek. To that, the answer is: 'The machine.'*

40 First part: Wretchedness of man without God.
Second part: Happiness of man with God.

———

otherwise

First part: That nature is corrupt, proved by nature itself.
Second part: That there is a Redeemer, proved by Scripture.

41 Letter to show the usefulness of proofs. By the machine.

Faith is different from proof. One is human, the other is a gift of God. *Justus ex fide vivit.* [The upright man finds life through faith (Rom. 1: 17).] It is this faith which God places in man's heart, and the proof is often the instrument. *Fides ex auditu.* [Faith comes from what is preached (Rom. 10: 17).] But this faith is in the heart and obliged to say not *Scio* [I know] but *Credo* [I believe].

42 *Order.* See what is clear and incontrovertible in the whole state of the Jews.

43 In the letter about injustice can come:
    The foolishness that the elder sons have everything. My friend, you were born on this side of the mountain. It is therefore right that your elder brother should have everything.
    Why are you killing me?

44 The wretchednesses of human life have upset all that. As they have realized that, they have taken to distractions.

45 *Order.* After the letter about the necessity of seeking God, put the letter about removing the obstacles, which is the argument of the machine, of preparing the machine to seek God through reason.

46 *Order.* Men despise religion, they hate it and are afraid it might be true. To cure that we have to begin by showing that religion is not contrary to reason. That it is worthy of veneration and should be given respect. Next it should be made lovable, should make the good wish it were true, then show that it is indeed true.
    Worthy of veneration because it has properly understood mankind.
    Worthy of affection because it promises the true good.

III. VANITY

47 Two faces which are alike, neither of which by itself makes us laugh, together make us laugh by their similarity.

48 True Christians nevertheless obey these madnesses, not because they respect them, but only the order of God which, to punish men, has subjected them to these madnesses. *Omnis creatura subjecta est vanitati. Liberabitur.* [It was not for any

fault on the part of creation that it was made unable to attain its purpose . . . but creation still retains the hope of being freed (Rom. 8: 20).] St Thomas explains in this way the reference in St James (2: 3) to the privilege of the rich, who think that if they do not show it in God's sight they leave the order of religion.

49 Perseus, king of Macedonia, Paulus Emilius.

Perseus was reproached for the fact that he did not kill himself.*

50 *Vanity*. That such an obvious thing as worldly vanity should be so little known that it would be both odd and surprising to say that it is foolish to seek greatness; that is remarkable.

51 *Inconstancy and strangeness*. To live by one's work alone, and to rule over the most powerful State in the world, are two quite different things. They are united in the person of the Grand Turk.*

52 A tip of a cowl puts 25,000 monks up in arms.*

53 He has four lackeys.

54 He lives across the water.

55 If you are too young you cannot judge things properly; similarly if you are too old.

If you do not think about it enough, or if you think about it too much, you become obstinate and blinkered.

If we look at our work immediately after completing it, we are still too much involved in it; too long afterwards and we cannot pick it up again.

Similarly with pictures seen from too far off, or from too close up. And there is only one indivisible point which is the right position. The others are too close, too distant, too high, or too low. Perspective determines it in the art of painting. But in truth and morality who will determine it?

56 The power of flies: they win battles, prevent our soul from activity, devour our body.

57 *Vanity of the sciences.* The knowledge of outward things will
not console me in times of affliction for the lack of moral rules,
but knowledge of the laws of morality will always console me
for lack of knowledge of the physical sciences.

58 *Man's condition.* Inconstancy, boredom, anxiety.

59 The experience of seeing kings accompanied by guards, drums,
officers, and all the paraphernalia which make the machine
yield to respect and terror means that, when kings are occasionally alone and without the trappings, their appearance im-
parts respect and terror into their subjects because their persons
are not separated in our minds from all that normally accompanies them. And people who do not know that this consequence follows from this experience believe that it is the result
of a natural force. From this comes the words: *The character of
divinity is imprinted on his face*, etc.

60 The might of kings is based on reason and the folly of the
people; indeed, much more on folly. The greatest and most
important thing on earth has weakness as its foundation. And
that foundation is wonderfully sure, since there is nothing
surer than that the people will be weak. What is based on reason alone is very ill-founded, like the appreciation of wisdom.

61 Man's nature is not to go forward all the time. It has its toings
and froings.
     Fever has its shivers and high temperatures. And the cold
shows the height of the fever's temperature as well as the heat
itself.
     The same is true of man's inventions from century to cen-
tury. The goodness and malice of the world likewise.
     Plerumque gratae principus vices. [Change is usually pleasing
to princes (Horace, *Odes*, 3. 29. 13, quoted by Montaigne, *The
Essays*, i. 42).]

62 *Weakness.* All man's activities are aimed at acquiring goods,
and they cannot have a title to show that they own goods by
right, since they can rely only on human fantasy, nor do they
have the strength to own them securely.
     It is the same with knowledge, since illness removes it.
     We are incapable of both truth and goodness.

63 *Ferox gens nullam esse vitam sine armis rati.* [A warlike people who think life is not worth living if they cannot bear arms (Montaigne, *The Essays*, i. 14, quoting Livy 24. 17)).] They prefer death to peace, others prefer death to war.

Any opinion can be preferable to life, love of which seems so strong and natural.

64 One does not choose the most highly born traveller to be the captain of the ship.

65 We do not worry about being looked up to in the towns we travel through, but if we have to live somewhere for a while, then we do. How long must it be? The time is in proportion to the length of our vain and puny existence.

66 *Vanity.* Respect implies: Give a helping hand.

67 What astonishes us most is to observe that everyone is not astonished at his own weakness. We go about our business seriously, and each person follows his own calling not because it is a good thing to do so since that is what custom demands, but as if everyone knew for certain where reason and justice lay. We are continually disappointed, and with ridiculous humility believe it is our fault, and not that of the cunning we always boast about. But it is a good thing for the reputation of Pyrrhonism that there are so many people in the world who are not Pyrrhonists, in order to demonstrate that we are quite capable of the most outrageous opinions, since we are capable of believing that we are not steeped in natural, inevitable weakness, and of believing that we are, on the contrary, in a state of natural wisdom.

Nothing strengthens Pyrrhonism more than the fact that there are some people who are not Pyrrhonists. If everyone were, they would be wrong.

68 This sect is strengthened not so much by its friends as by its enemies, because human weakness is much more apparent in those who do not recognize it than in those who do.

69 *Heel of a shoe.* How well shaped it is! How skilful that craftsman is! How brave that soldier is! Here is the source of our inclinations and our choice of situations. How much that man

drinks! How little that man drinks! That is what makes people sober or drunkards, soldiers, cowards, etc.

70 Anyone who does not see the vanity of the world is very vain himself.

And so who does not see it, apart from the young who are preoccupied with bustle, distractions, and plans for the future?

But take away their distractions and you will see them wither from boredom.

Then they feel their hollowness without understanding it, because it is indeed depressing to be in a state of unbearable sadness as soon as you are reduced to contemplating yourself, and without distraction from doing so.

71 *Occupations.* The sweetness of fame is so great that whatever we pin it to, we love, even death.

72 Too much and too little wine. If you give someone none, he cannot discover the truth. It is the same if you give him too much.

73 Men spend their time chasing after a ball, or a hare. It is the amusement of kings, too.

74 What vanity painting is, which attracts admiration by resembling things whose originals we do not admire!

75 When we read too quickly or too slowly we understand nothing.

76 How many kingdoms know nothing about us!

77 Little things comfort us because little things distress us.

78 *Imagination.** That is the part of the human being which dominates, this mistress of error and falsehood, and all the more treacherous because it is not consistently treacherous. For it would be an infallible rule of truth if it were an infallible one of lies. But while it is more often false, it gives no indication of its quality, indicating in the same way both truth and falsehood. I am not speaking of mad people, I am speaking of the wisest, and it is amongst them that imagination has the overriding right to change their minds. Reason may well complain, it cannot put a price on things.

This proud, powerful enemy of reason, which enjoys believing that it controls and dominates it to show how much it can achieve in every realm, has established a second nature in man. Imagination has those it makes happy and unhappy, its healthy and sick, its rich and poor. It makes reason believe, doubt, deny. It abrogates the senses, it brings them to life. It has its fools and its wise men, and nothing upsets us more than to see it satisfy its guests more fully and completely than reason. Those skilful in imagination are more pleased with themselves than the prudent can ever reasonably be pleased with themselves. They look imperiously on others, they argue boldly and confidently; the others only timidly and warily. Their vivacious expression often wins over the opinion of their listeners, such is the esteem those wise by imagination have with their like-minded judges.

It cannot make fools into wise men, but it can make them happy, unlike reason, which can only make its friends miserable, one enveloping them with glory, the other with shame.

Who dispenses reputation, who lends respect and veneration to people, to works, to laws, to the great, if it is not this imagining faculty? How inadequate are all the earth's riches without its connivance.

Would you not say that this judge, whose venerable old age makes him respected by all, governs his actions by pure, sublime reason, and that he judges things by their true nature without paying attention to the empty circumstances which damage only the imagination of the weak? See him go to listen to a sermon with truly devout zeal, reinforcing the soundness of his reason with the warmth of his charity. There he is, ready to listen with exemplary respect. If, when the preacher appears, nature has given him a hoarse voice and an odd kind of face, or his barber has shaved him badly and circumstances in addition have made him rather scruffy, whatever great truths he declaims, I will bet on our senator's loss of gravity.

If you put the world's greatest philosopher on a plank wider than he needs, but with a precipice beneath, however strongly his reason may convince him of his safety, his imagination will prevail. Many would be unable to contemplate the idea without going pale and sweating.

I do not want to list all the effects of the imagination. Who can be unaware that the sight of cats, of rats, or the crunching of a piece of coal can unhinge reason completely? The tone of voice affects the wisest, and changes the vigour of a speech or a poem. Love or hatred stands justice on its head. And how much more righteous does an advocate find the case he is pleading if he is well paid in advance? How much better does his bold gesture make his cause seem to judges, tricked by his appearance? Ludicrous reason that a wind can twist and turn! I should have to list almost all of human actions which are swung almost only by its buffeting. For reason has been forced to give way, and the wisest reason takes for its principles those which human imagination has foolhardily introduced everywhere. <We must, since reason so ordained, work all day for benefits recognized as imaginary. And, when sleep has refreshed us from the labours of our reason, we must immediately jump up to pursue the phantoms and erase the impressions created by this ruler of the world.>

Our judges have understood this mystery well. Their red gowns, the ermine skins which they wrap themselves in like stuffed cats, the courts where they pass judgment, their fleurs de lys, this whole impressive accoutrement was strictly necessary. And if doctors had no long robes or mules, if professors did not wear square caps and gowns four times too big, they would never have duped the world, which cannot resist such an authentic display. If they dispensed true justice, and if doctors knew the true art of healing, they would have no need of their square caps. The majesty of these sciences would be respected enough for its own sake. But being able to resort only to imaginary sciences they have to put on these empty symbols, which strike the imagination to which they must appeal. And in this way do indeed gain respect.

Only soldiers are not similarly got up in disguise, because their role is a more essential one. They establish themselves by force, the others by play-acting.

This is why our kings have not sought such disguises. They have not cloaked themselves in extraordinary costumes in order to be seen as such, but surround themselves with guards and foot soldiers. These armed troops have hands and strength only for them, the trumpets and drums which march before them and the regiments which surround them make the most unflinching tremble. It is not simply the apparel; they have the might. Reason at its most refined would have difficulty in looking on the Great Lord surrounded in his superb seraglio by 40,000 janissaries as just another man.

We cannot even see an advocate in cap and gown without forming a favourable opinion of his professional capacity.

Imagination orders everything. It is the spring of beauty, justice, and happiness which is the be-all and end-all of the world.

I would heartily like to see the Italian book of which I know only the title, *Dell 'opinione regina del mondo*,* which itself is worth many others put together. Without knowing it I accept what it says, except the evil in it, if there is any.

These, then, are roughly the effects of this misleading faculty which seems to have been implanted in us precisely to lead us into necessary error. We have many other principles of error.

Long-held impressions are not the only ones capable of misleading us; the attraction of novelty has the same power. All human arguments derive from these, with people blaming each other either for clinging to their false childhood impressions or for recklessly pursuing new ones. Has anyone found the middle path? Let him come forward and prove it. There is no principle, however natural it may seem even from childhood onwards, that cannot be treated as a false impression deriving either from being taught, or through the senses.

'Because', it is said, 'since childhood you have believed that a box was empty because you could not see anything in it, you have believed in the possibility of a vacuum.* This is an illusion of your senses, strengthened by habit, that science must correct.' And others say: 'Because you have been taught in the schools that there is no such thing as a vacuum, your common sense, which understood the notion of a vacuum perfectly well before receiving this false idea, has been corrupted and must be corrected by a return to your original state.' Which is doing the deceiving: the senses or the education?

We have another principle of error, illnesses. They impair

our judgement and feeling. If major illnesses obviously distort them, I have no doubt that lesser ones do so in proportion, too.

Our own interest is another wonderful means of pleasantly blinding ourselves. Not even the fairest man in the world is allowed to be the judge in his own case. I know people who, in order not to fall into the trap of self-interest,* have leant over backwards in the other direction. The surest method of losing an absolutely just case is to have it recommended to them by their own close relations. Justice and truth are two points so subtle that our instruments are too imprecise to locate them exactly. If they succeed, they blunt the point and press all round, more on the false than the true.

<Human beings are therefore so excellently fashioned that they have no exact principle of truth, and many excellent ones of falsehood. Let us see how many.

But the most entertaining cause of their errors is the battle between the senses and reason.>

Human beings are simply a subject full of natural error, which cannot be eradicated without grace. [Nothing] points them towards the truth. Everything deceives them. (The chapter about misleading powers must begin with this.*) These two principles of truth, reason and the senses, apart from the fact that each of them lacks sincerity, mutually deceive one another. The senses deceive reason through false appearances, and the very deceit they play on the soul is played back on them in return. Reason takes its revenge. The passions of the soul disturb the senses and give them false impressions. They lie and deceive themselves at will.

But apart from this error, which arises accidentally and from a lack of understanding between these heterogeneous faculties . . .

79 *Vanity*. Causes and effects of love. Cleopatra.

80 We never keep ourselves to the present moment. We look forward to the future as too slow in coming, as if to hasten its arrival, or we remember the past to hold it up as if it had happened too quickly. We are so undiscerning that we stray into times which are not our own and do not think of the only one that is truly ours, and so vain that we dream about those

which no longer exist and allow the present to escape without thinking about it. This is because the present usually hurts us. We hide it from sight because it wounds us, and if it is pleasant then we are sorry to see it pass. We try to buttress it with the future, and think of arranging things which are not in our power for a time we cannot be at all sure of attaining.

Everyone should study their thoughts. They will find them all centred on the past or the future. We almost never think of the present, and if we do it is simply to shed some light on the future. The present is never our end. Past and present are our means, only the future is our end. And so we never actually live, though we hope to, and in constantly striving for happiness it is inevitable that we will never achieve it.

81 The mind of this sovereign judge of the world is not so independent that it cannot be disturbed by the first nearby clatter. It does not need a cannon's roar to immobilize its thoughts, the noise of a weathercock or a pulley will do. Do not be surprised if he cannot gather his thoughts at the moment—a fly is buzzing in his ear. That is enough to make him incapable of giving sound advice. If you want him to reach the truth, then chase away the insect holding his reason in check, disturbing that mighty intellect which rules over cities and kingdoms.

What a ludicrous god he is! *O ridicolosissimo heroe!*

82 It seems to me that Caesar was too old to amuse himself by going off conquering the world. It was a fine enough pastime for Augustus or Alexander. They were young and difficult to stop. But Caesar ought to have been more mature.

83 The Swiss are affronted when they are called gentlemen, and prove their lower-class origins when they want to be considered fit for high office.*

84 'Why are you killing me?' 'Well, don't you live over the water? My good friend, if you lived on this side, I should be a murderer and it would be wrong to kill you. But because you live on the other side I am courageous, and it is right.'

85 *Good sense.* They are forced to say: 'You are not acting in good faith, we are not asleep.' etc. How I love to see this proud

reason humbled and begging!* Those are not the words of a man whose rights are disputed and who is defending them strongly, arms in hand. He does not waste time saying that his opponents are not acting in good faith, but punishes their bad faith by force.

IV. WRETCHEDNESS

86 Baseness of man going as far as submission to beasts, even to adoring them.

87 *Inconstancy*. Things have various qualities and the soul various impulses,* for nothing which offers itself to the soul is straightforward, and the soul offers itself straightforwardly to nothing. Hence we cry and laugh at the same thing.

88 *Inconstancy*. We think we are playing on an ordinary organ when we are playing on men. They are indeed organs, but they are odd, changing and volatile; <their pipes do not follow in a regular pattern. People who can only play an ordinary organ> would not be able to draw chords from them. We have to know where the keys are.

89 We are so unhappy that we can only take pleasure in something on condition that we should be allowed to become angry if it goes wrong. Thousands of things can, and do, hourly. Whoever finds out the secret of deriving pleasure from things that go right without becoming angry if they do go wrong will have made the right discovery. It is perpetual motion.

90 It is not good to be too free.

___

It is not good to have everything necessary.

91 *Tyranny*. Tyranny is wanting to have something in one way when it can only be had in another. We allow different claims for different sorts of merit, recognizing charm's claim to love, force for its claim to fear, science's claim to belief.

We have to allow these claims; we are wrong to deny them and wrong to seek others.

So it is false and tyrannical to say: 'I am handsome therefore I must be feared. I am strong therefore I must be loved. I am . . .' And it is equally false and tyrannical to say: he is not strong, therefore I will not admire him. He is not skilful, therefore I will not fear him.'

92   Tyranny consists in
                the universal desire
                to dominate, beyond
                one's station.

Various compartments; of strength, beauty, wit, and piety, in which each is supreme and nowhere else, and sometimes they overlap. Then strength and beauty foolishly fight it out to see which will master the other, for their mastery is of a different kind. They do not understand each other. Their mistake is to want to be supreme everywhere. Nothing can be, not even strength. It holds no sway over the kingdom of the intellect. It governs only external actions.

93 When it is a question of deciding whether to make war and kill so many men, to condemn so many Spaniards to death, it is one man's decision alone, and he is an interested one at that. It should be the decision of an impartial third party.

94 On what will he base the economy of the world he wants to rule? If left to each individual's whim, what confusion! If on justice, he does not know what it is. Certainly, if he did know, he would not have laid down that most common of all men's maxims, that a man must follow the customs of his own country. The glory of true equity would have held all the nations in its sway. And the legislators would not have taken the fanciful quirks of the Persians and Germans as their model instead of this steady justice. We should see it enacted by all the States of the world, in every age, instead of which we see nothing, just or unjust, which does not change in quality with a change in climate. Three degrees of latitude overthrow jurisprudence. A meridian determines the truth. Law has its periods; Saturn's entry into the house of the Lion marks the origin of a given crime. It is an odd kind of justice to have a river for its boundary. Truth lies on this side of the Pyrenees, error on the other.

They allow that justice does not reside in customs but in natural laws common to all countries. They would certainly uphold this stubbornly if the haphazard nature of chance, which scattered human laws, had managed to find at least one which was universal. But the joke is that men's whims are so widely diverse that there is not a single general law.

Larceny, incest, infanticide, and parricide have all been accounted virtuous deeds. Can there be anything more ludicrous than a man having the right to kill me because he lives over the water and his king has a quarrel with mine, even though I have none with him?

No doubt there are natural laws, but our fine reason having been corrupted, it corrupted everything. *Nihil amplius nostrum est, quod nostrum dicimus artis est. Ex senatusconsultis et plebiscitis crimina exercentur. Ut olim vitiis sic nunc legibus laboramus.* [Nothing more is ours what we call ours is by convention (Cicero, *About the ends of goods and evils*, 5. 21). It is by virtue of senatorial decrees and votes of the people that crimes are committed (Seneca, *Letter* 95, quoted by Montaigne, *The Essays*, iii. 1). Just as we once used to suffer for our vices, we now suffer for our laws (Tacitus, *Annals*, 3. 25).]

From this confusion derives the fact that one man will say the essence of justice is the legislator's authority, another the king's convenience, and a third, present custom. This last is the safest. Following reason alone, nothing is intrinsically just; everything moves with the times. Custom is the whole of equity for the sole reason that it is accepted. That is the mystical basis of its authority. Whoever tries to trace this authority back to its origin, destroys it. Nothing is faultier than laws which put right faults. Whoever obeys them because they are just is obeying a justice he merely imagines, but not the essence of the law. It is self-contained, it is the law and nothing more. Whoever wanted to examine the reason for this would find it so feeble and lightweight that, if he were unaccustomed to contemplating the feats of human imagination, he would marvel that in a century it had accumulated so much pomp and reverence. The art of criticizing and overthrowing States lies in unsettling established customs by delving to their core in order to demonstrate their lack of authority and justice. They say they have to go back to the fundamental and original laws of the State, which unjust custom has abolished. That is a sure way of losing everything; nothing will be just on those scales. However, people listen readily to such reasoning. They shake off the yoke as soon as they recognize it, and great men profit from this, to the ruin of the state and the ruin of those who are curious to examine established customs. That is why the wisest of legislators used to say that the good of mankind requires them to be deceived, and another sound politician: *Cum veritatem qua liberetur ignoret, expedit quod fallatur.* [When he asks about the truth that is to bring him freedom, it is a good thing that he should be deceived (Varro, quoted by Montaigne, *The Essays*, ii. 12, half remembering Augustine's *City of God*, N. 37).] He must not be allowed to be aware of the truth about the usurpation. It was introduced once without reason and has since become reasonable. He must be made to regard it as genuine and eternal, and its origins must be disguised if it is not to come to a swift end.

95 *Justice*. Justice, like finery, is dictated by fashion.

96 Could anyone who had had the friendship of the king of England, the king of Poland, and the queen of Sweden* ever have believed he would be without any place of refuge or asylum in the world?

97 *Glory*. Admiration spoils everything from childhood on. 'Oh! how well that was said, Oh! how well he has done it, how beautifully behaved he is,' and so on. The children of Port-Royal who are not given the spur of emulation and reward cease to care.

98 *Mine, yours*. 'This is my dog,' said those poor children. 'That is my place in the sun.' That is the origin and picture of universal usurpation.

99 *Diversity*. Theology is a science, but at the same time how many sciences is it? Man is a substance, but when analysed is he head, heart, stomach, veins, each vein, each portion of vein, blood, each one of the blood's humours?

From a distance a town is a town, and countryside countryside, but as you get closer there are houses, trees, tiles, leaves, grass, ants, ants' legs, to infinity. They are all included in the word 'countryside'.

100 *Injustice*. It is dangerous to tell the people that laws are not just, since they obey them only because they believe them to be just. That is why they must be told at the same time to obey them because they are laws, just as they must obey their superiors, not because they are just, but because they are their superiors. All sedition can thereby be prevented if people can be made to understand that, and that this is the proper definition of justice.

101 *Injustice*. Jurisdiction is not conceived in terms of the person holding it, but in that of the person subject to it. It is dangerous to tell the people that. But the people have too much faith in you: it will do them no harm and can be useful to you. It must therefore be publicized. *Pasce oves meas, non tuas*. [Feed my sheep. Not yours (John 21: 15–17).] You owe me pasture.

102 When I consider the short span of my life absorbed into the preceding and subsequent eternity, *memoria hospitis unius diei praetereuntis* [like the memory of a one-day guest (Wisd. 5: 15)], the small space which I fill and even can see, swallowed up in the infinite immensity of spaces of which I know nothing and which knows nothing of me, I am terrified, and surprised to find myself here rather than there, for there is no reason why it should be here rather than there, why now rather than then. Who put me here? On whose orders and on whose decision have this place and this time been allotted to me?

103 *Wretchedness*. Job and Solomon.

104 If our condition were truly happy, we should not have to divert ourselves from thinking about it.

105 *Contradiction*. Pride* counterbalancing all wretchedness. He either hides his wretchednesses or, if he unveils them, takes pride in knowing them.

106 We must know ourselves. Even if that did not help in discovering truth, it would at least help in putting order into our life. Nothing is more proper.

107 The feeling of the inauthenticity of present pleasures and our ignorance of the emptiness of absent pleasures causes inconstancy.

108 *Injustice*. They have never found another way of satisfying their concupiscence without harming others.

109 Job and Solomon.

110 *Ecclesiastes* shows that man without God knows nothing and remains inevitably unhappy. To be unhappy is to want to do something but to be unable to do it. He can want to be happy and certain of some truth; however he can neither know nor not want to know. He cannot even doubt.

111 <Is the soul still too noble a thing for the feeble enlightenment it possesses? Let us bring it to the level of the material world. Let us see if it knows what the body it inhabits is made of, and the others which it contemplates and moves about at will.

What have these great dogmatists known about this, who know everything?

393* Harum sententiarum. [On these opinions (Cicero, *Tusculan Discourses*, 1. 11).]

It would no doubt be enough if reason were reasonable. It is sufficiently so to admit that it has not yet been able to find anything stable, but it is not yet in despair of succeeding. On the contrary it is as keen as ever in the search, and believes it has the necessary strength for success.

It must therefore be achieved, and after examining its strengths in its effects, let us recognize them for what they are in themselves. Let us see whether reason has the strength and grip capable of establishing the truth.

13—But perhaps this subject goes beyond the compass of reason. So let us examine what it has discovered with its own strength. If there is anywhere where its own self-interest should have made it apply itself most seriously, it is in the search for its sovereign good. Let us see where these strong and far-seeing souls have placed it, and whether they agree about it.

One says that the sovereign good lies in virtue, another in

pleasure, another in following nature, another in truth, *Felix qui potuit rerum cognoscere causas* [Happy the man who could know the reasons for things (Virgil, *Georgics*, 2. 490)], another in happy ignorance, another in doing nothing, yet more in not being taken in by appearances, another in admiring nothing, *Nihil mirari prope res una quae possit facere et servare beatum* [To be surprised at nothing is almost the only way to find happiness and keep it (Horace, *Epistles*, 1. 6. I)] and these fine Pyrrhonists* with their Stoical ataraxia, doubt, and perpetual suspension of judgement, and others wiser still who say sovereign good cannot be found, not even by wishing it. We have been well served!

Transpose the following Article after the laws: Whether we must see if this fine philosophy has required no certainty after such long and hard work. Perhaps at least the soul will know itself. Let us listen to the rulers of the world on this subject. What have they thought about its substance?

395 Have they been luckier in placing it?

395 What have they found out about its origin, its duration, and its departure? 399>

V. BOREDOM AND QUALITIES ESSENTIAL TO MANKIND

112 *Pride*. More often than not curiosity is merely vanity. We only want to know something in order to talk about it. Otherwise we would not go on a sea voyage to say nothing about it, but simply for the pleasure of seeing things without ever hoping to describe them.

113 *Description of man*. Dependence, desire for independence, needs.

114 How irksome it is to give up those occupations to which we have become attached. A man lives happily with his family. If he sees an attractive woman, or gaily gambles for five or six days, he is miserable if he goes back to what he was doing before. It happens all the time.

VI. CAUSE AND EFFECTS

115 Respect means to go out of your way for others.

This is seemingly aimless but it is very true, for it means that I would certainly go out of my way if you needed it, since I do it anyway when you do not. Besides, respect distinguishes the great. If respect required only to be directed at those sitting in armchairs, we would respect everyone, and there would be no distinction made. But, having gone to some trouble, we can make the distinction very easily.

116 The only universal laws are the laws of the land in everyday things, and the majority will in the others. How has that come about? From the force that resides in them.

Hence kings, who have force, do not follow the majority will of their ministers.

Equality of possessions is no doubt right, but, being unable to ensure that force obeys justice, we have made it just to obey force. We cannot strengthen justice, so we justify strength, in order that from both together there could be peace, which is the sovereign good.

Wisdom leads us back to childhood. *Nisi efficiamini sicut parvuli.* [Unless you become as little children (Matt. 18: 3).]

117 The world judges a great number of things in a state of natural ignorance, the true seat of man. Science has two extremes, which meet. The first is the pure state of natural ignorance at birth. The other is the point reached by those with noble souls who, having explored everything man is capable of knowing, realize they know nothing and return to their original state of ignorance. But it is a wise ignorance of self-awareness. Those who are in between, who have discarded their original state of natural ignorance but who have not yet reached the other, have a smattering of sufficient knowledge, and presume to understand it all. They upset the world, and judge everything badly. Ordinary people and clever people make up the world; the first group scoff at the world and are scoffed at in return. They misjudge everything and the world does not.

118 <Descartes. It has to be said in general: 'That is done by figure

and movement', because it is true. But it is absurd to say
which, or to invent the machine, because that is useless, uncertain, and difficult. Even if it were true, we do not believe the
whole of philosophy to be worth one hour's effort.>

119 *Summum jus, summa injuria.* [The extreme of the law is the
height of injustice (Terence, *The Self Tormentor*, 4. 5. 47).]

Majority opinion is the best way because it is visible and has
the force to make itself obeyed. That is what the least clever
people think.

If it had been possible, force would have been entrusted to
justice, but because force cannot be manhandled as we wish,
being a palpable quality, whereas justice is a intangible one
which we can manipulate as we like and so has been given into
the control of force, we therefore call justice whatever might
can enforce.

Hence the right of the sword, because the sword gives a true
right.

Otherwise we would see violence on one side and justice on the
other. End of the twelfth *Provinciale*.

Hence the injustice of the *Fronde*,* which raises what it puts
forward as justice against might.

It is not the same within the Church, where there is true
justice and no violence.

120 *Veri juris.* [Of true justice (Cicero, *On Duty*, 3. 17, quoted by
Montaigne, *The Essays*, iii. 1).] We no longer have any. If we
did, we would not hold it as a rule of justice to follow the
customs of our country.* That is why, unable to find justice,
we found might.

121 The chancellor is grave-faced and wears badges of office because his position is a false one. Not so the king's, as he has
power. He has no need for our imagination. Judges, doctors,
etc. have only our imagination to rely on.

122 This is the effect of might, not custom, because people capable of originality are rare. The great majority only want to follow, and refuse respect to those who seek it through their originality. If they continue in their search for respect and scorn those who are not original, then the others might belittle them, and beat them. So this subtlety of mind should not be vaunted but be kept quiet.

123 *Cause and effects.* This really is to be wondered at: I am supposed not to bow to a man in brocade clothing followed by seven or eight lackeys. And if I do not, he will have me thrashed. His clothes are his power. It is the same with a horse in fine harness compared with another. It is odd that Montaigne does not see the difference, and innocently asks what, and for what reason, people find one. 'Really,' he says, 'how does it come about that . . .' etc.

124 *Cause and effects.* Gradation. The rank and file honour people of high birth. Those of middling intelligence despise them, saying that their birth is an advantage of chance, not of what they are. Clever men honour them, not in the way the rank and file do, but from deeper motives. Devout people with more zeal than knowledge despise them, despite the fact that they are honoured by clever men, because piety gives them a new light to judge them by. But perfect Christians honour them in a different, higher light.

So opinion follows opinion, for and against, depending on how much understanding you have.

125 *Cause and effects.* We must have deeper motives and judge everything by them whilst nevertheless using the language of the people.

126 *Cause and effects.* So it is true to say that everyone is under an illusion, because while the opinions of the people are sound, they are not thought out. They think truth lies where it does not. There is certainly truth in their opinions, but not as much as they think there is. It is true that gentlemen should be honoured, but not because birth is an effective advantage, etc.

127 *Cause and effects.* Constant switch between for and against. We

have shown that man is conceited by the value he puts on inessentials. All these opinions have been overturned.

We have gone on to show that all these opinions are quite sound and that as, therefore, all these emptinesses were well founded, the people are not so empty-headed as they have been made out. And so we have overturned the opinion which overturned theirs.

But we must now overturn the last proposition and show that it remains true that the people are empty-headed, even though their opinions are sound, because they do not put their finger on where the truth lies and, seeing it where it is not, their opinions must always be completely wrong and unsound.

128 *Sound opinions of the people.* The worst evil of all is civil war.

They are safe, if a reward for merit is sought, because everyone will say they have merit. The evil to fear when a fool succeeds through right of birth is neither so great, nor so certain.

129 *Sound opinions of the people.* To be finely turned out is not simple vanity, because it shows that a great number of people work for you. The way your hair is dressed shows you have a valet, a perfumer, etc., as do pleats, thread, braid, etc. But it demonstrates not simply your appearance or your accessories that you have several people working for you.

The more retainers you have, the more powerful you are. To be well turned out shows your power.

130 *Cause and effects.* Man's weakness is the reason for so many of the accepted forms of beauty, such as being able to play the lute well. <Not being able to play the lute> is an evil only because of our weakness.

131 *Cause and effects.* Concupiscence and force are the basis of all our actions. Concupiscence causes voluntary actions, force involuntary ones.

132 Why is it that a lame person does not annoy us when a lame mind does? It is because a lame person realizes that we walk straight, but a lame mind declares that it is we who are limping. Apart from that we would feel pity not anger. Epictetus

asks in much stronger terms: 'Why do we not get angry if we are told we have a headache, and we do get angry if we are told that we argue badly, or make the wrong choice?'

The reason for that is that we are quite certain that we do not have a headache and that we are not lame, but we are not so sure that we are making the right choice. As a result, we are surprised and astonished when we feel sure about something because we see it from our own point of view, that another should feel just the opposite, and even more so when a thousand other people make fun of our choice, because we must always have a preference for our own judgement over that of so many others. It is a daring and difficult thing to do. There is never such a contradiction of feeling over a lame person.

We are so made that by telling us that we are fools we believe it. The more we tell ourselves the same thing, the more we bring ourselves to believe it. For we alone hold an inner dialogue with ourselves, which must be kept properly in check. *Corrumpunt bonos mores colloquia prava.* [Bad friends ruin the noblest people (1 Cor. 15: 33).] We must keep silence with ourselves as much as possible, conversing only about God, who we know is the truth. That way we persuade ourselves that he is.

133 *Cause and effect.* Epictetus: those who say 'You have a headache'. It is not the same thing. We are aware of our health, not of what is right. Indeed his idea was silly.

However, he thought he could demonstrate it by saying: either in our power or not.

But he did not realize it is not in our power to regulate our heart, and he was wrong to conclude that it was because there were Christians.

134 The people have very sound opinions. For example:

1. Having chosen distraction, and the hunt rather than the kill. The half-learned make fun of this and delight in demonstrating the world's foolishness on account of it. But we are right in a way they cannot understand.

2. Having given distinction to men through outward signs such as nobility or possessions. Again the world takes

delight in demonstrating how unreasonable this is, and yet it is very reasonable. Cannibals laugh at an infant king.*

3. Taking offence at a slap, or coveting glory.* But that is very desirable because of the other essential benefits which come with it. A man who has been slapped without taking offence is subjected to insults and deprivation.

4. Working towards an unknown goal, making a sea voyage, walking over a plank.

135 *Justice, might.* It is just to follow justice. It is necessary to follow the strongest.

Justice without strength is powerless. Strength without justice is tyranical.

Justice without strength is a contradiction because there are always wicked people. Strength without justice is an indictment. So justice and strength must be joined, and for that, what is just must be made strong, or what is strong, just.

Justice lays itself open to wrangling. Strength is clearly recognizable and cannot be argued with. So we have been unable to combine strength with justice because strength has overturned justice, has said justice is unjust, and claimed justice for itself.

So, having been unable to strengthen justice, we have justified strength.

136 What a great advantage nobility is, giving an 18-year-old the position, recognition, and respect that anyone else would have earned at 50! That is an effortless start of thirty years.

VII. GREATNESS

137 If an animal did thinkingly what it does instinctively, and spoke thinkingly what it speaks instinctively in the hunt, warning its fellows that the prey has been lost or found, it would also certainly speak about the things that matter more, such as: 'Gnaw through that rope which is hurting me which I cannot reach.'

138 *Greatness*. The law of cause and effect demonstrates man's greatness through the construction of such a fine moral order drawn out of concupiscence.

139 The parrot's beak, which it wipes even though it is clean.

140 What is it within ourselves that feels pleasure? Is it the hand, the arm, flesh, blood? We will see that it has to be something outside the body.

141 *Against Pyrrhonism*. <It is strange that we cannot define these things without making them obscure.>* We suppose that everyone thinks of these things in the same way. But the assumption is mere conjecture, since we have no proof. I am aware that we use these words in the same situations, and that whenever two men see an object move they both talk about that object in the same words, both saying it has moved. From that identical set of words we draw the strong impression of an identical set of ideas. But that does not absolutely convince us with ultimate conviction, although we could well lay bets on it, since the same consequences can be drawn from different suppositions.

That is quite enough at least to muddle the issue. Not that it completely extinguishes the natural light which makes us certain about such things. Members of the Academy* would have wagered, but that dims the light and worries the dogmatists, to the delight of the tight-knit Pyrrhonist cabal who cling to that ambiguous ambiguity, and a certain dubious darkness from which our doubts cannot lift all brightness nor our natural light chase off all the shadows.

142 We know the truth not only by means of the reason but also by means of the heart.* It is through the heart that we know the first principles, and reason which has no part in this knowledge vainly tries to contest them. The Pyrrhonists who have only reason as the object of their attack are working ineffectually. We know that we are not dreaming, however powerless we are to prove it by reason. This powerlessness proves only the weakness of our reason, not the uncertainty of our entire knowledge as they claim.

For the knowledge of first principles such as space, time, movement, numbers is as certain as any that our reasoning can give us, and it is on this knowledge by means of the heart and instinct that reason has to rely, and must base all its argument. The heart feels that there are three dimensions in space and that there is an infinite series of numbers, and then reason goes on to prove that there are no two square numbers of which one is double the other. The principles are felt, and the propositions are proved, both conclusively, although by different ways, and it is as useless and stupid for the heart to demand of reason a feeling of all the propositions it proves, before accepting them.

So this powerlessness ought to be used only to humble reason, which would like to be the judge of everything, and not attach our certainty. As if argument alone were able to instruct us. Would to God that we never needed it and that we knew everything through instinct and feeling! But nature has denied us this benefit; on the contrary, it has given us very little of this kind of knowledge. All the other kinds can be acquired only through reason.

That is why those to whom God has granted faith through the heart are blessed and quite properly convinced of it. But to those to whom it has not been granted we can only give it through reason, until God grants it through the heart. Without that, faith is simply human, and worthless for salvation.

143 I can well imagine a man without hands, feet, or head, since only experience teaches us the head is more necessary than the feet. But I cannot imagine a man without the capacity for thought. He would be a stone, or a beast.

144 Instinct and reason, the mark of two different natures.

145 *Thinking reed.* It is not in space that I must look for my dignity, but in the organization of my thoughts. I shall have no advantage in owning estates. Through space the universe grasps and engulfs me like a pinpoint; through thought I can grasp it.

146 Man's greatness lies in his capacity to recognize his wretchedness.

A tree does not recognize its wretchedness.

So it is wretched to know one is wretched, but there is greatness in the knowledge of one's wretchedness.

147 Immateriality of the soul.   Philosophers who have subdued their passions, what material thing can have achieved it?

148 All these forms of wretchedness prove mankind's greatness. They are the wretchednesses of a great noble, the wretchedness of a dethroned king.

149 *Man's greatness*. Man's greatness is so obvious that it is drawn from his very wretchedness. For what is natural in animals we call wretchedness in man. From this we realize that, his nature now being like that of the animals, he has fallen from a better nature which previously was his.

For who can be wretched at not being a king except a dethroned king? Was Paulus Emilius miserable because he was not a consul? On the contrary, everyone thought that he was lucky to have been one, because the office was not a permanent one. But Perseus was thought to be so unhappy at no longer being king, because it was a permanent position, that people were surprised he managed to stay alive. Who is miserable for only having one mouth? And who would not be miserable for only having one eye? Perhaps we have never considered the idea of being distressed at not having three eyes, but without any at all we are inconsolable.

150 Man's greatness even in his concupiscence, from having known how to draw an admirable moral order from it and make it into an image of charity.

VIII. CONTRADICTIONS

151 After demonstrating the baseness and greatness of man.

Let us now know our own worth. Let us have self-esteem because we have within ourselves a nature capable of good, but let us not at the same time cherish the vileness of which we are capable. Let us despise ourselves because that capacity is hollow, but let us not despise our natural capacity on that account.

Let us hate ourselves; let us love ourselves. We have in ourselves the capacity for knowing truth and for enjoying happiness, but we have neither a truth which is constant nor one which satisfies.

So I would like to lead us to the point where we want to find it, to be ready and free from passions to follow it wherever we find it, knowing how much its knowledge is clouded by the passions. I would like us to hate concupiscence in ourselves, which exercises its own constraint, so that it would not blind us in our choice nor stop us when we have made it.

152 We are so presumptuous that we would like to be known throughout the world, and even by people who will be there even when we no longer are. And we are so vain that the esteem of five or six people who are close to us is enough to give us pleasure and happiness.

153 It is dangerous to make man too aware that he is on the same level as animals without demonstrating to him his greatness. It is also dangerous to make him too aware of his greatness without showing him his baseness. It is even more dangerous to leave him ignorant of either state, but very helpful to demonstrate both of them to him.

154 Man must not think he is on a level with either beasts or angels, and he must not be ignorant of those levels, but should know both.

155 *A.P.R* Greatness and wretchedness.* Since wretchedness and greatness can be concluded from each other, some people have preferred to conclude to human wretchedness, taking greatness as their proof, and others have even more strongly preferred to conclude to his greatness, with a strength greater because derived from wretchedness itself. Everything used by the first group to prove greatness has served the second as an argument to conclude to wretchedness, since the greater the wretched, the higher the level from which the fall took place. And the other group the other way round. They attack one another in an endless circle, for it is certain that the more awareness we have the more we will find both greatness and wretchedness in ourselves. In a word, we know that we are

wretched. Therefore we are wretched, because we are. But we are indeed great because we know it.

156 Contradiction, despising our existence, dying for nothing, hating our existence.

158 What are our natural principles if not those we are used to? And for children, are they not those taught by their fathers, as the instinct for the hunt is in animals?

Different customs give rise to other natural principles. That can be seen from experience. If there are some principles that cannot be eradicated by custom, there are also other customary principles contrary to nature and ineradicable from nature and from new customs. It depends on the disposition of the individual.

159 Fathers fear in case the natural love of their children is wiped out. So what is this nature capable of being wiped out?

Custom is a second nature which destroys the first.

But what is nature? Why is custom not natural?

I am very much afraid that nature is itself only a first custom, just as custom is a second nature.

160 Human nature can be considered in two ways. One according to our end, and then we are great and incomparable. The other according to the masses, in the same way the nature of a horse or a dog is by the masses, to see its speed ET ANIMUM ARCENDI [and how it wards off strangers]; and then we are low and vile. These are the two ways by which we are judged differently, and which make the philosophers argue so furiously.

For one way denies the supposition of the other. One claims: 'We were not born to this end, because all our actions deny it.' The other claims; 'We are distancing ourselves from the end when we commit these base acts.'

161 Two things teach us about our whole nature: instinct and experience.

162 *Occupation. Thoughts.* All is one, all is diverse. How many natures there are in us! How many occupations, and through what trick of fate! We all normally take up what we have heard praised. A well-turned heel.

163   If he praises himself, I belittle him.
           If he belittles himself, I praise him
           And continue to contradict him
           Until he understands
           That he is an unfathomable monster.

164 The main strengths of the Pyrrhonists—I shall leave aside the
     lesser ones—are that we can be in no way sure of the truths of
     these principles, apart from faith and revelation, except that
     we feel them to be natural to us. Now this natural feeling is not
     a convincing proof of their truth, since, having no certainty,
     apart from faith, about whether we were created by a bene-
     volent God, an evil demon, or by chance, it is open to doubt
     whether the principles given to us are true, false, or uncertain,
     depending on our origin.
        In addition, since none of us can be certain, apart from faith,
     whether we are awake or asleep, given that while asleep we
     believe as firmly as we do that we are awake. We think we see
     space, figures, movement. We feel the passage of time, we
     measure it; in short we behave just as we do when awake. The
     result is that, spending half our lives asleep, by our own admis-
     sion and whatever it seems like to us, we have not the slightest
     conception of the truth, as all our feelings during that period
     are illusions. Who knows if that other half of our lives when we
     assume we are awake is not another form of sleep, slightly
     different from the first kind, from which we awaken when we
     think we are sleeping? <As we often dream that we are dream-
     ing, piling one dream on top of another, is it not perfectly
     feasible that the half of our life when we think we are awake is
     just itself a dream on to which the others are grafted and from
     which we will awaken at our death? During that time we have
     as little grasp of the principles of truth and goodness as we do
     during natural sleep; all the passage of time and life and the
     various beings we feel to be alive, the different thoughts which
     stir us are perhaps only the same illusions of the passing of
     time and the worthless hosts of our dreams.>
        These are the principal strengths on both sides. I leave aside
     the minor ones, such as the speeches made by the Pyrrhonists
     about the influence of habit, education, native customs, and

similar things. Although they inform the behaviour of most ordinary people who only have these weak foundations on which to base their dogmas, they are brushed aside by the merest whisper from the Pyrrhonists. You only have to look at their books if you are not entirely convinced: you very soon will be, perhaps too soon.

I shall pause at the single strength of the dogmatists' argument, which is that, speaking in good faith and in all sincerity, we cannot doubt natural principles.

The Pyrrhonists counter this with the simple declaration that from the uncertainty about our origin derives the uncertainty about our nature. The dogmatists still have to find an answer to that, though they have been trying since the world began.

So there is open warfare between us and everyone must take sides, declaring either for dogmatism or for Pyrrhonism. Those who think they can remain neutral are Pyrrhonists *par excellence*. This neutrality is the essence of their conspiracy. Anyone who is not against them must be in the highest degree on their side. They are not even supporters, they are neutral, indifferent, totally detached from everything, including themselves.

What will we do in this state of mind? Shall we cast doubt on everything? Shall we doubt if we are awake if we are pinched, if we are burnt? Will we doubt whether we doubt? Will we doubt that we exist at all? We cannot get to that stage, and I am quite certain that no truly genuine Pyrrhonist has ever existed. Nature upholds powerlessness of reason and prevents it ever reaching that stage of lunacy.

So on the other hand will we say that we certainly know the truth when, given the slightest nudge, we cannot demonstrate the basis of this claim and we have to give way?

What a figment of the imagination human beings are! What a novelty, what monsters! Chaotic, contradictory, prodigious, judging everything, mindless worm of the earth, storehouse of truth, cesspool of uncertainty and error, glory and reject of the universe.

Who will unravel this tangle? <It is certainly beyond dogmatism and Pyrrhonism and the whole of human philosophy.

Man is beyond man. Let us allow the Pyrrhonists what they have so often claimed, that truth is neither within our grasp nor is it our target. It does not reside on earth but belongs in heaven, in God's bosom, and we can know it only as much as he is pleased to reveal. Let us then learn our true nature from the uncreated and incarnate truth.

You cannot be a Pyrrhonist without stifling nature, nor a dogmatist without repudiating reason.> Nature confounds Pyrrhonists and reason confounds dogmatists. What will then become of you, men who are looking for your true condition through your natural reason? You cannot avoid one of these sects nor survive in either.

Be aware then, proud men, what a paradox you are to yourselves! Humble yourself, powerless reason! Be silent, foolish nature! Learn that humanity infinitely transcends humanity and hear from your Master your true condition of which you are unaware.

Listen to God.

<Is it not as clear as day that man's condition is twofold? Indisputably.> For in the end, if man had never been corrupted, he would enjoy in his innocent state both truth and happiness with confidence. And if man had never been other than corrupted, he would have no notion of either truth or beatitude. But in the wretched state in which we are, more wretched even than if there were no dignity in our condition, we have an idea of happiness and we cannot achieve it, we feel an image of truth and we possess only untruth. We are incapable both of total ignorance and certain knowledge, so obvious is it that we were once in a state of perfection from which we have unhappily fallen.

It is astonishing however that the mystery furthest from our understanding is the transmission of sin, the one thing without which we can have no understanding of ourselves!*

Because there can be no doubt that nothing shocks our reason more than to say that the sin of the first man made guilty those who, so far from that source, seem incapable of having taken part in it. This contamination seems not only impossible to us, but also quite unjust. For what is more contrary to the laws of our wretched justice than eternally to damn a child with no will of its own for a sin in which the child had so small a part to play that it was committed six thousand years before the child came into existence? Certainly nothing shocks us more deeply than this doctrine. Nevertheless without this most incomprehensible of all mysteries we are incomprehensible to ourselves. Within this gnarled chasm lie the twists and turns of our condition. So, humanity is more inconceivable without this mystery than this mystery is conceivable to humanity.

<Hence it appears that God, wanting to keep to himself alone the right to teach us about ourselves, wanting to make the difficult explanation of our being unintelligible to ourselves, hid the knot so high, or rather, so low, that we were quite incapable of finding out about it ourselves. So it is not through the proud workings of our reason but the simple submission of reason that we can truly know ourselves.

These basic truths, solidly based on the inviolable authority of religion, tell us that there are two equally and constant truths of faith: one is that man in the state of creation or of grace is on a level above all nature, as if godlike and participating in the divinity. The other is that, corrupt and sinful, he has fallen from this state and been put on the level of the beasts. Both these propositions are equally solid and certain.

Scripture confirms them in several places: *Deliciae meae esse cum filiis hominum. Effundam spiritum meum super omnem carnem. Dii estis.* [Delighting to be with the sons of men (Prov. 8: 31); I will pour out my spirit on all mankind (Joel 2: 28); You too are gods (Ps. 82: 6).] Etc. And it says elsewhere: *Omnis caro foenum. Homo assimilatus est jumentis insipientibus et similis factus est illis. Dixi in corde meo de filiis hominum.—Eccl. 3.* [All flesh is grass (Isa. 40: 6); (Man) is one with the cattle doomed to slaughter (Ps. 49: 12); I also thought that mankind behaves like this so that God may show them up for what they are (Eccl. 3: 18).]

From this it is clear that, through grace, man is made as if on the level of God, participating in his divinity, and that without grace he is deemed the equivalent of brute beasts.>

IX. DIVERSION*

165 'If man were happy he would be even more so if he had less diversion, like the saints and God.' 'Yes, but does not happiness consist in being able to enjoy diversion?' 'No, because it comes from somewhere else, from outside, and so he is thereby dependent and liable to be disturbed by thousands of things which inevitably cause him distress.'

166 In spite of these wretchednesses he wants to be happy, he only wants to be happy, and cannot not want to be happy. But how will he set about it? The only way would be to become immortal. But he cannot, so has decided to stop himself from thinking about it.

Not having been able to conquer death, wretchedness, or ignorance, men have decided for their own happiness not to think about it (Montaigne, *The Essays*, i. 20).

167 I feel that I might never have existed, since my self consists in my thinking. So I who think would never have existed if my mother had been killed before my soul had been created. So I am not a necessary being. I am neither eternal nor infinite. But I can certainly see that in nature there is an essential, eternal, and infinite being.*

168 *Diversion*. On the occasions when I have pondered over men's various activities, the dangers and worries they are exposed to at Court or at war, from which so many quarrels, passions, risky, often ill-conceived actions and so on are born, I have often said that man's unhappiness springs from one thing alone, his incapacity to stay quietly in one room. If a man had enough to live on and if he knew how to stay happily at home, then he would not leave to go to sea, or besiege a town. You only buy a commission in the army, which is so expensive, if you cannot bear being unable to leave town. You only go out of your way to find conversation or card games if you cannot remain happily at home. Etc.

But when I thought more closely about it, and, having found the cause of all our unhappiness, wanted to discover the reason, I found that there was a truly powerful one which lies in the natural unhappiness of our feeble, mortal condition, so wretched that nothing can console us when we think about it closely.

Whatever position we imagine with all the conceivable wealth of which we can conceive for ourselves, royalty is the best station in the world. However, let us consider that position with every possible satisfaction which can go with it. If a king has no distractions and is allowed to consider and reflect on what he is, that fragile happiness will not sustain him. He will inevitably fall into thinking about situations which threaten him with rebellions, and finally about death and illness which are unavoidable. So, if he has nothing in the way of so-called distractions, he will be unhappy, unhappier even than the humblest of his subjects who can play games and enjoy themselves.

That is why gaming and the conversation of women, war, and great offices of state are so sought after. It is not that happiness lies in such things, nor that we suppose that true beatitude comes from the money we can win at the gaming table or hunting the hare; no one would accept such things as a gift. We are not looking for this soft, peaceful existence which allows us to think about our unfortunate condition, nor the dangers of war or the burden of office, but the bustle which distracts and amuses us—The reason why we prefer the hunt to the kill.

That is why we like noise and activity so much. That is why imprisonment is such a horrific punishment. That is why the pleasure of being alone is incomprehensible. That is, in fact, the main joy of the condition of kingship, because people are constantly trying to amuse kings and provide them with all sorts of distraction.—The king is surrounded by people whose only thought is to entertain him and prevent him from thinking about himself. King though he may be, he is unhappy if he thinks about it.

That is all that men have managed to invent to make themselves happy. And those who make themselves into philosophers about it, and who believe that people are quite unreasonable to spend a day hunting a hare that they would not even have wanted to buy, scarcely know our nature. The hare would not save us from the sight of death and the wretchednesses which distract us from it, but the hunt does.

A. And so, when they are taken to task because the nature of
what they are so ardently seeking inevitably fails to satisfy
them, if they replied as they ought if they thought about it
properly, that they were only seeking in all that a violent and
boisterous occupation to prevent them from thinking about
themselves, and that is why they choose an alluring object
which gratifies and strongly attracts them, their opponents
would have no answer . . . But that is not their response, because they do not themselves know themselves. They do not
know that it is only the hunt, not the kill, they are looking for.
They imagine that once they had obtained the post they could
lie back at ease, not realizing how insatiably covetous nature is.
They sincerely think they are seeking peace and quiet, whereas
they are really seeking agitation. They have a secret instinct
which leads them to look for distractions and occupations
elsewhere, which derives from their feelings of constant
wretchednesses. And they have another secret instinct, remaining from the greatness of our original nature, which tells them
that happiness lies only in repose, not frantic activity. From
these two opposite instincts arises a confused plan, hidden
from sight in the depths of their soul, which leads them to seek
repose through activity, and always to imagine that the satisfaction they do not presently enjoy will be achieved if, some
obvious difficulties having been overcome, they can thereby
open the door to peace.

The whole of life goes on like this. We seek repose by bat-
tling against difficulties, and once they are overcome, repose
becomes unbearable because of the boredom it engenders. We
have to get away from it, and beg for commotion. We think
about either our present afflictions or our future ones. Even
when we think we are protected on every side, boredom with
its own authority does not shrink from appearing from the
heart's depths, where it has its roots, to poison the mind.

The advice given to Pyrrhus* to take the rest which he was
about to expend much energy looking for, was very badly
received.

Dancing: you have to think where you are going to put your
feet.

The nobleman sincerely thinks that the hunt is a noble and royal pursuit, but his huntsman is not of that opinion.

B. Human beings are so unhappy that they would be bored even if they had no reason for boredom, simply because of their nature. They are so vain that with thousands of legitimate reasons for boredom the slightest thing like tapping a billiard ball with a cue is enough to distract them.

C. But, you will say, what is his object in all this? The chance the next day of boasting to friends that he played a better game than another. In the same way other people sweat in their study to demonstrate to mathematicians that they have proved a hitherto unresolved problem in algebra. Just as stupidly, in my opinion, even more people expose themselves to the utmost danger to boast about some stronghold they have taken. Then there are those who go to extraordinary lengths to know about all these things, not to become wiser but simply to show that they know about them. These are the worst fools of the bunch because they know what they are doing, whereas for the rest we can suppose they would not go on being foolish if they, too, knew.

Anyone can spend a life free from boredom by gambling just a little every day. If every morning you give them the money they would otherwise win, on condition that they do not gamble, you make them unhappy. You will say perhaps that they are looking for the entertainment, not the winnings. Make them therefore play for nothing; they will not become excited and will get bored. So it is not simply the entertainment they are looking for; tame uncommitted entertainment will bore them. They have to become excited and deceive themselves, imagining that they would be happy to win what they would not want to be given on the condition that they did not gamble. They work this up to a frenzy, pouring into it their desire, anger, and fear of the thing they have created, like children who take fright at the face they have just scribbled.

Why was this man, who lost his only son a month or two ago and who is overwhelmed with lawsuits and disputes so upset this morning, and yet now does not think about it at all? Do not be surprised, he is fully occupied looking to see which way the boar will go which the hounds have been chasing so eagerly for six hours. Nothing else is needed. However unhappy we are, if we can be persuaded to take up some distraction we will be perfectly happy for the time being. However happy we may be, if we have no absorbing hobby or entertainment to occupy us and prevent boredom from taking over, we will soon be fretful and unhappy. Without entertainment there is no joy. With it there is no sadness. That is also what constitutes the happiness of the high-ranking who have numerous people to entertain them, and have the power to remain in that state.

D. Make no mistake: what else does it mean to be Chief Secretary, Chancellor, or Chief Justice, if not to be in a position in which every morning large numbers of people come to them from all over, leaving them scarcely an hour in the day to think of themselves? When they are in disgrace, sent off to their houses in the country where they lack neither wealth nor servants to help them with their needs, they still feel miserable and unwanted because no one stops them thinking about themselves.

169 *Distraction.* Is the dignity of royalty not enough in itself for anyone who possesses it to be made happy at the very prospect of what it is? Does he need to be diverted from the thought of it, like ordinary people? I can see that we can be made happy by distracting ourselves from our domestic woes in filling our mind with the effort of dancing well, but is a king in the same position? Will he be happier if he pays more attention to these futile amusements than to the prospect of his greatness? What more satisfying preoccupation could his mind be given? Would it not therefore ruin his joy if he were made to think about suiting his step to the rhythm of the music, or skilfully placing a rod, instead of leaving him in peace to enjoy the contemplation of the glorious majesty which surrounds him? Let us try it out. If a king is left entirely alone, with no means of satisfying his senses, nothing to worry about, no company and only himself to think about, you will see that a king without distraction

is a man full of wretchednesses. So that situation is carefully avoided, and kings never lack a large number of courtiers who take care to make distraction follow upon business, and even make sure that their leisure hours are filled with pleasures and sport so that there is never an empty moment. That is to say a king is surrounded by people who take enormous pains to ensure that he is not alone and able to think about himself, as they know well it will make him miserable, king though he is.

I am not talking about Christian kings as Christians in all this, simply as kings.

170 *Distraction*. It is easier to put up with death without thinking about it, than with the idea of death when there is no danger of it.

171 *Diversion*. From childhood onwards people are entrusted with the care of their honour, their property, their friends, and even with the property of their friends. They are showered with duties, the need to learn languages and exercises. They are led to believe that they will never be happy if their health, honour, and wealth, and those of their friends, are not in a satisfactory state, and that if one element is amiss they will be unhappy. So they are given offices and duties which keep them hectically occupied from daybreak. You may well observe that it is an odd way to make them happy. What more could we do to make them unhappy? What do you mean, what could we do? We would only have to remove all these preoccupations from them because they would then see and think about what they are, where they come from, where they are going. So you cannot give them too much to do, too much to distract them, and that is why, after creating so many duties for them, if they have some spare time they are advised to amuse themselves, play games, keep themselves totally occupied.

How hollow and full of filth man's heart is.

X. PHILOSOPHERS

172 Even if Epictetus saw the way perfectly well he said to us: 'You are following the wrong one.' He shows that there is another

but does not lead us to it. It is wanting what God wants. Jesus
Christ alone leads to it. *Via, Veritas.* [I am the Way, the Truth
and the Life (John 14: 6).]

173   The vices of Zeno himself.*

174   *Philosophers.* All very well to shout out to someone who does
not know himself to make his own way to God! All very well
to tell it to a man who does not know himself!

175   *Philosophers.* They believe that God alone is worthy of love and
admiration, and wanted the love and admiration of humanity.
They are not aware of their corruption. If they are filled with
feelings of love and adoration for God, and if they find their
principal joy in him, then by all means let them think well of
themselves. But if they are hostile towards this, if their only inclination is to enjoy men's esteem, if their only perfection lies
in persuading men, without forcing them, that their happiness
lies in loving them, then I say that this perfection is obnoxious.
What, they have known God and did not solely desire that we
should love him, but that we should be content with them!
They wanted to be the object of men's longing for happiness.

176   *Philosophers.* We are full of things which propel us outwards.
Our instinct leads us to believe we must seek our happiness
outside ourselves. Our passions pull us outwards even when
objects to excite them are not there. External objects tempt us
in themselves and beguile us even when we are not thinking
about them. It is all very well for philosophers to say: 'Withdraw into yourselves, you will find your goodness there'; we
do not believe them. Those who do are the most hollow and
stupid of all.

177   What the stoics propose is so difficult and worthless.

────────

The stoics declare: All those who are not at the pinnacle of
wisdom are equally foolish and wicked, like those who are in
two inches of water (Montaigne, *The Essays*, ii. 2).

178   The three kinds of concupiscence* have formed three sects,
and all the philosophers have done is to follow one of them.

179 *Stoics.* They conclude that you can always do what you can sometimes do, and since the desire for glory makes those who have it successful in something or other, that everyone else could be successful as well.

These are feverish impulses which health cannot imitate.

Epictetus draws the conclusion from the fact that, because there are resolute Christians, everyone can be one.

XI. THE SOVEREIGN GOOD

180 Argument about Sovereign Good.

Ut sis contentus temetipso et ex te nascentibus bonis. [That you may be content with yourself and the good things innate in you (Seneca, *Epistles*, 20. 8).]

There is a contradiction, because they end up advising suicide.

Oh what a happy life, that we get rid of like the plague!*

181 *Second part.*
That man without faith can know
neither true good, nor justice.

All men are in search of happiness. There is no exception to this, whatever different methods are employed. They all aim for this goal. So while some go to war and others do not, the same desire is in both but from different viewpoints. The will never takes the slightest step except with that aim. This is the motive for men's every action, even those who are going to hang themselves.*

However no one without faith, over so many years, has yet achieved that target which everyone constantly aims for. All men complain, princes, subjects, noblemen, commoners, old, young, strong, weak, learned, ignorant, healthy, sick, in every country, every age, every condition.

Such a lengthy, continual, and universal test ought to convince us of our powerlessness to achieve good through our own efforts. But examples teach us little. They are never so exactly the same that some tiny difference does not exist, leading us to expect that we will not be disappointed this time as we were on the last occasion. So, never finding the present satisfactory, experience tricks us, and from one misfortune to another leads us towards death, which is its eternal consummation.

What does this greed and helplessness proclaim, except that there was once within us true happiness of which all that now remains is the outline and empty trace? Man tries unsuccessfully to fill this void with everything that surrounds him, seeking in absent things the help he cannot find in those that are present, but all are incapable of it. This infinite abyss can be filled only with an infinite, immutable object, that is to say, God himself.

He alone is our true good. From the time we have forsaken him, it is a curious thing that nothing in nature has been capable of taking his place: stars, sky, earth, elements, plants, cabbages, leeks, animals, insects, calves, snakes, fever, plague, war, famine, vice, adultery, incest. From the time he lost his true good, man can see it everywhere, even in his own destruction, though it is so contrary to God, reason, and nature, all at once.

Some seek the true good in authority, some in the intellectual quest for knowledge, yet others in pleasures.

Yet others, who indeed have comes closest to it, thought that the universal good which we all desire could not lie within any single thing which can be owned only by one person and which, if it is shared, causes more distress to its owner over the part the owner is denied than enjoyment over the part the owner has. They have understood that true good needs to be such that everyone could possess it at the same time, without diminution or envy, and that no one could lose it against his will. And their reason is that this desire, being natural to us, since it is of necessity in everyone and we cannot not have it, they conclude from this . . .

XII. A.P.R.

182   A.P.R. Beginning.

After explaining incomprehensibility.

Man's greatnesses and wretchednesses are so apparent that

true religion must instruct us that there is both some great principle of greatness and a great principle of wretchedness.

It must also give us a reason for these astonishing contradictions.

To make us happy it must show us that there is a God, that we are obliged to love him, that our happiness is in him, and our sole evil is in separation from him. It must acknowledge that we are full of darknesses which prevent us from knowing and loving him, and so, our duties obliging us to love God and our concupiscences turning us away from him, we are full of wrongs. It must give us the reasons for these resistances that we have to God and to our own good. It must teach us the remedies for our helplessness and the ways of acquiring them. Then let us examine all the religions in the world on all these points and let us see whether any other but Christianity will satisfy them.

Will the philosophers, who offer us as the only good the good within us? Is that the true good? Have they found the remedy for our ills? Is our presumption cured by putting us on the same level as God? Are those who have likened us to animals and Muslims, who have offered us only earthly pleasures as the only good, even in eternity, found the remedy for our concupiscences?

What religion will therefore teach us to cure pride and concupiscence? What religion will, at last, teach us about our good, our duties, the weaknesses which distract us from them, the cause of these weaknesses, the remedies which can cure them and how they can be obtained? All the other religions have been unable to do that. Let us see what God's wisdom will do.

'Humans', it says, 'do not expect either truth or consolation from humanity. It is I who made you. I created humanity holy, innocent, perfect. I filled him with light and intelligence. I showed him my glory and my wonders. Then the eyes of humanity saw God's majesty. He was not then in the darknesses which blind him, nor did he suffer the death and wretchednesses which afflict him. But humans were unable to sustain the burden of such glory without falling into presumption. Humans wanted to make themselves the centre of their own attention and to be independent of my help. They took themselves away from my dominion and, wanting to find happiness in making themselves my equal by finding their happiness in themselves, I left them to themselves. I turned into rebates all the creatures who were subject to them and provoked them with hostility, so that today human beings have become like beasts, and so far removed from myself that they scarcely have any confused idea of their maker left, so much has all other knowledge been extinguished or muddied. The senses, independent of reason and often in control of it, have won in the pursuit of pleasure. All creatures are a cause of pain or temptation and dominate human beings either by subduing them by their strength, or charming them with their gentleness, which is an even worse and more harmful domination.

'That is the state humanity is in today. They retain some ineffective inkling of the happiness of their first nature, and they are sunk in the wretchednesses of their blindness, and of their concupiscence which has become their second nature.'

A.P.R. For tomorrow. Prosopopoeia.*

'Humans, it is hopeless to look for the remedy for your wretchedness in yourselves. All your intelligence can only bring you to realize that it is not in yourselves that you will find either truth or good.

'Philosophers promised you this but they could not keep their promise.

'They do not know what your true good is, nor your true state. <I am the only one who can teach you what your true good is and what your true state is. I teach these things to those who listen to me, and the Books which I have given into the hands of humanity reveal them very clearly. But I did not want this knowledge to be so plain. I teach humanity about what can make them happy: why do you refuse to listen to me?

Do not look for satisfaction on earth, do not hope for anything from humanity. Your good is only in God, and ultimate happiness lies in knowing God, in becoming united with him for ever in eternity. Your duty is to love him with all your heart. He created you.> How could they have cured your weaknesses which they did not even know about? Your main weaknesses are pride, which takes you away from God, and concupiscence, which pins you down to the earth, and the philosophers have done nothing except sustain one of them. If they gave you God as something to strive for, it was simply to increase your pride. They made you think you were the same as he, and conformed to your nature. Those who saw the vanity of this pretension flung you on to the other precipice by making you think your nature was on a bestial level, and led you to seek your good amongst the pleasures shared by the beasts.

'That is not the way to cure you of your injustices which the sages did not know. Only I can make you understand who you are.' Etc.

('I do not ask you for blind faith.')
Adam. Jesus Christ.

If you are united with God, it is through grace, not nature.

If you are humbled, it is through penitence, not nature.

Hence this double potential:

You are not in the state of your creation.

These two states being assailable, it is impossible for you not to recognize them.

Watch your impulses, observe yourself, and see if you do not find in yourself these two natures.

Would so many contradictions be found in a simple subject?

Incomprehensible. Everything that is incomprehensible does not cease to be. Infinite number, an infinite space equal to the finite.

Incredible that God should unite himself to us. This consideration is drawn only from the realization of your lowness, but, if you hold it sincerely, follow it as far as I do and admit that we are in fact so low that by ourselves we are incapable of knowing if his mercy may not make us worthy of him. For I would like to know where this animal who recognizes how weak he is gets the right to measure God's mercy and set limits to it suggested by his own imagination. He knows so little about what God is that he does not know what he is himself. And so, bewildered by the consideration of his own state, he dares to say that God cannot make him capable of communicating with him, and why he believes that God cannot make himself knowable and lovable to him since man is by nature capable of love and knowledge. There is no doubt at least that he knows he exists and that he loves something. So, if he sees something in the darkness in which he exists, and if he finds some object of love amongst earthly things, why, if God reveals some inkling of his existence to him, is he incapable of knowing and loving him in the way he is pleased to communicate to us? There is no doubt, therefore, an intolerable presumption in these things, though they appear to be based in humility, which is neither sincere nor reasonable unless it makes us confess that, not knowing by ourselves who we are, we can only learn it from God.

'I do not mean you to believe in one with no reason, and I do not intend to hold you tyranically in thrall. Neither do I intend to give you an explanation for everything. To reconcile these contradictions I intend to make you see clearly, through convincing proofs of divine marks in one which will convince you of what I am, and to demonstrate my authority through miracles and proofs which you will be unable to refute. Thereafter you will believe the things I teach you, and will find no reason for rejecting them other than your own inability to know whether or not they are true.'

God wanted to redeem men and open the path of salvation to those who seek it. But we make ourselves so unworthy of it that God rightly refuses to some, because of their callousness, what he grants to others through a mercy which they do not deserve.

If he had wanted to overcome the obstinacy of the most hardened, he would have been able to by revealing himself so clearly that they could not have doubted the truth of his essence, as he will appear at the last day with such violent thunderings and violences of nature that the risen dead and the blindest shall see him.

This is not the way he wished to appear in his sweet coming, but because so many make themselves unworthy of his clemency he wanted to leave them deprived of the good they do not want. It was not, therefore, just that he should appear in an obviously divine manner, totally capable of convincing all men. But nor was it just that he should come in such an obscure way that he could not be recognized by those who sincerely sought him. He wanted to be perfectly recognizable to them. And so, wanting to appear without disguise to those who sought him with their heart, and hidden from those who flee from him with all their heart, he has modified.*

<A.P.R. for tomorrow.   2

modified our recognition of him, giving visible signs to those who seek him and none to those who do not.

There is enough light for those who desire to see, and enough darkness for those of a contrary disposition.>

XIII. BEGINNING

183 Unbelievers who swear that they follow reason must be extraordinarily strong on reason.

So, what do they say?

'Do we not see', they say, 'animals living and dying like men, and Turks like Christians? They have their ceremonies, their prophets, their teachers, their saints, their holy men like us,' etc.

Is this contrary to Scripture, does it not say all that?

If you scarcely care about knowing the truth, that is enough to leave you in peace. But if you profoundly want to know it, the details have not been looked at closely enough. It would be enough for a philosophical question, but here, where everything is in question . . .

However, after lightly considering the matter, we enjoy ourselves, etc. We should find out about this religion; even if it does not explain this obscurity, perhaps it will teach us about it.

184 We are fools to rely on the company of our equals as wretched and helpless as we are. We will die alone.

We must therefore behave as if we were alone. We would then build splendid houses, etc. We would unhesitatingly seek the truth. And if we refuse, it is a sign that we rate humans' esteem higher than the search for truth.

185 Between us and hell or heaven there is only life, the most fragile thing in earth.

186 What, finally, are you promising me—for ten years is what we decided—but ten years of *amour propre*, of trying hard to please without succeeding, not to mention inevitable pain?

187 *Stakes.* We must live in this world according to these different suppositions:

If we could always be here.

If it is certain that we will not long be here, and uncertain whether we will be here one hour.

This last supposition is ours.

Heart.

Instinct.

Principles.*

188 Pity the atheists who are searching. For are they not unhappy enough? Revile those who boast about it.

189 Atheism,* sign of strength of mind but only up to a certain point.

190 According to the odds, you must take the trouble to seek the truth, because if you die without worshipping the true principle you are lost. 'But,' you say, 'if he had wanted me to adore him, he would have left some signs of his will.' And so he has, but you have ignored them. So look for them, it is worth your while.

191 If we have to give up a week of our life, we ought to give up a hundred years.

192 There are only three kinds of people: those who serve God
having found him; others who spend their time seeking him
who have not found him, and the rest who live without seeking
him nor having found him. The first are reasonable and happy,
the last are lunatic and unhappy, those in the middle are unhappy and reasonable.

193 Atheists have to say things that are perfectly clear. But it is not
perfectly clear that the soul is material.*

194 Begin by pitying unbelievers. They are unhappy enough in
their condition.
  They must not be abused, except if it helps them. But it
harms them.

195 A man in a prison cell, not knowing whether his sentence has
been passed and with no more than an hour to learn the result,
this hour being sufficient if he knows it has been passed to
have it revoked, it would be unnatural if he did not spend that
hour finding out whether the sentence was passed, rather than
playing piquet.
  And so it is supernatural that man, etc. It is a weighing-
down of the hand of God.
  So it is not only the zeal of those who seek God which
proves God, but the blindness of those who do not seek him.

196 Beginning.
Prison cell.

———

I think it is a good thing that Copernicus' opinion is not
explored further, but this:

———

It matters to the whole of life to know whether the soul is
mortal or immortal.

197 The last act is bloody, however wonderful the rest of the play.
At the end, earth is thrown on the head, and that is the last of
it.

198 We run carelessly over the precipice after having put something in front of us to prevent us seeing it.

XIV. SUBMISSION AND USE OF REASON IN WHICH TRUE CHRISTIANITY CONSISTS

199 How I hate those stupidities: of not believing in the Eucharist, etc. If the Gospel is true, if Jesus Christ is God, where does the difficulty lie?

200 I would not be a Christian without the miracles, said St Augustine.*

201 We must <have three qualities, Pyrrhonist, mathematician, Christian. Submission. Doubt. They all interlink.> know where to doubt, where to affirm and where to submit when necessary. Whoever does not do this does not understand the force of reason. There are some who fall short of these three principles, either by affirming that everything can be demonstrated, lacking all knowledge of the demonstration, or doubting everything, lacking the knowledge of where to submit, or by submitting to everything, lacking the knowledge of where to discriminate.

202 *Susceperunt verbum cum omni aviditate, scrutantes Scripturas si ita se haberent.* [They welcomed the word very readily; every day they studied the scriptures to check whether it was true (Acts 17: 11).]

203 The way of God, who disposes all things gently, is to implant religion into our mind through reason and into our heart through grace. But to want to implant it into our mind and heart* with force and threats is to implant not religion, but terror, *terrorem potius religionem* [terror rather than religion].

204 If we submit everything to reason, our religion will contain nothing mysterious or supernatural. If we shock the principles of reason, our religion will be absurd and ridiculous.

205 St Augustine. Reason would never submit unless it perceived that there are occasions when it should submit.*
　　It is right, therefore, that it should submit when it perceives that it ought to submit.

206 It will be one of the curses of the damned to see that they will

be condemned by their own reason with which they claimed to condemn the Christian religion.

207 Those who do not love truth find their excuse in the arguments and the numbers of those who deny it, and so their error arises only from their dislike of truth and charity. So they have no excuse.

208 Contradiction is a bad indication of truth.

Several things that are certain are contradicted.

Several false things pass without contradiction.

Contradiction is not an indication of falsehood and the absence of contradicton is not a sign of truth.

209 See the two sorts of men under the title 'Perpetuity'.

210 There are few true Christians. Even as far as faith goes. There are many who believe, but through superstition. There are many who do not believe, but through licentiousness. There are few in between.

———

I do not include those who lead a truly devout life, nor all those who believe through a feeling of the heart.

211 Jesus Christ performed miracles, then the apostles and the early saints in great numbers; because the prophecies were not yet accomplished by men and were being fulfilled by them, nothing could be a witness apart from the miracles. It was foretold that the Messiah would convert the nations: how could this prophecy be fulfilled without the conversion of the nations? And how could the nations be converted to the Messiah, not seeing the final effect of the prophecies which prove him? So before he had died, risen again, and converted the nations, everything had not been accomplished, and so the miracles were necessary during the whole of this time. Now there is no more need of them against the Jews and unbelievers, for the prophecies which have been fulfilled are a constant miracle.*

212 Piety is different from superstition.

———

To uphold piety to the point of superstition is to destroy it.

Heretics reproach us for this superstitious submission. That is to do what they reproach us for.

———

Impiety of not believing the Eucharist on account of what cannot be seen.

———

Superstition of believing some propositions, etc.

———

Faith, etc.

213 There is nothing so consistent with reason as the denial of reason.

214 *Two excesses*. Excluding reason, allowing only reason.

215 We would not have sinned in not believing in Jesus Christ with no miracles.

216 *Videte an mentiar*. [As man to man I will not lie (Job 6: 28).]

217 Faith states clearly what the senses do not, but not the opposite of what they see. It is above them, not against.*

218 You abuse the belief people have in the Church and delude them.

219 People not infrequently have to be cautioned against being too docile. It is a natural vice, like incredulity, and just as pernicious. Superstition.

220 Reason's last step is to recognize that there is an infinite number of things which surpass it. It is simply feeble if it does not go as far as realizing that.

———

If natural things surpass it, what will we say about supernatural things?

XV. EXCELLENCE OF THIS WAY OF PROVING GOD

221 God through Jesus Christ.
       We only know God through Jesus Christ. All contact with

God is removed without this mediator; through Jesus Christ we know God. All those who claimed to know God and to prove him without Jesus Christ only had impotent proofs. But to prove Jesus Christ we have the prophecies which are solid, palpable proofs. Being fulfilled and proved by his coming, these prophecies underline those truths, and consequently the proof of Jesus Christ's divinity. In him and through him we therefore know God. Apart from that and without Scripture, without original sin, without the necessary mediator who was promised, and arrived, we cannot absolutely prove God, nor teach either correct doctrine nor correct moral values. But through and in Jesus Christ we can teach morality and doctrine. Jesus Christ is therefore the true God of mankind.

But at the same time we know our wretchedness, for this God is, quite simply, the healer of our wretchedness. Hence we can only know God fully by knowing our own iniquities. Those who knew God without knowing their wretchedness did not glorify him, but were glorified by him. *Quia non cognovit per sapientiam, placuit Deo per stultitiam praedicationis salvos facere.* [If it was God's wisdom that human wisdom should not know God, it was because God wanted to save those who have faith through the foolishness of the message that we preach (1 Cor. 1: 21).]

222 *Preface.* The metaphysical proofs of God are so far removed from man's reasoning, and so complicated, that they have little force. When they do help some people it is only at the moment when they see the demonstration. An hour later they are afraid of having made a mistake.

———

Quod curiositate cognoverunt, superbia amiserunt. [What they gained through curiosity they lost by pride (St Augustine, *Sermons,* cxli. 1–2).]

223 Pride is what is produced by knowing God without Jesus Christ, which is communicating without a mediator with the God known without a mediator.

Whereas those who have known God through a mediator know their own wretchedness.

224 Not only is it impossible to know God without Jesus Christ, it is also useless. They are not drawn away from him, but closer. They have not been humbled but *quo quisque optimus eo pessimus si hoc ipsum quod sit optimus ascribat sibi.* [The better one is the worse one becomes if one ascribes this excellence to oneself (St Bernard, *Sermons on the Canticles*, LXXXIV).]

225 Knowing God without knowing our wretchedness leads to pride.

Knowing our wretchedness without knowing God leads to despair.

Knowing Jesus Christ is the middle course, because in him we find both God and our wretchedness.

XVI. TRANSITION FROM KNOWLEDGE OF MAN TO KNOWLEDGE OF GOD

226 *Prejudice leading to error.* It is deplorable to see everyone deliberating only over the means, not the end. Every individual ponders over how to be true to his social position, but the choice of position or country is dictated by fate.

It is pitiful to see so many Turks, heretics, and unbelievers following in their fathers' footsteps simply because they have all been imbued with the belief that it is the best way. That is what determines each individual's career as locksmith, soldier, etc.*

That is why savages do not fit in Provence.

227 Why are limits imposed on my knowledge, my height, my life held to a hundred rather than to a thousand years? For what reason did nature so order it, and choose this mid-point rather than any other from all infinity, when there is no more reason to choose one rather than another, none more alluring than another?

228*<Since we cannot achieve universality by knowing everything that there is to know about everything, we must know a little

about everything. For it is much better to know something about everything, than everything about something. That universality is the finer. If we could have both it would be even better. But if we have to choose, we must choose that one. The world feels it and chooses it, for the world is often a good judge.

It is a whim on my part that makes me hate someone who croaks, or who breathes heavily while eating.

Whims carry great weight. What good will it do to us if we incline towards its weight because it is natural? Nothing; we should rather resist it.

Nothing demonstrates man's vanity better than looking at the cause and the effects of love, for they change the whole world. Cleopatra's nose.>

229 H.5.* On contemplating our blindness and wretchednesses, and on observing the whole of the silent universe, and humanity with no light abandoned to itself, lost in this nook of the universe not knowing who put us there, what we have come to achieve, what will become of us when we die, incapable of all knowledge, I become frightened, like someone taken in his sleep to a terrifying, deserted island who wakes up with no knowledge of what has happened, nor means of escape. At that point I am astonished that we do not despair at so wretched a state. I see others around me whose nature is the same as mine, and I ask them if they are better informed than I am. They say they are not. Then these wretched, lost people, having looked around and seen some agreeable enough objects, gave themselves to them and became attached to them. For my part I have not been able to find such an attachment, and considering how much more probable it is that there is something more that I cannot see, I have sought to find whether this God has not left some mark of himself.

I see several opposing religions, all except one of them false. Each wants to be believed on its own authority and threatens those who do not believe. I therefore do not believe them on that account. Anyone could say the same. Anyone can call himself a prophet. But I see the Christian religion, where I find prophecies, and that is not something which anyone can do.

230 H. *Disproportion of man.* <That is where natural knowledge leads us. If it is not true, there is no truth in mankind, and if it is, they find there a great source of humiliation, forced to humble themselves one way or another.

And since we cannot exist without believing it, I would like before embarking on a greater search into nature, to consider it for once seriously and at leisure. I would like us to look also at ourselves and decide whether we have some kind of proportion with it, by comparing what we would do with these two things.>

So let us contemplate the whole of nature in its full and mighty majesty, let us disregard the humble objects around us, let us look at this scintillating light, placed like an eternal lamp to illuminate the universe. Let the earth appear a pinpoint to us beside the vast arc this star describes, and let us be dumbfounded that this vast arc is itself only a delicate pinpoint in comparison with the arc encompassed by the stars tracing circles in the firmament. But if our vision stops there, let our imagination travel further afield. Our imagination will grow weary of conceiving before nature of producing. The whole of the visible world is merely an imperceptible speck in nature's ample bosom, no idea comes near to it. It is pointless trying to inflate our ideas beyond imaginable spaces, we generate only atoms at the cost of the reality of things. It is an infinite sphere whose centre is everywhere and its circumference nowhere.* In the end it is the greatest perceivable sign of God's overwhelming power that our imagination loses itself in this thought.

Let us, having returned to ourselves, consider what we are, compared to what is in existence, let us see ourselves as lost within this forgotten outpost of nature and let us, from within this little prison cell where we find ourselves, by which I mean the universe, learn to put a correct value on the earth, its kingdoms, its cities, and ourselves.

What is man in infinity?

But to present ourselves with an equally astonishing wonder, let us search in what we know for the tiniest things. In its minuscule body a mite shows us parts incomparably tinier: legs with joints, veins in its legs, blood in its veins, humours in its blood, drops in its humours, vapours within the drops. Subdividing these last divisions, we will exhaust ourselves. Let the last object at which we can arrive be the subject of our discussion. We will think that there, perhaps, is the ultimate microcosm of nature.

I want to make us see within it a new abyss. I want to depict for us not only the visible universe, but the immensity of what can be conceived about nature within the confines of this miniature atom. Let us see in it an infinity of universes, of which each has its own firmament, planets, and earth in the same proportion as in the visible world, in this land of animals, and ultimately of mites, in which we will find the same as in the first universe, and will find again in others the same thing, endlessly and perpetually. Let us lose ourselves in these wonders, which are as startling in their minuteness as others are in the vastness of their size. For who will not be amazed that our body, which was not perceptible in an imperceptible universe within the whole, is now a giant, a world, or rather an everything, in comparison with this nothingness we cannot penetrate?

Whoever looks at himself in this way will be terrified by himself, and, thinking himself supported by the size nature has given us suspended between the two gulfs of the infinite and the void, will tremble at nature's wonders. I believe that, our curiosity turning to admiration, we will be more disposed to contemplate them in silence than arrogantly search them out. For in the end, what is humanity in nature? A nothingness compared to the infinite, everything compared to a nothingness, a mid-point between nothing and everything, infinitely far from understanding the extremes; the end of things and their beginning are insuperably hidden for him in an impenetrable secret. <What can he therefore imagine? He is> equally incapable of seeing the nothingness from where he came, and the infinite in which he is covered.

What will we do, then, apart from noting some appearance of a mid-point, in eternal despair at knowing neither our beginning nor our end? All things derive from a void and are swept on to the infinite. Who can follow these astonishing processes? The author of these wonders understands them. No one else can do so.

For lack of having contemplated these infinities we have presumptuously delved into nature as if we had some proportion with it.

It is a strange thing that we have wanted to understand the principles of things and from them know everything, with a presumption as infinite as the aim of our search. For there is no doubt that such a plan cannot be conceived without presumption, or a capacity as infinite as nature's.

When we have learnt more, we understand that nature has stamped its own and its author's image on everything, and almost all things therefore derive from its double infinity. This is why we see that every science is infinite in the scope of research. Who can doubt that mathematics, for example, has an infinity of infinities of propositions to expound? They are also infinite in the multiplicity and subtlety of their principles. For who cannot see that the principles we claim to be the ultimate ones cannot stand on their own, but depend on others, which are themselves supported by others, so there can be no possibility of an ultimate principle?

But we treat as the ultimate principles those which seem to our reason to be ultimate, just as we do in material things. We call that point indivisible beyond which our senses can see no further, even though it is, in its nature, infinitely divisible.

Of these two scientific infinities we are much more aware of that of size, and that is why few people have claimed to know everything. 'I am going to speak about everything,' Democritus would say. <But apart from the fact that it is of small account simply to speak about it, without proof and knowledge, it is nevertheless impossible to do so, as the infinite number of things hidden from us make anything we can express in speech or thought only an invisible speck of the whole. Hence the vanity, absurdity and ignorance of the title of some books, *De omni scibili*.* [Of everything knowable.]

We see immediately that only arithmetic offers numberless properties, and each science likewise.>

But the infinitely tiny is much less visible. The philosophers have been ready to claim to have achieved it, and that is where they have all stumbled. This has given rise to all the familiar titles: *Of the principles of things, Of the principles of philosophy,** and other similar ones, as ostentatious in purpose, though seemingly less so, than that other blindingly obvious one, *De omni scibili.*

By nature we believe we are much more capable of delving to the centre of things than of comprehending their circumference, and the visible extent of the world is visibly greater than us. But since we are greater than little things, we think we are more capable of fathoming them, yet it does not require less capacity to penetrate into nothingness than it does into the whole. It has to be infinite to do either. It seems to me that whoever has understood the ultimate principles of things could also achieve understanding of the infinite. One depends on the other, and leads to the other. These extremes touch and join because they have gone so far in opposite directions, meeting in God and God alone.

Let us then acknowledge our range: we are something, and we are not everything. What we have of being hides from us the knowledge of the first principles which emerge from nothingness. The scant being that we have hides from us the sight of infinity.

Our intelligence holds the same rank in the order of intelligible things as does our body in the whole vastness of nature. Limited in every respect, this state in the mid-point between two extremes is apparent in all our faculties. Our senses can perceive nothing extreme. Too much noise deafens us, too much light blinds us, being too far away or too close up prevents us from seeing properly. A speech which is too long or too short impairs its message, too much truth confuses us. I know people who cannot grasp that subtracting four from zero leaves zero. First principles are too self-evident for us. Too much pleasure upsets us, too much harmony in music is unpleasant, and too many kindnesses irritate us. We want to be able to repay the debt with interest. *Beneficia eo usque laeta sunt dum videntur exsolvi posse, ubi multum antevenere pro gratia odium redditur.* [Kindness is welcome to the extent that it seems the debt can be paid back. When it goes too far gratitude turns into

hatred (Tacitus, *Annals*, 4. 18, from Montaigne, *The Essays*, iii.
8).] We can feel neither extreme heat nor extreme cold, we find
the extremes of qualities hostile and cannot perceive them; we
no longer feel them, we suffer them. Extreme youth or old age
shackles the mind with too much or too little education. It is as
if the extremes do not exist for us, and we in turn do not exist
for them; they escape us and we them.

That is our true state. That is what makes us incapable of
certain knowledge or absolute ignorance. We are wandering in
a vast atmosphere, uncertain and directionless, pushed hither
and thither. Whenever we think we can cling firmly to a fixed
point, it alters and leaves us behind, and if we follow it, it slips
from our grasp, slides away in eternal escape. Nothing remains
static for us, it is our natural state yet it is the one most in
conflict with our inclinations. We burn with desire to find a
firm foundation, an unchanging, solid base on which to build
a tower rising to infinity, but the foundation splits and the
earth opens up to its depths.

So let us not look for certainty and stability. Our reason is
always disappointed by the inconstant nature of appearances;
nothing can fix the finite between the two infinites which both
enclose and escape it.

That being understood, I think we can each remain peacefully in the state in which nature has placed us.

This mid-point which has fallen to our share, being midway
between the extremes, what does it matter if another understands things better? If he has, and if he goes a little more
deeply into them, is he not still infinitely wide of the mark?
Even if we live ten years longer, is our life span not equally
tiny compared with infinity?

Within the scope of these infinities all finites are equal, and
I do not see why we settle our thoughts on one rather than the
other. Simply comparing ourselves to the finite distresses us.

If we were first of all to take stock of ourselves, we would
realize how incapable we were of progressing further. How
could a part possibly know the whole? But we will perhaps
aspire to knowing at least those parts on our own level. But the
parts of the world are so connected and interlinked with each

other that I think it would be impossible to know one without the rest.

We are, for example, connected to everything we know: we need place to circumscribe ourselves, time to give duration to our life, activity in order to live, elements to constitute our body, heat and food to nourish us, air to breathe. We see light, we feel bodies; everything, in short, comes within our compass. In order to understand humans, therefore, we have to know why we need air to live, and to understand air we have to know the connection between it and our ability to live, etc.

Fire cannot exist without air. So in order to understand one we have to understand the other.

Everything is therefore caused and causal, aided and aiding, direct and indirect, and all are held together by a natural, impeccable link which ties the most distant and differing things together. I maintain that it is no more possible to know the parts without knowing the whole than to know the whole without knowing the parts individually.

<The eternity of things in themselves or in God must always be a source of amazement compared to our own short span.

The fixed and constant immobility of nature, compared with the continual flux within ourselves, must have the same effect.>

And what completes our inability to understand things is that they are not so simple in themselves, and we are made up of two different kinds of opposing natures, body and soul. For it is impossible that the part of us which reasons is other than spiritual. And if it were claimed that we are simply bodies we would be even further deprived of the knowledge of things, there being nothing so inconceivable as to say that matter understands itself. We cannot possibly know how matter could know itself.

And in this way, if we are simple, material, we can know nothing at all of anything. If we are made up of mind and matter, we can never totally understand simple things <since the instrument which helps this understanding is partly spiritual. And how would we clearly understand spiritual

substances, having a body which weighs us down and drags us towards the earth?>, spiritual and corporeal.

For this reason almost all philosophers confuse the ideas of things, and speak spiritually of corporeal things and corporeally of spiritual ones. They boldly say that bodies are pulled downwards, that they tend towards their centre, that they flee their destruction, that they fear emptiness. They say bodies have inclinations, sympathies and antipathies, things which belong only to spiritual beings. And when speaking of minds, they consider them as if they were in a particular place, and attribute to them the powers of movement from one place to another, a function purely of bodies.

Instead of accepting the idea of these things in their pure state, we tint them with our qualities, and imprint our composite nature on to all the simple things we see.

Who would not believe, seeing us compose everything of spirit and matter, that we could understand this mixture? Nevertheless it is what we understand least. To human beings, a human being is nature's most stupendous work. They cannot understand what the body is, far less the spirit, and least of all how the body can be combined with the spirit. That is the worst of their difficulties, and yet it is their own existence. *Modus quo corporibus adhaerent spiritus comprehendi ab homine non potest, et hoc tamen homo est.* [The way in which minds are attached to bodies is beyond man's understanding, and yet this is what man is (St Augustine, *City of God*, xxi. 10).]

<That is part of the reason why human beings are so slow in understanding nature. It is infinite in two ways, they are finite and limited. Nature endures and keeps itself perpetually alive, humanity is transient and mortal. Things in particular disintegrate and transform all the time: human beings only see them momentarily. Things have their origin and their end: humans cannot conceive of either. They are simple, and humans are made up of two different natures.>

Finally, to complete the proof of our weakness, I will end with these two considerations.

231 H.3. A human being is only a reed, the weakest in nature, but he is a thinking reed. To crush him, the whole universe does

not have to arm itself. A mist, a drop of water, is enough to kill him. But if the universe were to crush the reed, the man would be nobler than his killer, since he knows that he is dying, and that the universe has the advantage over him. The universe knows nothing about this.

232 All our dignity consists therefore of thought. It is from there that we must be lifted up and not from space and time, which we could never fill.

So let us work on thinking well. That is the principle of morality.

233 The eternal silence of these infinite spaces terrifies me.

234 Take comfort; it is not from yourself that you must expect it, but on the contrary by expecting nothing from yourself that you should expect it.

XVII. NATURE IS CORRUPT AND FALSENESS OF OTHER RELIGIONS

235 *Falseness of other religions.* Muhammad without authority.

His arguments must therefore have been very powerful, since they had only their own power.

So what did he say? That he must be believed.

236 *Falseness of other religions.* They have no witnesses. These ones do.

God challenges other religions to produce such signs. *Isa.* 43: 9–44: 8.

237 Whether there is a single principle of everything. A single end of everything. Everything through him, everything for him. True religion must therefore teach us to worship only him and love only him. But as we find it impossible to worship something we do not know, or to love something other than ourselves, the religion which teaches us these duties must also teach us about our inability. It must also instruct us about the remedies. It tells us that all was lost through a man, that the link between God and ourselves was broken, and that through a man the link was repaired.

We are born so opposed to this love of God, and it is so necessary that we must be born guilty, or God would be unjust.*

238 *Rem viderunt, causam non viderunt.* [They have seen our true state but they have not seen the cause (St Augustine,* *Against Pelagius,* iv. 60).]

239 *Against Muhammad.* The Koran is no more Muhammad's than St Matthew's Gospel, for it is quoted by several authors from century to century. Even its enemies, Celsus and Porphyry,* never denied it.

The Koran says that St Matthew was a good man. So Muhammad was a false prophet either by calling good men wicked, or by disagreeing with what they said about Jesus Christ.

240 Without this divine knowledge, what have human beings been able to do other than to raise themselves on the inner feeling remaining from their past greatness, or abase themselves at the sight of their present weakness? For, unable to see the whole truth, they have been unable to achieve a perfect virtue, some considering nature as corrupt, and others as irreparable. They have been unable to escape pride or sloth,* the two sources of all the vices, since they can only either give way through cowardice or escape through pride. For, if they knew human excellence, they were unaware of its corruption, so that they avoided sloth but became lost in pride, and if they understood nature's weakness they ignored its dignity, so that they could avoid vanity but thereby threw themselves into despair.

Hence there are various sects of stoics, epicureans, dogmatists, and academicians, etc.

The Christian religion alone has been able to cure these two vices, but not by one chasing out the other through earthly wisdom, but by chasing out both through the simplicity of the Gospel. For it teaches the just, whom it exalts even to participation in the divinity,* that in this sublime state they still carry the source of all corruption which throughout their lives makes them prone to error, wretchedness, death, and sin, and it cries out to the most ungodly that they are capable of receiving their

Redeemer's grace. Making those that it justifies tremble, and consoling those that it condemns, it tempers fear with hope so judiciously through this double potentiality for grace and sin, common to all, that it abases infinitely more than reason can do, but without despair, and raises up infinitely more than natural pride, but without excess, making it thereby obvious that, alone free from error and vice, the right to teach and correct men belongs only to the Christian religion.

Who then can refuse to believe and worship such heavenly enlightenment? For is it not clearer than daylight that we feel within ourselves the ingrained marks of excellence, and is it not equally true that we perpetually endure the effects of our deplorable condition?

What else then does this chaos and monstrous confusion trumpet, if not the truth about these two states, in so powerful a voice that it is impossible to resist?

241*Difference between Jesus Christ and Muhammad.* Muhammad not foretold. Jesus Christ foretold.

Muhammad by killing. Jesus Christ by having his followers killed.

Muhammad by forbidding reading, the apostles by commanding reading.

242 They are diametrically opposed. If Muhammad took the path of success in the human sense, Jesus Christ took the path of death in the human sense, and instead of concluding that, since Muhammad achieved success, Jesus Christ could have done so too, we must conclude that, since Muhammad succeeded, Jesus Christ had to die.

243 All men naturally hate each other. We have used concupiscence as best we can to make it serve the common good. But that is only pretence, and a false picture of charity. In the end it comes down to hatred.

244 We have founded upon and drawn from concupiscence admirable laws of administration, morality, and justice.

But at heart, at the wicked heart of humanity, this FIGMENTUM MALUM* [evil element (Gen. 8: 21).] is only covered up, not removed.

245 Jesus Christ is a God whom we approach without pride, and before whom we humble ourselves without despair.

246 *Dignior plagis quam osculis non timea quia amo.* [More deserving of blows than kisses, I am not afraid because I love (St Bernard, *Sermons on the Canticles*, LXXXIV).]

247 The true religion should have as its characteristic the obligation to love its God. That is fair, and yet none has ordered it. Ours has.

It ought to have known concupiscence and powerlessness. Ours has.

It ought to have produced remedies for these things. One is prayer. No religion has asked of God to love him and follow him.

248 After understanding man's whole nature, in order for a religion to be true it must have known our nature. It must have understood its greatness and pettiness, and the reason for both. What other than Christianity has understood this?

249 True religion teaches us our duties, our weakness, pride and concupiscence, and the remedies, humility, mortification.

250 There are some clear and conclusive figures, but there are others which seem a little far-fetched, and which only provide proof for those already persuaded. They are like those of the Apocalyptical tradition. But the difference is that they have none which are totally reliable, so much so that there is nothing more unworthy than when they show that they are as soundly based as some of ours. For they do not have any that are conclusive, as some of ours are. The game is not therefore equal. We must not put these things on equal terms and confuse them because they seem to be similar in one stage, when they are so different in another. It is the enlightenments which, when they are divine, merit respect for what is obscure.

251 It is not by what is obscure in Muhammad and what can gain acceptance as a mystical sense that I want him to be judged, but by what is obvious: his paradise, and everything else. That is where he is absurd. That is why it is wrong to take his enigmas for mysteries, given that his visions are absurd. It is

not the same with the Gospels. I accept that there are equally enigmatic obscurities in them, as in Muhammad's writings, but there are wonderful elucidations and prophecies, evident and fulfilled. The game is not therefore equal. We must not put on equal terms things which are not alike except in their obscurity, rather than their illuminations, which merit respect for their obscurities.

252 Other religions, like those of the pagans, are more popular because of their external trappings, but they are not for educated people. A purely intellectual religion would be better suited to them, but it would not do for the people. Only the Christian religion suits everyone as it combines the external and the internal. It lifts up the people inwardly, and humbles the proud outwardly. Without both it is not perfect, for the people must understand the spirit of the letter, and the educated must submit their spirit to the letter.

253 No other religion has held that we should hate ourselves. No other religion can therefore please those who hate themselves and who are looking for a being who can be loved wholeheartedly. And they, if they had never heard of the religion of a humiliated God, would embrace it at once.

XVIII. TO MAKE RELIGION ATTRACTIVE

254 Jesus Christ for all.

Moses for one people.

Jews blessed in Abraham. 'I will bless those who bless you' (Gen. 12: 3 and 22: 18), but all nations are blessed through his seed.

Parum est ut, etc. Isaiah. [It is not enough for you to be my servant (Isa. 49: 6).]

Lumen ad revelationem gentium. [A light to enlighten the pagans (Luke 2: 32).]

Non fecit taliter omni nationi [He never does this for other nations (Ps. 147: 20).], said David, speaking of the Law. But speaking of Jesus Christ we must say *Fecit taliter omni nationi, Parum est ut*, etc. Isaiah.

And so it is for Jesus Christ to be eternal. The Church itself offers the sacrifice only on behalf of the faithful. Jesus Christ offered the sacrifice of the cross for all.*

255 Carnal Jews and pagans have wretchedness, and Christians too. There is no redeemer for the pagans, for they do not even hope for one. There is no redeemer for the Jews; they hope for him in vain. There is only a redeemer for the Christians. See 'Perpetuity'.

XIX. FOUNDATIONS OF RELIGION AND ANSWER TO OBJECTIONS

256 In the chapter 'Foundations' must be put what is in the chapter 'Figurations' about the reason for figures. Why Jesus Christ prophesied in his first coming, why prophesied in an unclear way.

257 The incredulous the most credulous. They believe the miracles of Vespasian,* so they do not believe in Moses'.

258 Just as Jesus Christ remained unrecognized by his fellow men, so his truth remains hidden among ordinary thinking, with no outward difference. Just like the Eucharist and ordinary bread.

———

The whole of faith consists in Jesus Christ and Adam, and the whole of moral activity in the workings of concupiscence and grace.

259 What do they have to say against the resurrection and the birth of a child to a virgin? That it is more difficult to produce or reproduce a human or an animal? If they had never seen a particular species of animal, could they have guessed whether they reproduced entirely on their own?

260 What do the prophets say of Jesus Christ? That he will obviously be God? No. Rather that he is *a truly hidden God*, that he will be unrecognized, that no one will think he is who he is, that he will be a stumbling block for many to fall over, etc.

We should not be accused of a lack of clarity any longer, therefore, since that is what we lay claim to. But people say that there are areas of uncertainty, and without them we would not have stumbled on Jesus Christ. And this is one of the strict intentions of the prophets. *Excaeca*. [Make the heart of this people gross (Isa. 6: 10).]

261 What human beings have acquired through their great wisdom has been taught by this religion to its children.

262 Everything that cannot be understood does nevertheless not cease to exist.

263 <If you want to say that man is too feeble to deserve communication with God, you have to be very elevated to be the judge of that.>

264 We understand nothing about God's works unless we take as the basis that he wanted to blind some and enlighten others.

265 Jesus Christ does not say that he was not from Nazareth in order to leave sinful people blinded, nor does he deny that he is Joseph's son.

266 God wants to motivate the will more than the mind. Absolute clarity would be more use to the mind and would not help the will.
   Humble their pride.

267 Jesus Christ came to blind those who see clearly and give sight to the blind, to heal the sick and allow the healthy to die, to call sinners to repent and justify them and leave the righteous in their sinfulness, to feed the poor and *send the rich away hungry*.

268 *To blind, to enlighten*. St Augustine, Montaigne, Sebond.
   There is enough light to enlighten the elect and enough darkness to humble them. There is enough darkness to blind the damned and enough light to condemn them and leave them without excuses.

   ———

Jesus Christ's lineage in the Old Testament is mixed up with so many other unconnected ones that it cannot be traced. If Moses had accounted only for Jesus Christ's ancestors, it would have been extremely clear. If he had not written down Jesus Christ's lineage, it would not have been clear enough. But, after all, those who look closely enough see Jesus Christ's ancestry perfectly well from Thamar, Ruth, etc.*

Those who ordered these sacrifices knew they were useless, and those who declared their uselessness did not stop practising them.

If God had allowed only one religion it would have been clearly recognizable. But if you look carefully at this you can easily see the true religion in this confusion.

Principle: Moses was a clever man. If he was then governed by his intelligence, he could never have put down anything directly contrary to intelligence.

So all obvious weaknesses are strengths. For example, the two genealogies in St Matthew and St Luke. What could demonstrate more clearly that they were not done in collaboration?

269   If Jesus Christ had come only to sanctify, the whole of Scripture and everything else would lean towards that view and it would be quite easy to convince the unbelievers. If Jesus Christ had come only to blind, his whole behaviour would be obscure and we would have no way of converting the unbelievers. But since he came *in sanctificationem et in scandalum* [to be a sanctuary and a stumbling-stone (Isa. 8: 14)], as Isaiah said, we cannot convert unbelievers, nor can they convert us, yet by that way we do convert them, since we say that there is nothing in his behaviour which converts one way or another.

270   *Figures.* Wanting to deprive his people of perishable things, and to show that it was not through lack of power, God made the Jewish people.

271   Man is not worthy of God, but he is not incapable of being made worthy of him.

It is unworthy of God to associate himself with man's wretchedness, but not unworthy of him to extricate man from his wretchedness.

272   *Proof.* Prophecy with fulfilment.

What preceded and what followed Jesus Christ.

273 *Source of contradictions.* A God humbled to the point of death on the cross. Two natures in Jesus Christ. Two comings. Two states of the nature of man. A Messiah triumphing over death through his own death.

274 A.P.R. for Tomorrow. <Wishing to appear openly to those who seek him whole-heartedly, and to remain hidden from those who single-mindedly avoid him, God> qualified the way he might be known so that he gave visible signs to those who seek him, and none to those who do not.

There is enough light for those whose only desire is to see, and enough darkness for those of the opposite disposition.

275 That God wanted to be hidden.

If there were only one religion, God would be clearly manifest.

If there were martyrs only in our religion, the same.

————

God being therefore hidden, any religion which does not say that God is hidden is not true. And any religion which does not give the reason why does not enlighten. Ours does all this. VERE TU ES DEUS ABSCONDITUS.* [Truly, God is hidden with you (Isa. 45: 15).]

276 The pagan religion has no foundation <today. It is said that previously it did have in the oracles which spoke. But where are the books to prove this to us? Are they so worthy of being believed because of the virtue of their authors? Have they been kept so carefully that we can confirm for ourselves that they are uncorrupt?>

The Muslim religion has its foundation in the Koran and Muhammad. But was this prophet, who was supposed to be the world's last hope, foretold? And what distinguishes him from any other man who wants to call himself a prophet? What miracles does he say that he himself has performed? What mystery did he teach, according to his own tradition? What morality and what happiness?

The Jewish religion must be regarded differently in the tradition of its sacred writings and in the tradition of its people. Morality and happiness are ridiculous in the tradition of its people, but admirable in the traditions of the sacred writings. The foundation is admirable. It is the oldest and most authentic book in the world, and whereas Muhammad tried to preserve his book by forbidding anyone to read it, Moses tried to preserve his by ordering everyone to read it. It is the same for all religions, for Christianity is very different in the holy books and in those of the casuists.

Our religion is so divine that another divine religion provides only its foundation.

277 Objections of atheists.
'But we have no light.'

XXII. PERPETUITY*

311 From one saying of David or of Moses, such as 'God will circumcise their hearts' (Deut. 30: 6), we can form an opinion of the quality of their mind. All their other arguments may well be ambiguous and cast doubt on whether they are philosophers or Christians, but in the end one saying like this determines all the others, just as a saying of Epictetus brings all the rest into order in the opposite way. There is ambiguity up to that point, and none after it.

312 States would cease to exist if laws were not often bent where necessity dictated,* but religion has never permitted nor made use of that. So either compromises or miracles are necessary.

It is not strange to preserve existence by yielding, but properly speaking neither is it preservation. And even so, in the end they do cease entirely to exist. Not a single one has lasted a thousand years. But for this religion always to have been preserved, and inflexibly . . . that shows its divinity.

313 *Perpetuity.* This religion, which consists in the belief that we have fallen from a state of glory and communion with God to a state of melancholy, penitence, and separation from God, but that after this life we would be restored by a Messiah who was to come, has always existed on earth. Everything has ceased to

be, but this, on account of which everything else exists, has endured.

In the first age of the world men were led into all sorts of misbehaviour, and yet there were saints like Enoch, Lamech, and others who awaited patiently the Christ promised since the beginning of the world. Noah saw men's wickedness at its highest point, and he had the merit to save the world in his own person through the expectation of the Messiah, of whom he was a prefiguration. Abraham was surrounded by idolators when God made known to him the mysteries of the Messiah, whom he acclaimed from afar. In the time of Isaac and Jacob abomination was spread over all the earth, but these saints lived in their faith, and Jacob, while blessing his children as he was dying, cried out rapturously, in a way which caused him to interrupt his speech: *I trust in your salvation, Yahweh, Salutare tuum exspectabo Domine* (Gen. 49: 18).

The Egyptians were infested with idolatry and magic, and even God's people were led astray by their example, but Moses, however, and others, saw the one whom they did not see, and worshipped him, contemplating the eternal gifts he was preparing for them.

Then it was the Greeks and the Romans who erected false deities, the poets made up of a hundred different theologies,* the philosophers split into a thousand different sects. And yet, in the heart of Judaea there were always chosen men who foretold the coming of the Messiah, who was known only to themselves. He eventually came in the fullness of time, and since then we have seen so many schisms and heresies emerge, so many States overthrown, so many changes of every kind, and this Church which worships the one who has always been worshipped has existed without interruption. What is astonishing, incomparable, and wholly divine is that this religion which has always survived has always been attacked. It has been on the edge of total destruction a thousand times, and each time that it has been in that position God has lifted it up with extraordinary manifestations of his power. The amazing thing is that it has continued without giving way or yielding to the will of tyrants, for it is not strange that a State should

survive when its laws are sometimes made to give into necessity. But for that SEE THE CIRCLE IN MONTAIGNE.*

314 *Perpetuity*. The Messiah has always been believed in. The tradition of Adam was still new in Noah and Moses. Since then
the prophets have foretold him while always foretelling other
things, and those events which took place from time to time for
humanity to see established the truth of their mission, and
consequently of their promises concerning the Messiah. Jesus
Christ performed miracles, as did the apostles, which converted all the pagans, and so with the fulfilment of all the
prophesies the Messiah has been proven for ever.

315 The six ages, the six fathers of the six ages, the six wonders at
the beginning of the six ages, the six dawns at the beginning of
the six ages.*

316 The only religion against nature, against common sense, against
our pleasures, is the only one which has always existed.

317 If the ancient Church was in error, the Church is a fallen one.
If it should be in error today, it is not the same thing because
it always has the ultimate principle of the tradition of the faith
of the ancient Church. And so this submission and conformity
to the ancient Church prevails, and corrects everything. But
the ancient Church did not presuppose and look to the future
Church, as we presuppose and look to the ancient one.

318 *2 sorts of men in each religion*. Amongst the heathen, those who
worship animals, and the others who worship a single god in
natural religion.
    Amongst the Jews, the carnal and the spiritual, who were
the Christians of the ancient Law.
    Amongst the Christians, the unspiritual, who are the Jews of
the new Law.
    The carnal Jews awaited a carnal Messiah, and the unspiritual
Christians believe that the Messiah has dispensed them from
loving God. The true Jews and the true Christians worship a
Messiah who makes them love God.

319 Anyone who tries to judge the religion of the Jews by the
unspiritual will understand it poorly. It can be seen in the

sacred Books and in the tradition of the prophets, who made it clear enough that they did not interpret the Law literally. In the same way our religion is divine in the Gospel, the apostles, and the tradition, but absurd in those who misuse it.

According to the carnal Jews, the Messiah has to be a great earthly prince. According to carnal Christians, Jesus Christ came to dispense us from loving God, and to give us sacraments which are fully efficacious without our intervention. Neither is either the Christian or the Jewish religion.

True Jews and true Christians have always awaited a Messiah who would make them love God and through this love overcome their enemies.

320 Moses, *Deut.* 30, promises that God will circumcise their hearts to make them capable of loving him.

321 Carnal Jews are half-way between Christians and pagans. Pagans do not know God and only love earthly things; Jews know the true God and only love earthly things; Christians know the true God and do not love earthly things. Jews and the pagans love the same possessions, Jews and Christians know the same God.

Jews were of two kinds: one kind had pagan sensitivities, the other Christian ones.

XXIV. PROOFS OF JESUS CHRIST

329 *Order*—against the objection that Scripture has no order.

The heart has its order, the mind has its own, which is based on principles and demonstration. The heart has another one. We do not prove that we ought to be loved by setting forth the causes of love; that would be absurd.

———

Jesus Christ and St Paul have the order of charity, not of the intellect, for they wanted to edify, not to instruct.

St Augustine the same. This order consists mainly in digressing on each point which relates to the end, in order always to keep it in sight.

339 The infinite distance between body and mind points to the infinitely more infinite distance between mind and charity, for charity is supernatural.*

All the brilliance of greatness has no attraction for people who are involved in pursuits of the mind.

The greatness of intellectual people is invisible to kings, the rich, captains, to all those great in a material sense.

The greatness of wisdom, which is nothing if it does not come from God, is invisible to carnal and to intellectual people. They are three different orders. Of kind.

Great geniuses have their power, their brilliance, their greatness, their victory, and their attraction, and have no need of carnal greatness, where they have no place. They are recognized not with the eyes but with the mind: that is enough.

Saints have their power, their brilliance, their victory, their attraction, and have no need of carnal or intellectual greatness, where these have no place since they neither add nor subtract anything. They are recognized by God and the angels, and not by bodies nor curious minds. God is enough for them.

Archimedes in obscurity would still be venerated. he did not fight battles for the eyes to see, but he furnished every mind with his discoveries. How brilliantly he shone in those minds!

Jesus Christ without worldly goods, and with no outward show of knowledge, has his own order of holiness. He made no discoveries, he did not reign, but he was humble, patient, holy, holy, holy* to God, terrible to devils and without sin at all. With what great pomp and and with what prodigious magnificence he came to the heart's eyes which see wisdom!

It would have been pointless for Archimedes to act the prince in his mathematical books, even though he was one.

It would have been pointless for Our Lord Jesus Christ, in order to shine in his reign of holiness, to come as a king. But he truly came in brilliance in his order.

It is quite absurd to be shocked at the lowliness of Jesus Christ, as if that lowliness was of the same order as that of the greatness which he came to reveal.

Let us consider that greatness in his life, in his passion, in his obscurity, in his death, in the choice of his disciples, in their desertion, in his secret resurrection, and in the rest. We will see that it is so great that we will have no reason to be shocked by a lowliness which was not there.

But there are some who can only admire carnal greatness, as if there were no such thing as greatness of the mind. And others who only admire greatness of the mind as if there were not infinitely higher greatness in wisdom.

All bodies, the firmament, the stars, the earth, and its kingdoms are not worth the lowest of minds. For it knows all of them, and itself, and bodies know nothing.

All bodies together, and all minds together, and all their products are not worth the least impulse of charity. That is of an infinitely higher order.

Out of all bodies together we could not succeed in making one little thought. It is impossible, and of another order. Out of all bodies and minds we could not draw one impulse of true charity. It is impossible, and of another, supernatural, order.

XXVII. CHRISTIAN MORALITY*

383 Christianity is strange: it requires human beings to recognize that they are vile and even abominable, and requires them to want to be like God. Without such a counterweight this elevation would make them execrably vain, or this abasement execrably despicable.

384 Wretchedness provokes despair.
Pride provokes presumption.
The Incarnation shows man the greatness of his wretchedness
through the greatness of the remedy which was required.

385 Neither an abasement which makes us incapable of good, nor
a holiness free from evil.

386 There is no doctrine more suited to man than that which
teaches him his double capacity to receive and to lose grace
because of the double dangers to which he is always exposed,
of despair or of pride.

387 Of everything that is on the earth he only participates in the
sorrows, not the pleasures. He loves those close to him, but
his charity is not confined by these limits and spreads to his
enemies, and then to God's.

388 What difference is there between a soldier and a Carthusian
with regard to obedience? For they are equally obedient and
dependent, in equally difficult circumstances. But the soldier
always hopes to become his own master and never does, because captains and even princes are always slaves and dependent, but still he aspires to become his own master, and
continually works towards it, whereas the Carthusian takes a
vow never to be anything other than dependent. So they do
not differ in their perpetual servitude, which they both under-
go always, but in the hope which the one has always, and the
other never.

389 No one is so happy as a true Christian, nor so reasonable, so
virtuous, or so deserving of love.

390 With what little pride does a Christian believe himself united
to God! With what lack of abjectness does he compare himself
to an earthworm! What a way to confront life and death, good
and evil!

391 The examples of noble deaths of Spartans and others scarcely
affect us. For where is the benefit to us?
But the example of the death of martyrs affects us, because
they are our members.* We have a common bond with them.

Their resolution can strengthen ours not only by example, but because it has perhaps merited our own.

There is nothing like this in the examples of pagans. We have no link with them. Just as we do not become rich by seeing a stranger who is, but much more by having a father or husband who is.

392 *Morality.* Having made heaven and earth, which are not conscious of the happiness of their existence, God wanted to create beings who would know it and who would make up a body of thinking members. For our members are not conscious of the happiness of their union, their astonishing understanding, the care taken by nature to imbue their minds and to make them grow and last. How happy they would be if they could be aware of this and see it! But to do that they would need understanding to be aware of it, and good will to accept that of the universal soul. But if, having been given understanding, they used it to keep the nourishment to themselves without letting it pass on to the other members, they would not only be unjust but wretched, and would hate rather than love themselves, their bliss as much as their duty consisting in their agreement to the conduct of the whole soul to which they belong, which loves them more than they love themselves.

393 Are you less of a slave for being loved and flattered by your master? You are certainly well off, slave, your master flatters you. Shortly he will beat you.

394 The will itself will never provide satisfaction, even if it had power over all it wanted. But we are satisfied as soon as we give it up. Without it we cannot be unhappy, though we cannot be happy.

395 They allow concupiscence a free field and rein in scruple, whereas they ought to do the opposite.

396 It is superstitious to put one's hopes in formalities, but arrogant not to want to submit to them.

397 Experience shows us an enormous difference between devotion and goodness.

398 Two kinds of men in every religion.
   See 'Perpetuity'.

399 Superstition, concupiscence.

400 *Not formalists.* When St Peter and the apostles debated abol-
   ishing circumcision, where it was a question of going against
   God's law, they do not study the prophets, but simply the
   reception of the Holy Spirit in the person of the uncircumcised.
      They judge it more certain that God approves those whom
   he fills with his spirit rather than that the Law must be
   observed.

   _____

   They knew that the only purpose of the Law was the Holy
   Spirit, and that, since it could be received without being cir-
   cumcised, it was not NECESSARY.

401 *Members.* Begin with this.
      To regulate the love we owe ourselves we have to think of a
   body full of thinking members, for we are members of the
   whole, and to see how all members ought to love themselves,
   etc.

   _____

   Republic. The Christian and even the Jewish republic has only
   had God as master, as Philo the Jew remarks, ON MONARCHY.
      When they fought it was only for God and their main hope
   was in God alone, they regarded their towns as belonging only
   to God and preserved them for God. *1 Chr.* 19: 13.

402 To make the members happy they must have a will, and ensure that it conforms to the body.

403 Imagine a body full of thinking members!

404 To be a member is to have no life, being, or movement except
   through the spirit of the body and for the body. The member
   which is cut off, no longer seeing the body to which it belongs,
   has only a withering and moribund being left. Yet it thinks
   itself to be a whole, and seeing no body on which it depends,
   it thinks it depends only on itself and wants to make itself its
   own centre and body. But having no principle of life in itself,
   it only becomes lost and bewildered at the uncertainty of its

existence, quite aware that it is not a body, yet not seeing that it is a member of a body. Eventually, when it comes to know itself, it is as if it had come home, and only loves itself from then on as part of the body. It deplores its past misdeeds.

By its own nature it could not love anything other than for itself and to make that thing subject to itself, because everything loves itself more than anything else. But in loving the body it loves itself, because it has no being except in itself, through itself and for itself. *Qui adhaeret Deo unus spiritus est.* [But he that is joined unto the Lord is one spirit (1 Cor. 6: 17).]

The body loves the hand, and the hand, if it had a will, ought to love itself in the same way that the soul loves it. Any love that goes further than that is wrong.

Adhaerens Deo unus spiritus est. We love ourselves because we are members of Jesus Christ. We love Jesus Christ because he is the body of which we are a member. All is one. One is in the other. Like the three Persons.

405 We must love only God and hate only ourselves.

If the foot had never known that it belonged to the body and that there was a body on which it depended, if it had had only knowledge and love of itself, and then came to know that it belonged to a body on which it depended, how sorry, how ashamed of its past life, it would be to have been of no use to the body which infused it with life, which would have destroyed it if it had rejected and cut itself off, as the foot cut itself off from the body! What prayers would be said for it to be kept! And how submissively it would allow itself to be governed by the will which directs the body, to the point of allowing itself to be amputated if necessary! Otherwise it would lose its status as a member. For every member must be willing to die for the sake of the body, for whom alone everything else exists.

406 If the feet and the hands had a will of their own, they would only ever be well ordered by submitting their own will to the

antecedent will which governs the whole body. When that is not the case, they are disorganized and miserable. But in desiring only the good of the body they achieve their own good.

407 Philosophers have made vices holy by attributing them to God himself. Christians have made virtues holy.

408 Two laws are sufficient to govern the whole Christian republic better than all the political laws.

XXVIII. CONCLUSION

409 What a distance there is between knowing God and loving him.

410 'If I had seen a miracle,' they say, 'I would be converted.' How can they affirm what they would do about something of which they know nothing? They imagine that this conversion consists in worshipping God, seeing it as some kind of transaction or conversation. True conversion consists in self-abasement before the universal being whom we have so often angered and who could legitimately destroy us at any time, in recognizing that we can do nothing without him and that we have deserved nothing from him but our disgrace. It consists in knowing that there is an irreconcilable opposition between God and ourselves, and that without a mediator there can be no transaction.

411 Miracles do not serve to convert but to condemn. I p. q. 113, a. 10, ad 2.*

412 Do not be astonished to see simple people believing without argument: God gives them the love of himself and the hatred of themselves, he inclines their hearts* to believe. We will never believe, with a belief which is efficacious and belongs to faith, unless God inclines our hearts. And we will believe from the moment he does so incline them.

And that is what David knew very well. *Inclina cor meum, Deus, in,* etc. [Turn my heart to your decrees (Ps. 99: 36).]

413 Those who believe without having read the Testaments do so because they have a truly holy inward disposition, and because

what they have heard about our religion accords with it. They feel that a God made them. They want to love only God, they want to hate only themselves. They feel that they are not strong enough by themselves, that they are incapable of approaching God, and that if God does not come to them they are incapable of any communication with him. They hear our religion say that we must love only God and hate only ourselves, but that since we are all corrupt and incapable of God, God became a man to unite hiself with us. It takes no more than this to persuade men who have this disposition within their hearts, and who have this understanding of their duty and their unworthiness.

414 *Knowledge of God.* Those we see to be Christians without knowing the prophecies and the proofs are no less able judges than those who do know them. They judge with their hearts,* as others judge with their minds. It is God himself who inclines them to believe, and it is this way that they are most efficaciously convinced.

<It will be argued that the unbelievers will say the same thing. But my answer to that is that we have proofs that God truly inclines those he loves to believe the Christian religion, and that heretics have no proof at all of what they say. And so, although our propositions are similar in their statements, they differ in that the one has no proof at all and the other is very soundly proved.>

I freely admit that one of these Christians who believe without proof will perhaps not have the means of convincing an unbeliever who will say as much for himself. But those who know the proofs of religion will prove effortlessly that this believer is truly inspired by God, although he cannot prove it himself.

For since God said in his prophets (who are unquestionably prophets) that in the reign of Jesus Christ he would spread his spirit over the nations, and that the sons, daughters, and children of the Church would prophesy, there can be no doubt that God's spirit is upon them and that it is not upon the others.

421 *5. Miracles. Beginning*. Miracles distinguish between doctrine, and doctrine distinguishes between miracles.

There are false ones and true ones. There must be a sign in order to recognize them, otherwise they would be useless.

But they are not useless, on the contrary they are fundamental.

But the rule we are given must be such that it does not destroy the proof that the true miracles give of the truth, which is the principal purpose of miracles.

Moses gave two: that the prophesy is not realized (*Deut.* 18). And that they do not lead to idolatry (*Deut.* 13). And Jesus Christ gave one.

If doctrine determines miracles, miracles are useless for doctrine.

If miracles determine . . .

Objection to the rule. Distinction of time, one rule in Moses' time, another now.

Any religion is false which, in its faith, does not worship one God as the principle of all things and which, in its morality, does not love one God as the object of all things.

422 *Reason for not believing*.

John 12: 37: *Cum autem tanta signa fecisset, non credebant in eum. Ut sermo Isaiae impleretur: Excaecavit*, etc.

Haec dixit Isias quando vidit gloriam ejus et locutus est de eo. [Though they had been present when he gave so many signs, they did not believe in him; this was to fulfil the words of the prophet Isaiah: . . . 'He has blinded their eyes.' Isaiah said this when he saw his glory, and his words referred to Jesus.]

Judaei signa petunt, et Graeci sapientiam quaerunt. Nos autem Jesum crucifixum. [The Jews demand miracles, and the Greeks look for wisdom, here we are preaching a crucified Christ (1 Cor. 1: 22).]

Sed plenum signis, sed plenum sapientia.

Vos autem Christum, non crucifixum, et religionem sine miraculis et sine sapientia.

[But full of signs and full of wisdom.

But you preach Christ not crucified and a religion without miracles and without wisdom. (Pascal's Latin comment.)]

The reason men do not believe in true miracles is lack of charity. *John: Sed vos non creditis quia non estis ex ovibus.* [But you do not believe, because you are no sheep of mine (John 10: 26).]

The reason they believe in false ones is lack of charity. *2 Thess.* 2.

Foundation of religion. It is miracles. What! Does God speak against miracles, against the foundations of the faith we have in him?

If there is a God, faith in God had to exist on earth. But Jesus Christ's miracles were not foretold by the Antichrist, but the Antichrist's miracles were foretold by Jesus Christ. And so if Jesus Christ were not the Messiah he would certainly have led us into error. But the Antichrist cannot lead us into error.

When Jesus Christ foretold the Antichrist's miracles, did he think he was destroying faith in his own miracles?

There is no reason for believing in the Antichrist which is not a reason for believing in Jesus Christ. But there are reasons for believing in Jesus Christ which are not reasons for believing in the other.

Moses foretold Jesus Christ and commanded us to follow him. Jesus Christ foretold the Antichrist and forbade us to follow him.

It was impossible in Moses' time to believe in the Antichrist, who was unknown to them. But it is perfectly easy, in the Antichrist's time, to believe in Jesus Christ, who is already known.

423 The prophecies, even the miracles and proofs of our religion, are not of such a nature that they can be said to be absolutely

convincing, but they are also such that it cannot be said unreasonable to believe them. So there is evidence and obscurity, to enlighten some and obscure the others. But the evidence is such that it exceeds, or at least equals, the evidence to the contrary, so that it cannot be reason which decides us not to follow it. Therefore it can only be concupiscence and wickedness of heart. And so there is enough evidence to condemn, and not enough to convince, in order that it should be obvious that grace and not reason moves those who follow it, and in those who flee it, it is concupiscence, not reason, which moves those who shun it.

———

VERE *discipuli*, VERE *Israelita, Vere liberi*, VERE CIBUS. [You will indeed be my disciples. There is an Israelite who deserves the name. You will be free indeed. My flesh is real food (John 8: 31; 1: 47; 8: 36; 6: 55).]

———

I assume we believe in miracles.

———

You corrupt religion either for the benefit of your friends or for the distress of your enemies. You make use of it as you please.

424 If there were no false miracles there would be no certainty.
    If there were no rule for distinguishing between them, miracles would be useless and there would be no reason to believe.
    But, in a human sense, there is no human certainty, only reason.

———

The Jews, who were called to subdue nations and kings, have been slaves to sin. And Christians, whose vocation was to serve and to be subjects, are free children.

———

Judg. 13: 23: *If the Saviour had wanted to kill us, he would not have shown us all these things.*

———

Hezekiah, Sennacherib.

———

Jeremiah: Ananias, the false prophet, dies in the seventh month.

2 *Macc.* 3. The temple, about to be sacked, rescued miraculously. 2 *Macc.* 15.

---

3 *Kgs.* 17. The widow to Elijah, who had raised the child to life: *By this I know that your words are true.*

3 *Kgs.* 18. Elijah, with the prophets of Baal.

Never, in the dispute about the true God or the truth of religion, has there been a miracle on the side of error and not on that of truth.

425 This is not the land of truth. It wanders unknown among men. God has covered it with a veil that keeps it from being understood by those who do not recognize his voice. The place is open to blasphemy, even about truths which are at least quite obvious. If the truths of the Gospel are proclaimed, the opposite are then proclaimed, and the arguments are so clouded that the people cannot distinguish between them. People ask: 'What do you have to make us believe you rather than the rest? What signs can you give us? You have only words, and so do we. If you had miracles, that would be fine.' It is true that doctrine ought to be supported by miracles, which are abused to blaspheme against doctrine. And, if miracles take place, then it is said that miracles are not enough without doctrine. And this is another truth, used to blaspheme against miracles.

Jesus Christ healed the man who was born blind, and performed numerous miracles on the Sabbath, thereby blinding the Pharisees, who said that miracles had to be judged by doctrine.

<We have Moses, but as for him we do not know where he comes from.

That is what is wonderful, that you do not know where he comes from and yet he performs such miracles.>

Jesus Christ was speaking neither against God nor against Moses.

The Antichrist and the false prophets foretold by both Testaments will speak openly against God and against Jesus Christ.

Whoever is not against, whoever would be a secret enemy, God would not allow him to perform miracles openly.

In a public dispute where both parties claim to stand for God, Jesus Christ, and the Church, miracles are never on the side of the false Christians, and the other side has none.

<He has a devil. John 10: 21: And the others said: can the devil open the eyes of the blind?>

The proofs which Jesus Christ and the apostles draw from Scripture are not conclusive. For they say only that Moses said that a prophet would come, but they do not prove from this that it would be this one, and that was the whole question. These passages therefore only serve to show that there is nothing contrary to Scripture, nor anything which is inconsistent with it, but not that there is agreement. But that is sufficient: inconsistency excluded, and also miracles.

426 Jesus Christ says that the Scriptures bear witness to him. But he does not show how.

Even the prophecies could not prove Jesus Christ during his life. And therefore no one would have been guilty of not believing in him before his death, if miracles had not been sufficient without doctrine. But those who did not believe in him while he was alive were sinners, as he said himself, and had no excuse. Therefore they must have had a proof which they resisted. But they did not have Scripture, only miracles. So they are sufficient when doctrine does not contradict them. And they must be believed.

John 7: 40. Dispute among the Jews as among Christians today.

Some believe in Jesus Christ, others do not believe in him because of the prophecies which said that he was to be born in Bethlehem. They should have taken more care about whether he was not from there, for his miracles were convincing; they ought to have made very sure of the supposed contradictions between his doctrine and Scripture. This obscurity did not excuse them, it blinded them. So those who refuse to believe in the miracles of today on some so-called, imaginary contradiction have no excuses.

The people who believed in him for his miracles are told by the Pharisees: *This people who do not know the Law are cursed. Is there a prince or a Pharisee who has believed in him?* For we know that *no prophet comes out of Galilee. Nicodemus answered: Does our Law judge a man before he has been heard?*

427 Our religion is wise and foolish. Wise, because it is the most learned and firmly based on miracles, prophecies, etc. Foolish, because it is not all these things which make us belong. They certainly condemn those who do not belong, but do not make those who do belong believe. What makes them believe is the cross. *No evacuata sit crux.* [And not to preach in terms of philosophy in which the crucifixion of Christ cannot be expressed (1 Cor. 1: 17).]

And so St Paul, who came with wisdom and signs, said that he came with neither wisdom nor signs: for he came to convert. But those who only come to convince can say they come with wisdom and signs.

_____

There is a great difference between not being for Jesus Christ and saying so, and not being for Jesus Christ and pretending to be. The first can perform miracles, not the others. For it is clear of some that they are against the truth, not of the others. And so the miracles are clearer.

_____

The Church is in a fine state when it is no longer supported except by God.

428 There is a mutual obligation between God and men. This word must be forgiven. *Quod debui.* [What could I have done (Isa. 5: 4).] *Accuse me*, says God in *Isaiah*.

God must fulfil his promises, etc.

Men owe it to God to receive the religion he sends them.

God owes it to human beings not to lead them into error.

But they would be led into error if the performers of miracles proclaimed a doctrine which does not seem patently false to the light of common sense, and if a greater performer of miracles had not already warned them not to believe these men.

So, if there were a division in the Church, and the Arians, for example, who claimed they were based on Scripture like the Catholics, had performed miracles and the Catholics had not, people would have been led into error.

For just as someone who proclaims God's secrets is unworthy of being believed on his personal authority, and that is why unbelievers doubt him, if someone, as a sign of his communication with God, raises the dead, foretells the future, parts the seas, heals the sick, not a single unbeliever would resist. And the unbelief of Pharoah and the Pharisees is the effect of a supernatural hardening.

So when we see, therefore, miracles and a doctrine above suspicion together on one side, there is no difficulty. But when we see miracles and a suspect doctrine on the same side, then we have to see which is the clearer. Jesus Christ was suspect.

Bar-Jesus blinded. God's strength overcomes that of his enemies.

The Jewish exorcists set upon by devils, saying: '*I command you by the Jesus whose spokesman is Paul . . . but who are you?*' (Acts 19: 13–16).

Miracles exist for the sake of doctrine and not doctrine for miracles.

If miracles are true, can any doctrine be capable of convincing? No. For it will not happen.
    Si angelus. [Or an angel from heaven . . . (Gal. 1: 8).]
    Rule. Doctrine must be judged by miracles. Miracles must be judged by doctrine. All that is true, but it is not contradictory.

For ages must be distinguished.

How pleased you are to know the general rules, thinking you can thereby cause trouble and make everything worthless. You will be prevented from doing this, Father. Truth is indivisible and firm.

Through God's duty it is impossible for someone, covering up an evil doctrine and revealing only a good one, and professing himself true to God and the Church, to perform miracles in order to disseminate imperceptibly a false and subtle doctrine. That cannot happen.

And even less that God, who knows our hearts, should perform miracles for the benefit of such a person.

429 Jesus Christ proved that he was the Messiah, never by proving his doctrine from Scripture or the prophecies, always by his miracles.

He proves that he forgives sins by a miracle.

Do not rejoice that the spirits submit to you, said Jesus Christ, *rejoice rather that your names are written in heaven* (Luke 10: 20).

If they will not listen either to Moses or to the prophets, they will not be convinced even if someone should rise from the dead (Luke 16: 31).

Nicodemus recognizes by his miracles that his doctrine is from God: *Scimus quia venisti a Deo magister, nemo enim potest facere quae tu facis nisi Deus fuerit cum illo.* [Rabbi, we know that you are a teacher who comes from God; for no one could perform the signs that you do unless God were with him (John 3: 2).] He does not judge miracles by doctrine, but doctrine by miracles.

The Jews, who were forbidden to believe in all performers of miracles, and furthermore were instructed to refer to the high priests and to follow what they said, had a doctrine of God, as we have one of Jesus Christ. And so all the reasons we have to refuse to believe in performers of miracles applied to them with regard to their prophets. However, they were very wrong to reject the prophets because of their miracles, and Jesus Christ, and would not have been blameworthy if they had not seen the miracles. *Nisi fecissem, peccatum non haberent.* [If I had not performed such works . . . they would be blameless (John 15: 24).]

All belief therefore rests on miracles.

———

Prophecy is not called miracle. As St John speaks of the first miracle at Cana, then of what Jesus Christ says to the Samaritan woman who reveals all her hidden life, and then heals the son of a noble. St John calls this *the second sign.* (John 2 and 4: 54.)

430 By pointing out truth we make people believe it. But by pointing out the injustice of ministers we do not correct it. A good conscience is preserved by pointing out falsehood; no money is made by pointing out injustice.

———

Miracles and truth are necessary because the whole human being must be convinced, body and soul.

———

Charity is not a figurative precept. It is horrible to say that Jesus Christ, who came to remove figures and replace them with truth, only came to erect the figure of charity where its reality previously stood.

If, then, the light inside you is darkness, what darkness that will be! (Matt. 6: 23).

431 There is a great difference between tempting and leading into error. God tempts but does not lead into error. To tempt is to instigate opportunities in which, under no compulsion, if we do not love God, we do a certain thing. To lead into error is to compel a man to connive in and follow a falsehood.

432 *Si tu es Christus, dic nobis.*
Opera quae ego facio IN NOMINE PATRIS MEI,

Haec testimonium perhibent de me.
Sed vos non creditis, quia non estis ex ovibus meis.
Oves meae vocem meam audiunt.

[If you are the Christ, tell us plainly. The works I do in my Father's name are my witness: but you do not believe, because you are no sheep of mine. The sheep that belong to me listen to my voice (John 10: 24).]

John 6: 30: *Quod ergo tu facis signum, ut videamus et credamus tibi. Non dicunt: quam doctrinam praedicas?** [What sign will you give to show us that we should believe in you? They do not say: what doctrine do you preach?]

———

Nemo potest facere signa quae tu facis, nisi Deus fuerit cum illo. [For no man could perform the signs that you do unless God were with him (John 3: 2).]

2 Macc. 14: 15: *Deus qui signis evidentibus suam portionem protegit.* [God who had established his people for ever and had never failed to support his own heritage by his direct intervention.]

———

Volumus signum videre, DE CAELO TENTANTES eum. Luke 11: 16. [Others asked him, as a test, for a sign from heaven.]

Generatio prava signum quaerit, et non dabitur. [It is an evil and unfaithful generation that asks for a sign! The only sign it will be given is the sign of the prophet Jonah (Matt. 12: 39).]

Et ingemiscens ait: quid generatio ista signum quaerit? Mark 8: 12. [And with a sigh that came straight from his heart he said, 'Why does this generation demand a sign?'] They asked for a sign with evil intention.

Et non poterat facere. [And he could work no miracle there (Mark 6: 5).] And nevertheless he promises them the sign of Jonas, the great and incomparable sign of his resurrection.

———

Nisi videritis signa, non creditis. [So you will not believe unless you see signs and portents! (John 4: 48).] He does not blame them for not believing unless there are miracles, but for not believing unless they see them themselves.

———

The Antichrist: *in signis mendacibus* [a deceptive show of signs and portents], says St Paul, 2 *Thess.* 2. *Secundum operationem Satanae. In seductione iis qui pereunt eo quod charitatem veritatis non receperunt ut salvi fierent. Ideo mittet illis Deus operationes erroris ut credant mendacio.* [Satan will set to work . . . and everything evil that can deceive those who are bound for destruction because they would not grasp the love of the truth which could have saved them . . . The reason why God is sending a power to delude them and make them believe what is untrue.] As in the passage of Moses: *Tentat enim vos Deus utrum diligatis eum.* [Yahweh your God is testing you to know if you love Yahweh your God (Deut. 13: 3).]

———

Ecce praedixi vobis. Vos ergo videte. [There; I have forewarned you. So stay awake (Matt. 24: 25, 42).]

XXXII. MIRACLES 3

443 The five propositions condemned, no miracle. For the truth was not attacked. But the Sorbonne, the bull . . .*

———

It is impossible for those who love God with all their hearts not to recognize the Church, so evident is it.

It is impossible for those who do not love God to be convinced of the Church.

———

Miracles carry such strength that God had to warn people not to think about them in opposition to him. It is so clear that there is a God. Otherwise they might have been capable of causing trouble.

And so these passages, *Deuteronomy, 13*, are so far from diminishing the authority of miracles that nothing could further underline their power. And the same for the Antichrist: *Enough to deceive even the chosen; if that were possible* (Matt. 24: 24).

444 *Atheists*. What reason have they for saying that one cannot rise from the dead? Which is more difficult: to be born or to rise

from the dead? That what has never been should be, or that what has once been still is? Is it more difficult to come into being than to come back? Habit makes us find one easy, lack of habit makes the other impossible. A way of judging which belongs to the crowd!

———

Why can a virgin not bear a child? Does not a hen produce eggs without a cock? What distinguishes them on the outside from the others, and who told us that a hen cannot create the seed of an egg as well as the cock?

———

There is such disproportion between someone's imagined merit and their stupidity, that it is unbelievable how far they misjudge themselves.

———

After so many signs of piety they still endure persecution, which is the surest sign of piety.

445 It is a good thing that they should commit injustices, for fear of allowing the Molinists* to seem to have acted justly. And so they must not be spared, they are worthy of committing them.

———

Pyrrhonist for obstinate.

———

Descartes useless and uncertain.

———

Nobody uses the word courtier apart from those who are not, nor pedant if they are not, nor provincial if they are not. And I would be willing to bet that it was the printer who put the word into the title of *Letters to a provincial*.

———

Thoughts. In omnibus requiem quae sivi. [Among all these I searched for rest (Eccles. 24: 7).]

If our condition were truly happy we would not have to take our minds off thinking about it in order to make ourselves happy.

———

All men's efforts are spent in pursuing their own possessions. And they cannot justly claim to possess them, nor have they the strength to secure their possession. It is the same with knowledge, and pleasures. We have neither truth nor the possessions.

———

Miracle. This is an effect which exceeds the natural power of the means employed. And non-miracle is an effect which does not exceed the natural power of the means employed. So those who heal by invoking the devil are not performing a miracle, for it does not exceed the natural power of the devil. But . . .

448 The three signs of religion: perpetuity, a holy life, miracles. They destroy perpetuity by probability, a holy life by their morality, miracles by destroying either their truth or their importance. If we believe them, the Church will have no use for perpetuity, holiness, and miracles.

———

In the same way heretics, too, deny them or deny their importance. But we would have to have no sincerity if we denied them, or have taken leave of our senses if we denied their importance.

———

Religion is adapted to all sorts of minds. The first stop simply at its establishment, and this religion is such that its establishment alone is enough to prove its truth. Others go as far as the apostles. The most learned go as far back as the beginning of the world. Angels see it even better and from an even greater distance.

———

My God, these are stupid arguments: would God have made the world in order to damn it? Would he ask so much of such weak people? etc. Pyrrhonism is the cure for this illness and will break down their vanity.

———

COMMINUENTES COR [Humbling my heart. (Acts 21: 13)]; St Paul: this is the Christian character. ALBE VOUS A NOMMÉ, JE NE VOUS CONNAIS PLUS [Alba has nominated you, I no longer know you], Corneille* (*Horace*, II. iii); this is the character of inhumanity. The character of humanity is the opposite.

———

No one has ever had himself martyred for miracles which he claimed to have seen; for, in the case of those which the Turks believe by tradition, man's folly goes perhaps as far as martyrdom, but not for those which have in fact been seen.

Jansenists resemble heretics in the reformation of their behaviour, but you resemble them in evil.

Those who wrote that in Latin speak French.

The harm having been done by putting these things in French, good should have been done by condemning them.

There is only one heresy which is explained differently in the schools and in the world.

449 Miracles distinguish between things in which there is doubt: between Jewish and heathen people, Jews and Christians, Catholics and heretics, the slandered and the slanderers, between the two crosses.*

But miracles would be useless to the heretics, for the Church, given authority by the miracles which have exercised our belief, tells us that they do not have the true faith. There is no doubt that they do not belong, since the Church's first miracles preclude faith in theirs. So miracle is set against miracle. The first and the greatest are on the Church's side.

These women, astonished at being told that they are on the path to perdition, that their confessors are leading them to Geneva, implanting the idea that Jesus Christ is not present in the Eucharist nor on the right hand of the Father, know all that to be false. They therefore offer themselves to God in this way: *Vide si via iniquitatis in me est.* [Make sure I do not follow pernicious ways (Ps. 139: 24).] What happens thereafter? This place which is said to be the devil's temple God makes his own temple; it is said that the children must be taken away, God heals them there; it is said to be the arsenal of hell, God makes it the sanctuary of his grace; finally they are threatened with all the anger and vengeance of heaven, and God overwhelms them with his favours. One would have to have taken leave of one's senses to conclude that they are therefore on the path to perdition.

No doubt we have the same signs as St Athanasius.*

450*The stupid idea that you have of your Society's importance has set you on these horrible paths. It is quite obvious that this is what made you employ slander, since you blame my slightest deceptions as being atrocious while you excuse them in yourselves, because you regard me as an individual and yourselves as the IMAGO.

It is obvious that what you praise are the follies of the foolish, like the privilege of not being damned.

Is it an encouragement to your children to condemn them when they serve the Church?

––––––

It is a device of the devil for diverting somewhere else the arms with which these people* would attack heresies.

––––––

You are bad politicians.

––––––

Pyrrhonism. Everything here is true in part, false in part. The essential truth is not like that, it is wholly pure and wholly true. This mixture dishonours and destroys it. Nothing is purely true, and so nothing is true in the sense of pure truth. You will say that it is true that murder is wrong. Yes, for we know what is evil and false very well. But what will be said to be good? Chastity? I say not, for the world would come to an end. Marriage? No, continence is better. Not to kill? No, for there would be appalling disorder, and the wicked would kill all the good. To kill? No, for that destroys nature. We have the true and the good only in part, mixed up with the bad and the false.

––––––

The story of the man born blind.

––––––

What does St Paul say? Does he constantly refer to the prophecies? No, but to his miracle.*

––––––

What does Jesus Christ say? Does he refer to the prophecies?
No. His death had not yet fulfilled them. But he says: *Si non
fecissem.* [If I had not performed such works . . . (John 15:
24).] *Believe in the work I do* (John 10: 38).

———

Two supernatural foundations of our wholly supernatural religion: one visible, the other invisible.

Miracles with grace, miracles without grace.

The synagogue, which has been treated with love as a figure
of the Church and with hatred because it was only a figure, was
restored when it was about to collapse, when its standing with
God was good, and was in this way a figure.

———

Miracles prove the power God has over our hearts by that
which he exercises over our bodies.

The Church has never approved a miracle amongst the
heretics.

———

Miracles, mainstay of religion. They distinguished the Jews.
They have distinguished Christians, saints, the innocent, the
true believers.

———

A miracle amongst the schismatics is not so much to be feared.
For the schism, which is more visible than the miracle, is an
obvious sign of their error. But when there is no schism
and the error is disputed, the miracle distinguishes between
them.

———

Si non fecissem quae alter no fecit. [If I had not performed such
works among them as no one else has ever done (John 15: 24).]

———

These unhappy people who have made us talk of miracles.

———

Abraham, Gideon.*
Confirm faith by miracles.

———

Judith: God speaks at last during the final oppressions.

———

If the cooling off of charity leaves the Church almost without *true worshippers*, miracles will rousc them. They are the ultimate efforts of grace.

If there were a miracle among the Jesuits.

When a miracle confounds the expectation of those in whose presence it occurs, and there is a discrepancy between the state of their faith and the nature of the miracle, then it should induce them to change, but, etc. Otherwise there would be as much reason for saying that if the Eucharist brought a dead man to life you would have to become a Calvinist rather than remain a Catholic. But when it crowns their expectations, and those who hoped that God would bless the remedies see themselves cured without remedies . . .

———

Unbelievers.

No sign has ever occurred on the devil's side without a more powerful one on God's side. Not, at least, without it having been foretold that it would happen.

SERIES
XXXIII

454*Montaigne is wrong: custom only has to be followed because it is custom, not because it is reasonable or just. But people follow it for the sole reason that they think it just. Otherwise they would not follow it any more, even though it were custom. For we only want to be subject to reason or justice. Without that, custom would be seen as tyranny, but the rule of reason and justice is no more tyrannical than that of pleasure. These are naturally human principles.

It would therefore be a good thing if the laws and customs were obeyed because they were laws, that we knew that there were no true and just law to be introduced, that we know nothing about it, and that therefore we should follow only those already accepted: this way we would never waver from them. But the people are not open to this doctrine. And so, as they believe that truth can be found and that it lies in laws and customs, they believe them and take their antiquity as a proof of their truth (and not simply of their authority, without truth). So they obey them, but are likely to revolt as soon as they are shown to be worthless, which can be shown of all laws and customs when looked at from a certain point of view.

Evil is easy, it appears in countless ways: good is almost unique. But a certain kind of evil is as difficult to find as what is called good, and often this particular evil is passed off as good in this way. It even takes as extraordinary a greatness of soul to achieve it as it does to achieve good.

We take examples to prove other things, and if we wanted to prove the examples we would take the other things to be their examples.

For, as we always think the difficulty lies in what we want to prove, we find clearer and more helpful examples to demonstrate it. So when we want to prove a general fact, we must give the particular rule for a case. But if we want to prove a particular case, we have to begin with the particular rule. For we always find the thing we want to prove obscure, and clear what we use to prove it. For when we put forward something to be proved, we are initially convinced that it is therefore obscure, whereas the thing that is to prove it is clear, and so we understand it easily.

I do not take well to such civilities as: 'I've given you a lot of trouble. I'm afraid of troubling you. I'm afraid it might take too long.' One is either persuasive or irritating.

How difficult it is to offer something of another's judgement without affecting his judgement by the way we do it. If you say: 'I think it's wonderful, I think it's obscure,' or something of that sort, you either influence his imagination to agree with you, or you irritate it to go in the other direction. It is better to say nothing, and then he judges it the way it stands, that is, what it is then and according to how the other circumstances over which we have no control could have affected it. But at least we will not have added anything. That is, unless our silence has some effect, according to the twist or interpretation someone may be inclined to give it, or according to what they guessed from our movements and facial expression, or tone of voice, depending on how good they are at judging faces. It is so difficult not to knock a judgement off its natural foundation, or rather, there are so few of these which are firm and stable.

455 Our entire reasoning comes down to surrendering to feeling.

———

But fantasy is like and not like feeling, so that we cannot distinguish between these opposites. One person says my feeling is fantasy, another that his fantasy is feeling. We need a rule. Reason is available, but it is pliable in any direction.

And so there is no rule.

456 These things which so concern us, like hiding the few possessions we have, often amount to practically nothing. They are a void which our imagination transforms into a mountain: a different turn of the imagination makes us easily discover it.

457 *Pyrrhonism*. I will write down my thoughts here in no order, but not perhaps in aimless confusion. It is the true order and will still show my aim by its very disorder.

I would be deferring too much to my subject if I treated it in an orderly way, since I want to show that the subject does not admit of order.

———

We imagine Plato and Aristotle only in long pedants' gowns. They were upright people like everyone else, laughing with their friends. And when they were amusing themselves by writing their *Laws* and their *Politics* they did it light-heartedly. It was the least philosophical and serious part of their lives, the most philosophical part being to live simply and calmly. If they wrote about politics, it was as if to provide rules for a madhouse. And if they pretended to treat it as something important, it is because they knew the madmen they were talking to thought they were kings and emperors. They connived with their delusions in order to restrain their madness to as mild a form as possible.

———

Those who judge a work without a rule of measurement stand in relation to others as do those with a watch to others without.

One man says: 'Two hours ago.' Another says: 'Only three-quarters of an hour ago.' I look at my watch and say to the first: 'You are bored,' and to the other: 'You hardly notice the time passing, because it has been an hour and a half.' And I dismiss people who say that I find time passing slowly and that I judge it whimsically.

They do not know that I am judging it by my watch.

There are some vices which only have a grip on us through other ones, and which, when we take the trunk away, are dispersed like the branches.

458 God and the apostles, foreseeing that the seeds of pride would give birth to heresies, and not wishing to give them the occasion to arise from the actual words, put into Scripture and the prayers of the Church the opposite words and seeds to bear their fruit in due season.

In the same way he gives charity to morality to bear fruit against concupiscence.

_____

When wickedness has reason on its side, it becomes proud, and shows off reason in all its lustre.

_____

When austerity or stern choice has not succeeded in achieving true good and we have to go back to following nature, it becomes proud of this reversal.

_____

The man who knows what his master wants will receive a greater thrashing because of what he can do with that knowledge (Luke 12: 47). *Qui justus est justificetur adhuc* [Let those who are holy continue to be holy (Rev. 22: 11)], because of the power justice gives him.

To him who has been given most, the strictest account will be demanded because of the power he has with that help.

There is a universal and essential difference between acts of will and all others.

_____

The will is one of the principal organs of belief, not because it creates belief, but because things are true or false according to the aspect by which we judge them. The will, which prefers one aspect to another, turns the mind away from contemplating the qualities of the one it does not wish to see. Thus the mind, in step with the will, keeps looking at the aspect the will likes, and so judges it by what it sees there.*

_____

All the good maxims exist in the world: we only fail to apply them.

For example, no one doubts that they should risk their life to defend the common good, and many do so, but not for religion.

_____

Inequality must necessarily exist between men. That is true, but having granted it, the door is open not only to the most overt domination but also to the most overt tyranny.

The mind must be relaxed a little, but that opens the door to the greatest excesses.

Let us set out the limits. There are no boundaries in things: laws want to impose some, and the mind cannot withstand it.

461 *Pray not to be put to the test* (Luke 22: 40). It is dangerous to be tempted. And those who are, are tempted because they do not pray.

_____

Et tu conversus confirma fratres tuos. [And once you are recovered, you in your turn must strengthen your brothers (Luke 22: 32).] But previously, *conversus Jesus respexit Petrum* [the Lord turned and looked straight at Peter (Luke 22: 61)].

_____

St Peter asks permission to strike Malchus, and strikes before hearing the answer. And Jesus Christ answers afterwards. (See Luke 22: 48–51.)

_____

The word GALILEE which the crowd of the Jews spoke as if by chance, accusing Jesus Christ before Pilate, gave Pilate a reason to send Jesus Christ to excuse Herod. In this way the mystery was accomplished by which he was to be judged by the Jews and the Gentiles. What was apparently fortuitous was the cause of the accomplishment of the mystery.

_____

The imagination enlarges small objects, exaggerating their significance by fantasy until they fill our souls, and with reckless insolence cuts down great things to its own size, as when speaking of God.

———

Lustravit lampade terras. [He lit the earth with his lamp (*Odyssey*, xviii. 136, quoted in Latin by Montaigne, *The Essays*, ii. 12).] The weather and my mood have little in common: I have my fogs and fine weather inside me. Whether my affairs themselves go well or badly has little to do with it. I sometimes struggle of my own accord against fortune: the achievement of mastering it makes me do so cheerfully, whereas I sometimes appear disgusted when fortune shines.

462 Write against those who delve too deeply into the disciplines. Descartes.

463 Power is the mistress of the world, not opinion.* But it is opinion which exploits power.

It is power that makes opinion. Weakness is estimable, in our opinion. Why? Because whoever wants to dance on the tightrope will be on his own.* And I will gather together a stronger group of people who will say that it is not estimable.

465 Languages are ciphers in which letters are not changed into letters, but words into words. So an unknown language is decipherable.

———

Diversity is so great that all the tones of voice, ways of walking, coughing, blowing one's nose, sneezing (are different). We distinguish grapes from among fruits, then from them muscat grapes, and then those from Condrieu, and then those from Desargues,* and then the particular graft. Is that all? Has it ever produced two bunches the same? And has a bunch produced two grapes the same? And so on.

I have never judged something in exactly the same way. I cannot judge a work while doing it: I have to do as painters do, and stand back, but not too far. How far then? Guess.

477 A miracle, we say, would strengthen my belief. We say so when we do not see one. The reasons, seen from far off, seem

to restrict our view, but when we have reached there we begin to see even further: nothing stops the giddiness of our intellects. There is no rule, we say, to which there is no exception, nor any truth so general that does not lack something. It is enough that it should not be absolutely universal to allow us to apply the exception to the subject in hand and to say: this is not always true, so there are cases when it is not. It only remains to show that this is one of them. And in that case we are very clumsy or very unlucky if we do not find some dodge.

479 Two contrary reasons. We must begin with that: without it we understand nothing, and everything is heretical. And even at the end of each truth, we must add that we are remembering the opposite truth.

480 If we had to do nothing except what was certain, we should do nothing for religion, for it is not certain. But how many things we do that are uncertain: sea voyages, battles! So I say we ought to do nothing at all, for nothing is certain, and there is more certainty in religion than that we will see the light tomorrow.

For it is not certain that we shall see tomorrow, but it is certainly possible that we shall not. We cannot say the same about religion. It is not certain that it exists, but who will dare to say that it is certainly possible that it does not? Now when we work for tomorrow, and the uncertain, we are acting reasonably.

_____

For we ought to work for the uncertain, according to the laws of probability, which are conclusive.

_____

St Augustine saw that we take chances with the uncertain: at sea, in battle, etc., but he did not see the law of probabilities which proves that we ought to. Montaigne saw that we are offended by a lame mind and that anyone can achieve everything, but he did not see the reason for this.

All these people have seen the effects but have not seen the causes. They are on the same level as those who have discovered the causes, like those who have only eyes compared with those who have minds: for the effects can be felt by the senses, and the causes are perceived only by the mind. And although these effects can be seen by the mind, this mind bears the same relationship to the mind which sees the causes as the relationship of the bodily senses to the mind.

481 Eloquence is a painting of thought. And so those who, having finished a likeness, add still more to it are producing a picture instead of a portrait.

486 There is a certain model of attractiveness and beauty which exists in a certain relation between our nature, weak or strong, whichever it is, and the thing we find attractive.

Everything which conforms to this model attracts us: whether it be a house, a song, speech, verse, prose, a woman, birds, rivers, trees, rooms, clothes, etc.

Everything which does not conform to this model displeases those who have good taste.

And, just as there is an exact relationship between a song and a house based on this good model, because both resemble this single model, though each in its own way, so, there is in the same way an exact relation between things based on a bad model. It is not that the bad model is unique, for there are innumerable ones. But each bad sonnet, for example, whatever false model it is based on, is exactly like a woman dressed in accordance with that model.

Nothing gives a better idea of how absurd a false sonnet is than to consider its nature and model, and then to picture a woman or a house based on that same model.

Poetic beauty. Just as we talk of poetic beauty, we also ought to talk of mathematical beauty and medicinal beauty. But we do not, and the reason why is that we know very well what the object of mathematics is, and that it consists in proofs, and what the object of medicine is, that is, cure. But we do not know what constitutes the attraction which is the object of poetry. We do not know what this natural model is that we must imitate, and for want of this knowledge we have invented certain bizarre terms: 'golden age', 'marvel of our times', 'fatal', etc. And we call this jargon poetic beauty.

But anyone trying to imagine a woman on that model, which consists in saying trivial things in big words, will see a pretty girl covered in mirrors and chains, which will make him laugh, because we know more about where a woman's attractions lie than where verse's attractions do. But people who are not connoisseurs would admire her in that get-up, and there are many villages where she would be taken for the queen. That is why we call sonnets on this model 'village queens'.

———

No one is widely accepted as a connoisseur of poetry unless he displays the badge of a poet, mathematician, etc. But universal people want no such badge and make scarcely any distinction between the expertise of a poet and an embroiderer.

Universal people are not called poets or mathematicians, etc. But they are all these things and make judgements about them all. No one could guess what they are. They will discuss whatever was being discussed before they came in. No one quality is more noticeable in them than another, until such time as it becomes necessary to employ it. But then we remember it. For it is equally characteristic that they are not described as good speakers when no question of language arises, but they are spoken of in that vein when it does.

It is, therefore, false praise to say of someone when he enters that he is very knowledgeable about poetry. And it is a bad sign when a man is not called upon when opinions are being sought about verses.

487 Faith is a gift of God. Do not think that we said it was a gift of reasoning. The other religions do not say that of their faith; they gave only reasoning to arrive at it, and nevertheless it does not lead there.*

XXXIV

494 The self is hateful.* You cover it up, Mitton, you do not take it away for all that: you are therefore still hateful.

'Not at all. For by behaving obligingly as we do towards everyone, people have no more cause to hate us.' That is true, if only we hated in the self the unpleasantness it causes us.

But if I hate it because it is unjust, because it makes itself the centre of everything, I will always hate it.

In a word, the self has two characteristics: it is unjust in itself, in that it makes itself the centre of everything; it is a nuisance to others, in that it wants to assert itself over them, for each self is the enemy, and would like to be tyrant to all the others. You take away the nuisance, but not the injustice.

And so you do not make it pleasing to those who hate its injustice. You make it pleasing only to the unjust, who no longer see it as their enemy. And so you remain unjust, and can please only unjust people.

495 What spoils it for us in comparing what happened within the Church in former times with what happens now is that usually we regard St Athanasius, St Theresa, and the others as crowned with glory and <. . .> judged almost divine before our time. Now that time has clarified things, that seems to be the case. But at the time when they were being persecuted this great saint was a man called Athanasius, and St Theresa a mad-woman. Elias was a man like us, subject to the same passions as us, as St Peter says (in fact, James 5: 17) to rid Christians of the false idea which makes us reject the example of the saints as bearing no relation to our state: they were saints, we say, not like us. So what happened then? St Athanasius was a man called Athanasius, accused of several crimes, condemned by such and such a council for such and such a crime: all the bishops are in agreement, and eventually the Pope. What is said to those who dissent? That they are disturbing the peace, causing schism, etc.

Zeal, light. Four sorts of person: zeal without knowledge, knowledge without zeal, neither knowledge nor zeal, both zeal and knowledge.

The first three condemn him, the last absolve him and are excommunicated from the Church, but nevertheless save the Church.

496 But is it probable that probability brings certainty?

Difference between tranquillity and peace of conscience. Nothing apart from truth brings certainty. Nothing apart from the sincere quest for truth brings tranquillity.

497 The corruption of reason can be seen in so many different and extravagant customs. Truth had to appear so that man should stop living for himself.

498 Casuists* submit decisions to corrupted reason and the choice of decisions to corrupted will, so that everything which is corrupt in man's nature takes part in his conduct.

499 You want the Church to judge neither the interior, because that belongs only to God, nor the exterior, because God is concerned only with the interior. And so, removing from him all choice of human beings, you keep within the Church the most dissipated, and those who so enormously dishonour it that the Jewish synagogues and the philosophical sects would have expelled them as unbelievers.

500 Anyone who wants can be ordained a priest, as under Jeroboam (3 Kgs. 12: 31).

It is an appalling thing that the discipline of the Church today is represented to us as so excellent, that to want to change it is treated as a crime. In former times it was infallibly excellent, and we find that it could be changed without committing a sin. But now, such as it is at present, can we not even want to see it changed?

It has certainly been allowed to change the custom whereby a priest could only be ordained with such circumspection that scarcely any were worthy of it. And will it not be permitted to deplore the custom which produces so many unworthy ones?

—————

Abraham took nothing for himself, but only for his servants (Gen. 14: 12–14). In the same way the just person takes nothing for himself from the world or from the applause of the world, but only for their passions which they use as a master, saying to one: *Go*, and to another *Come* (Luke 7: 8). *Sub te erit appetitus tuus.* [(Is not sin at the door like a crouching beast hungering for you,) which you must master (Gen. 4: 7).] The passions dominated in this way become virtues: avarice, jealousy, anger, even God attributes them to himself; and they are just as much virtues as mercy, pity, constancy, which are also passions. They must be used like slaves and, given their nourishment, prevent the soul from feeding from it. For when the passions are in control they become vices, and then they give the soul their nourishment, and the soul feeds off it and is poisoned.

501 *Church, Pope. Unity/multiplicity.* Considering the Church as a unity, the Pope, who is its head, represents the whole. Considering it as a multiplicity, then the Pope is only a part. The Fathers considered it sometimes one way and sometimes the other, and so spoke of the Pope in different ways.

St Cyprian, SACERDOS DEI* [the priest of God].

But in establishing one of these two truths, they have not excluded the other. Multiplicity which is not reduced to unity is confusion. Unity which does not depend on multiplicity is tyranny.

———

France is now almost the only place where it is permissible to say that the council is above the Pope.*

502 We are full of needs. We only love those who can satisfy them all. He is a good mathematician, we will say, but I have no need of mathematics: he would take me for a proposition. He is a good soldier: he would take me for a place under siege. So what I need is an upright person,* who can adapt himself generally to all my needs.

———

A true friend is such a valuable thing, even for the greatest nobleman, so that he can speak well of them and uphold them even in their absence, that they ought to do all they can to acquire one. But they must choose carefully! For if they expend all their efforts on fools, it will be useless, whatever good they say about them; and even then they will not speak well of them, if they find themselves on the weaker side, for they have no authority, and thus will speak ill of them in order to keep in with the rest.

505 There can be no doubt that whether the soul is mortal or immortal ought to make the whole difference in ethics. And

yet philosophers have drawn up their ethics independently of this!*

———

They debate to pass the time.

———

Plato, to attract towards Christianity.

508 *Figurative.* Nothing is so like charity as cupidity,* and nothing is so contrary. And so the Jews, loaded with possessions which flatter their cupidity, were very like Christians, and just the opposite of them. In this way they had the two qualities which they had to have, to be very like the Messiah, in order to prefigure him, and very unlike, in order not to be suspect witnesses.

509 Concupiscence has beome natural for us and has become our second nature. There are therefore two natures in us: one good, the other bad. Where is God? Where you are not. And *The kingdom of God is within you* (Luke 17: 21; Louvain translation). Rabbis.

510 Whoever does not hate the self-love within him, and this instinct which leads him to make himself into God, is truly blind. Who cannot see that nothing is so contrary to justice and truth? For it is wrong that we deserve this, and unjust and impossible to achieve it, since everyone demands the same thing. It is therefore manifestly an unjustness in which we are born, which we cannot get rid of and which we must get rid of.

However no religion has observed that it was a sin, or that we were born in it, or that we are obliged to fight it, and no religion has thought of giving us the remedy, either.

511 If there is a God, we have to love only him and not transitory last creatures. The argument of the unbelievers in *Wisdom* is based solely on assuming that there is no God. 'That said,' they say, '*let us enjoy what good things there are*' (Wisd. 2: 6). That is the last resource. But if there were a God to love, he would have reached not this conclusion, but quite the opposite one. And the conclusion of the wise is: 'There is a God, let us not therefore delight in creatures.'

———

So everything which impels us to become attached to creatures is bad, since it prevents us either from serving God, if we know him, or from seeking him, if we do not know him. But we are full of concupiscence, and we are therefore full of evil, so we ought to hate ourselves and everything which incites us to any other attachment but God.

512 All their principles are true, the Pyrrhonists', the stoics', the atheists', etc. But their conclusions are wrong, because the contrary principles are also true.

513 Man is obviously made for thinking. It is his whole dignity and his whole merit, and his whole duty is to think as he ought. But the order of thought is to begin with oneself and with one's author and one's end.

But what does the world think about? Never about that! But about dancing, playing the lute, singing, writing verse, tilting at the ring, etc., about fighting, becoming king, without thinking about what it is to be a king or to be a human being.

514 Internal war in human beings between reason and passions.

If there were only reason without passions.

If there were only passions without reason.

But having both they cannot be without war, not being able to have peace with one without being at war with the other.

So they are always divided and in contradiction with themselves.

515 *Boredom*. Nothing is so intolerable for man as to be in a state of complete tranquillity, without passions, without business, without diversion, without effort. Then he feels his nothingness, his abandonment, his inadequacy, his dependence, his helplessness, his emptiness. At once from the depths of his soul arises boredom, gloom, sadness, grief, vexation, despair.

516 If it is a supernatural blindness to live without trying to find out what one is, it is a horrific blindness to live a bad life believing in God.

517 *Prophecies*. That Jesus Christ will be at his right hand while God subdues his enemies (Ps. 109: 1–2). Therefore he will not subdue them himself.

518 *Injustice.* That presumption should accompany wretchedness is an extreme injustice.

519 *Search for the true good.* The ordinary sort of man places his good in wealth and external possessions, or at least in diversion.

The philosophers have shown the vanity of all that and have placed it where they could.

520*Vanity is so anchored in the human heart that a soldier, a cadet, a cook, a kitchen porter boasts, and wants to have admirers, and even philosophers want them, and those who write against them want the prestige of having written well, and those who read them want the prestige of having read them, and I, writing this, perhaps have this desire, and those who will read this . . .

521 Of the desire to be esteemed by those in whose company one is.

———

Pride takes hold of us so naturally in the midst of all our wretchedness, errors, etc., that we even lose our lives joyfully, provided people talk about it.

———

Vanity: gaming, hunting, visits, theatre, false perpetuity of one's name.

522 The dual nature of humanity is so obvious that there are some who have thought we have two souls.

A simple being seeming to them to be incapable of such great and sudden variations: from boundless presumption to appalling dejection.*

523 Man's nature is: wholly nature. *Wholly animal.*

There is nothing that cannot be made natural. There is nothing natural that cannot be lost.

524 It is good to be weary and tired from the useless search for the true good, in order to stretch one's arms out to the Redeemer.

525 Human sensitivity to little things and insensitivity to the greatest things: sign of a strange disorder.

526 Despite the sight of all the wretchednesses which afflict us and hold us by the throat, we have an instinct which we cannot repress, which lifts us up.

527 The most important thing in our life is the choice of a career: chance decides it. Custom makes masons, soldiers, slaters. He is an excellent slater, they say. And speaking of soldiers: They are quite mad, they say. And others, on the contrary: There is nothing so great as war, the rest are all rogues. From hearing from our childhood on these careers praised, and all the others despised, we make our own choice. For naturally we love virtue and hate folly. These very words stir us, we only make a mistake in applying them. So great is the force of custom that, of those whom nature has merely made men, we make all conditions of men.

For in some places everyone is a mason, in others everyone a soldier, etc. Doubtless nature is not so uniform. It is therefore custom which does this, for it constrains nature. Sometimes nature overcomes it, and keeps us within our instincts, despite all customs, good or bad.

XXXV

529 *Quench the brand of sedition*: too flowery.

———

The restlessness of his genius: two bold words too many.

———

When we are well we wonder how we should manage if we were ill. When we are ill we happily take medicine: the illness takes care of that; we no longer have the passions and desires for distractions and outings prompted by good health, and which are incompatible with the demands of illness. Nature then prompts the passions and desires appropriate to our present state. It is only the fears that we inspire in ourselves, and not by nature, which disturb us, because they link the state in which we are with the passions of the state in which we are not.

———

Because nature always makes us unhappy in whatever state we are, our desires paint a happy state for us, because they link the state in which we are with the pleasures of the state in which we are not. And even if we did attain these pleasures, we would not thereby be happy, because we should have other desires appropriate to our new state.

This general proposition must be reduced to the particular.

___

If those people who are always optimistic when something is going wrong, and who rejoice when it turns out well, are not equally distressed by bad fortune, they are likely to be suspected of being pleased at its failure; they are delighted to find such excuses for hope as they can to show that they care, and to cover, by the joy they pretend to have, their real joy at seeing the affair fail.

___

Our nature consists in movement. Absolute stillness is death.

___

Mitton sees clearly that nature is corrupt and that mankind is opposed to integrity. But he does not know why it cannot fly higher.

___

Fine deeds kept secret are the most admirable. When I see some of them in history, such as on p. 184,* I am very pleased; but of course they were not entirely secret, because they have become known. And although everything possible was done to keep them secret, the little by which they have come to be known has spoiled everything. For the finest thing about them was wanting to keep them secret.

___

Can it be anything but the willingness of the world that makes you find things probable? Will you delude us into believing it is the truth, and that, if the fashion of duelling did not exist, you would find it probable that one could fight duels, looking at the thing in itself?

530 Justice is what is established. And so all our established laws will necessarily be held to be just without examination, since they are established.

531 *Feeling*. Memory, joy are feelings. And even mathematical propositions become feelings, for reason makes feelings natural and natural feelings are blotted out by reason.

532 *Honnête homme*.* We must be able to say of him, not that he is a mathematician, or a preacher, or eloquent, but that he is an upright man. This universal quality is the only one which pleases me. When on seeing a man it is his book we remember, that is a bad sign. I would like no quality to be noticed until we come up against it and there is the opportunity to make use of it, NE QUID NIMIS [nothing in excess], for fear of one quality predominating and being used as a label. Let us not think of him as a good speaker unless it is relevant to be a good speaker. But then we should think of him.

534 *Montaigne*. What is good in Montaigne can only be acquired with difficulty. What is bad in him, and I am not talking about his morals, could have been swiftly corrected if he had been warned that he was too long-winded and talked too much about himself.*

536 Memory is necessary for all the operations of reason.

When a natural style is used to depict a passion or an effect, we find within ourselves the truth of what we hear, which we did not know was there, with the result that we are inclined to like the person who made us feel it, for he has not pointed out what he possesses, but what we do. And thus this kindness makes him agreeable to us, not to mention that the understanding we have in common with him necessarily moves our heart to like him.

539 Speeches about humility are a matter of pride for those who care for reputation, and of humility for the humble. In the same way speeches about Pyrrhonism allow the positive to be positive. Few speak humbly of humility, chastely of chastity, doubtingly of Pyrrhonism. We are nothing but lies, duplicity, contradiction, and we hide and disguise ourselves from ourselves.

540 When I am writing down my thought it sometimes escapes me, but that reminds me of my weakness, which I am continually

forgetting. This teaches me as much as my forgotten thought, for I am only concerned with knowing my nothingness.

542 *Conversation.* Big words about religion: 'I deny it.'
Conversation. Pyrrhonism helps religion.

547 Anyone condemned by Escobar really will be condemned!
Eloquence. There must be both the pleasing and the real, but what is pleasing must itself be drawn from what is true.

All are everything to themselves, for once dead, everything is dead for them. Hence all think they are everything to everyone. We must not judge nature according to ourselves, but according to its own standards.

554 *Style.* When we see a natural style, we are quite astonished and delighted, for we were expecting to see an author and we find a person. Whereas those with good taste who think they will find a person when they see a book are quite surprised to find an author: PLUS POETICE QUAM HUMANE LOCUTUS ES. [You have spoken more as a poet than a man (Petronius. *Satyricon*, 90).] These people pay tribute to nature who show it that it can talk of anything, even theology.

555 The world must be truly blind, if it believes you.

556 The Pope hates and fears scholars who have not taken vows to obey him.

557 Man is neither angel nor beast, and unhappily whoever wants to act the angel, acts the beast.*

558 *Provincial Letters.* Those who love the Church complain that morals are being corrupted: but at least the laws survive. But these people corrupt the laws. The model is spoilt.

559 *Montaigne.* Montaignes's faults are great. Licentious words: that does not matter, despite Mademoiselle de Gournay.* Credulous: PEOPLE WITHOUT EYES. Ignorant: SQUARING THE CIRCLE, BIGGER WORLD. His views on deliberate homicide, on death. He inspires indifference about salvation, WITHOUT FEAR AND WITHOUT REPENTANCE. As his book was not written in order to inspire piety, he was not obliged to do so; but we are always obliged not to discourage it. We can excuse his rather

free and licentious opinions on some circumstances in his life—
730. 331—but we cannot excuse his completely pagan views on
death. For we must renounce all piety if we do not wish at least
to die as a Christian. But he only thinks of a cowardly and easy
death throughout his book.

560 I do not admire the excess of a virtue, like courage, unless I
see at the same time an excess of the opposite virtue, as in
Epaminondas, who possessed extreme courage and extreme
kindness (Montaigne, *The Essays*, iii. 1). Otherwise it is not to
rise up but to sink. We do not show greatness by being at one
extreme, but rather by touching both at once and filling all the
space in between.

But perhaps it is only a sudden movement of the soul from
one extreme to the other and that in fact it is only one point,
like the spark of a fire. Agreed, but at least that shows the
soul's agility, even if it does not show its range.

561 *Infinite movement.* Infinite movement, the point which fills everything, movement at rest, infinity without quantity, indivisible and infinite.

562 *Order.* Why should I decide to divide my ethics into four
rather than six? Why should I establish virtue in four rather
than two or one? Why as ABSTINE ET SUSTINE [abstain and
sustain] rather than FOLLOW NATURE,* or DISCHARGE YOUR PRI-
VATE BUSINESS WITHOUT INJUSTICE, like Plato, or anyone else?

But there you are, you will say, everything summed up in a
word. Yes, but that is no use unless you explain it. And when
you come to explain it, as soon as you delve into this precept
which contains all the others, they all come out in the initial
confusion you wanted to avoid. So when they are all enclosed
in one, they are hidden and useless, as if they were in a box,
and only ever appear in their natural confusion. Nature has
established them all without enclosing one inside the other.

563 *Order.* Nature has made all her truths self-contained. Our art
encloses some within others, but this is not natural. Each has
its own place.

564 *Glory.* Animals do not esteem each other. A horse does not
esteem its companion. That is not to say they will not race

against each other, but it is of no consequence, for in the stable the heavier and less prepossessing horse does not give up its oats to the other, as humans want others to do to them. Their own virtue is sufficient.

565 When they say that heat is only the movement of certain glob-ules and light the CONATUS RECEDENDI [centrifugal force] that we feel, we are amazed. What! is pleasure nothing more than a ballet of spirits? We had such a different idea of it! And these feelings seem so far removed from the ones we say are the same ones we compare them to! The feeling of fire, that heat which affects us in quite a different way from touch, the recep-tion of sound and light, all seem mysterious to us, and yet it is as down-to-earth as being hit by a stone. It is true that the smallness of the spirits entering the pores touch other nerves, but they are still nerves which have been touched.

566 I had spent a long time in the study of abstract sciences, and I had been put off them by realizing how little one could discuss them. When I began the study of humanity, I saw that these abstract sciences are not proper to humanity, and that I was moving further away from my condition by going into them than were others by being ignorant of them. I forgave others for knowing little about them. But I thought I would at least find many companions in the study of humanity, since it is the true study which is proper to mankind.* I was mistaken: there are even fewer who study it than mathematics. It is only be-cause they do not know how to study that subject that they research the rest. But is it not the case that this is still not the knowledge mankind ought to have, and that it is better for them not to know themselves in order to be happy?

567 What is the self?
A man who sits at the window to watch the passers-by; can I say that he sat there to see me if I pass by? No, for he is not thinking of me in particular. But someone who loves a person because of her beauty, does he love her? No, because smallpox, which will destroy beauty without destroying the person, will ensure that he no longer loves her.
And if someone loves me for my judgement, for my memory,

is it me they love? No, because I can lose these qualities without losing myself. Where is the self, then, if it is neither in the body nor in the soul? And how can you love the body or the soul except for its qualities, which do not make up the self, since they are perishable? For would we love the substance of a person's soul in the abstract, whatever qualities it contained? That is impossible, and would be unjust. Therefore we never love a person, only qualities.

So let us stop mocking people who are honoured for their appointments and offices. For we love no one except for his borrowed qualities.

568 It is not in Montaigne but in myself that I find everything I see there.*

569 *May God not impute our sins to us* (cf. Ps. 31: 2): that is to say, all the consequences and results of our sins, which are frightful, even of our slightest faults, if we want to follow them mercilessly.

570 *Pyrrhonism.* Pyrrhonism is the truth. For, after all, men before Jesus Christ did not know where they had got to, nor if they were great or small. And those who said one or the other knew nothing about it, and were guessing, irrationally and at random, and indeed they were always wrong by excluding one or the other.

Quod ergo ignorantes quaeritis, religio annuntiat vobis. [Adapted from Acts 17: 23: The God whom I proclaim is in fact the one whom you already worship without knowing it.]

571 *Montalte.** Lax opinions are so beloved of human beings that it is strange that theirs are not. It is because they have exceeded all limits. Moreover, many people see the truth and cannot attain it, but few do not know that the purity of religion is contrary to our corruptions. Ridiculous to say that an eternal reward is offered to Escobar's morals.

572 The easiest conditions to live in from the world's point of view are the most difficult from God's. On the other hand, nothing is so difficult from the world's point of view as the religious life, and nothing is easier than leading it from God's. Nothing

is easier than to have high office and great possessions, according to the world. Nothing is more difficult than to lead such a life in God's way without taking interest and pleasure in it.

573 *Order*. I could well have taken this discourse in an order like this, to show the vanity of all sorts of conditions: showing the vanity of ordinary lives, then the vanity of philosophical lives, Pyrrhonist and stoic ones. But the order would not have been kept. I know a bit about it, and how few people understand it. No human science can keep to it. St Thomas did not keep to it. Mathematics keeps to it, but it is useless as it is so profound.

574 Original sin is folly in men's eyes, but it is presented as such. You should not therefore reproach me for the lack of reason in this doctrine, since I present it as being without reason. But this folly is wiser than all men's wisdom, *sapientius est hominibus* [is wiser than human (wisdom) (1 Cor. 1: 25)]. For without it, what are we to say what man is? His whole state depends on this imperceptible point. And how could he have become aware of it through his reason, since it is something contrary to his reason, and his reason, very far from finding it out through its own ways, draws back when presented with it.

575 Let no one say that I have said nothing new: the arrangement of the material is new. When playing tennis, both players hit the same ball, but one of them places it better.

I would just as soon be told that I have used old words. As if the same thoughts did not form a different form of discourse by being differently arranged, just as the same words make different thoughts by being differently arranged.

576 Those who lead disordered lives say to those who lead ordered ones that it is they who stray from nature, and believe themselves to follow it; like those on board ship think people on shore are moving away. Language is the same on all sides. We need a fixed point to judge it. The harbour judges those on board ship. But where will we find a harbour in morals?

577 *Nature copies itself*. Nature copies itself: a seed cast on good ground bears fruit; a principle cast into a good mind bears fruit.

Numbers, which are so different by nature, copy space.

Everything is made and directed by the same master: the root, branches, fruit, principles, consequences.

When everything is moving at the same pace, nothing appears to be moving, as on board ship. When everyone is going in the direction of depravity, no one seems to be doing so: the one person who stops shows up the haste of the others, like a fixed point.

578 *Generals*. It is not enough for them to introduce such behaviour into our temples, TEMPLIS INDUCERE MORES. [To bring their customs into the temples.] Not only do they want to be tolerated in the Church, but, as if they had become the most powerful members, they want to drive out those who do not belong to them . . .

MOHATRA,* ONE IS NOT A THEOLOGIAN TO BE ASTONISHED BY IT.

Who could have told your generals that a time was so close that they would offer such behaviour to the universal Church and would call the rejection of this disorderly behaviour an act of war, TOT ET TANTA MALA PACEM [(they give) such massive ills the name of peace (Wisd. 14: 22)].

579 When we want to reprove someone usefully and show him that he is wrong, we have to see from what point of view he is approaching the matter, for it is usually correct from that point of view, and allow him that truth, but we must show him the point of view from which it is wrong. He will be content with that, for he will see that he was not wrong and only failed to see all sides of the matter. But we are not annoyed at not seeing everything, but we do not like to be wrong. Perhaps this comes from the fact that by nature we cannot see everything, nor by nature can we be wrong from the point of view we take up, as the perceptions of the senses are always right.

580 Movements of grace, hardness of heart, external circumstances.

581 *Grace*. Rom. 3: 27: glory excluded. *By what law? By works? No, but by faith.* Faith is therefore not in our power as are the works of the Law, and it is given to us in another way.

584 *Binding and loosing*. God did not want to allow absolution
without the Church: as it is involved in the offence, he wants
it to be involved in the pardon. He associates it with this
power, as do kings their parliaments. But if it absolves or binds
without God, it is no longer the Church. The same with parliament: for while the king may have pardoned someone, it
must be registered; but if parliament registers without the king
or if it refuses to register on the king's orders, it is no longer
the king's parliament, but a rebellious body.

585 They cannot have perpetuity, yet they seek universality. For
that they make the whole Church corrupt, so that they can be
saints.

586 *Popes*. Kings control their empire, but popes cannot control
theirs.

587 We know ourselves so little that many people think they are
about to die when they are quite healthy, and many people
think they are quite healthy when they are close to death, not
aware of their approaching fever or the abscess ready to form.

588 *Language*. The mind must not be distracted elsewhere except
for relaxation, and at a time when that is appropriate: to relax
it when necessary and not otherwise. For if it relaxes at the
wrong time, it becomes weary; and if it becomes weary at the
wrong time, it relaxes and we give everything up. Malicious
concupiscence takes such delight in producing quite the opposite of what people want to obtain from us without giving us
any pleasure, which is that for which we barter everything that
people want.

589 *Strength*. Why do we follow the majority? Is it because they are
more right? No, but stronger.
     Why do we follow ancient laws and ancient opinions? Are
they the soundest? No, but they are unique, and remove the
roots of disagreement.

590 Someone told me one day that he felt great joy and confidence
when he had come from confession. Another told me that he
was still afraid. I reflected that one good man could be made
from putting those two together, and that each one was lacking

by not having the feelings of the other. The same thing often happens in other situations.

591 It is not absolution by itself which remits sins in the sacrament of penance, but contrition, which is not authentic unless it seeks the sacrament.

In the same way it is not the nuptial benediction which takes away the sin from procreation, but the desire to procreate children for God, which is genuine only in marriage.

And as a contrite person without the sacrament is more fit to receive absolution than an impenitent one with the sacrament, so the daughters of Lot, for example, who wanted only to have children, were purer without marriage than married people with no desire for children.*

XXXVI

617 When we are accustomed to using the wrong reasons to prove effects of nature, we no longer want to accept the right ones, when they have been discovered. The example given was about the circulation of the blood, to explain why the vein swells below the ligature.

We are more easily convinced, usually, by reasons we have found by ourselves than by those which have occurred to others.

Liancourt's story about the pike and the frog: they always behave like this, and never otherwise, nor any other sign of intellect.*

Truth is so darkened nowadays, and lies so established, that unless we love the truth we will never know it.*

Weak people are those who know the truth, but who maintain it only as far as it is in their interest to do so. Beyond that, they abandon it.

The adding machine produces effects which are closer to thought than anything done by animals. But it does nothing to justify the assertion that it has a will, like animals.

Even when people's interests are not affected by what they say, we must not definitely conclude from this that they are not lying. For there are people who lie simply for the sake of lying.

_____

There is pleasure to be on board a ship battered by a storm, when we are certain that it will not perish: the persecutions buffeting the Church are of this kind.

618   When we do not know the truth about something, it is a good thing that there should be a common error on which people can concentrate their minds, such as the moon, for example, to which we attribute the changing of the seasons, the progress of illnesses, etc. For mankind's chief malady is its uneasy curiosity about things it cannot know. And it is not so bad for it to be wrong as so vainly curious.

_____

The style of writing of Epictetus, Montaigne, and Salomon de Tultie* is the commonest, which is most persuasive, which stays longer in the memory, and which is most often quoted, because it is entirely composed of thoughts born out of ordinary, everyday conversations; as, when people speak of the commonly accepted error that the moon is the cause of everything, they never fail to say that Salomon de Tultie says such and such; when they do not know the truth about something, it is a good thing that there should be some common error, etc., which is the thought of the other side.

622   How disordered is the judgement by which no one puts himself above the rest of the world, or prefers his own good and the duration of his happiness and his survival to that of all the rest of the world!

_____

Cromwell was about to ravage all of Christendom, the royal family was lost, and his own set to be ever-powerful, but for a little grain of sand which lodged in his bladder. Even Rome was about to tremble beneath him. But once this little piece of gravel was there, he died, his family fell into disgrace, peace reigned, and the king was restored.

————

Those who are accustomed to judge by feeling understand nothing about things which involve reasoning. For to start with they want to get to the heart of things at a glance and are not accustomed to look for principles. The others, on the contrary, who are accustomed to reason from principles, understand nothing about things which involve feelings, since they search for principles and are unable to see at a glance.

————

Two sorts of people make everything the same, like holidays and working days, Christians and priests, all the sins between one another, etc. And from this some people conclude that what is bad for priests is also bad for Christians, and the others that what is not bad for Christians is permissible for priests.

626 *Thought*. All mankind's dignity consists in thought. But what is this thought? How foolish it is!

Thought, therefore, is an admirable and incomparable thing by its very nature. It must have had strange faults to have become contemptible. But it does have such faults that nothing is more ridiculous. How great it is by its nature, how lowly it is by its faults.

Draining away. It is a horrible thing to feel that all that we possess is draining away.

627 *Light, darkness*. There would be too much darkness if truth did not have some visible signs. One such admirable sign is that it has always resided in a visible Church and congregation. There would be too much light if there were only one feeling in this Church. That which has always existed is the true one. For the true one has always been there, and no false one has always been there.

628 Thought constitutes the greatness of mankind.

630*All the principal kinds of entertainment are dangerous for Christian life. But among all those which the world has invented there is none more to be feared than the theatre. It gives us such a natural and delicate representation of the passions that it arouses and engenders them in our hearts, especially that of love, mainly when it is represented as very chaste and very virtuous, for the more innocent it seems to innocent souls, the more liable they are to be moved by it. Its violence flatters our self-esteem, which at once forms a desire to produce the same effects that we see so well staged. And at the same time our conscience is conditioned by the propriety of the feelings that we see there, which remove the fear from pure souls, who imagine that it does not offend the purity of loving with a love which seems to them to be so clear-sighted.

And so we go from the theatre with our hearts so full of the beauty and sweetness of love, and our souls and minds so convinced of its innocence, that we are quite prepared to receive our first impressions, or rather to look for the opportunity of arousing them in someone else's heart, so that we may receive the same pleasure and the same sacrifices that we have seen so well portrayed in the theatre.

XXXVII

637 Nothing appeals to us except the contest; not the victory.

We like to watch animals fighting, not the victor tearing into the vanquished. What did we want to see, if not the final moment of victory? And when it comes we are sickened by it. It is the same with gaming, the same with the pursuit of truth: we like to see the clash of opinions in an argument, but not at all to contemplate the truth when it is found. For it to be enjoyed, it must be seen to arise from the argument. Similarly with the passions there is pleasure to be had in seeing two opposites collide, but when one overwhelms the other, it becomes simple brutality. We never seek such things themselves, only the pursuit of them. And so it is in the theatre that happy, unclouded scenes are ineffective, as are those of extreme and hopeless misery, and brutish love affairs, and harsh cruelties.

643 People are not taught how to be upright, yet they are taught all the rest. And they are never so proud of knowing anything else

as they are of being upright. They are only proud of knowing the one thing they have never learned.

Children who are frightened of the face they have scribbled are just children. But what is the way of making someone as weak as a child become strong indeed as an adult? We have to change only our imagination. Everything that improves progressively also declines progressively. Nothing that was ever weak can ever be absolutely strong. It is no good saying: 'He has grown up, he has changed'; he is still the same.

644*Preface to the first part*. Discuss those who have written about self-knowledge; Charron's depressing and wearisome division; the confusion in Montaigne: the fact that he clearly felt the defect of a correct method, that he avoided it by jumping from one subject to another, that he wanted to appear in a good light.

What a foolish project he had to paint his own portrait!* And not even as a digression and against his principles, as anyone might mistakenly do, but following his own principles and as his prime and main intention. For talking nonsense by accident or through weakness is a common failing. But to say such things intentionally is intolerable. And to talk such nonsense as this . . .

Preface to the second part. Discuss those who have written about this subject.

I admire the boldness with which these people set about speaking of God. In addressing their arguments to unbelievers, their first chapter is about proving the existence of God from the works of nature. I would not be surprised about their venture if they were addressing their arguments to the faithful, for it is clear that those with a keen faith in their hearts can see straightaway that everything which exists is the work of the God they worship. But for those in whom this light has been extinguished and in whom these authors are trying to rekindle it, these people deprived of faith and grace who, scrutinizing with all their intelligence everything they see in nature which can lead them to this knowledge, but finding only obscurity

and darkness; to say to them that they only have to look at the
least of the things surrounding them and they will see God
revealed there, and then to give them as a complete proof of
this great and important matter the course of the moon and the
planets, and to claim to have achieved a proof with such an
argument, is to give them cause to believe that the proofs of
our religion are indeed weak. I see by reason and experience
that nothing is more likely to arouse their contempt. This is
not how Scripture, which understands better the things which
are God's, speaks of them. It says on the contrary, that God is
a hidden God; and that since the corruption of nature, he has
left men in a blind state from which they can emerge only
through Jesus Christ, without whom all communication with
God is barred: *Nemo novit Patrem, nisi Filius, et cui Filius
voluerit revelare.* [Just as no one knows the Father except the
Son and those to whom the Son chooses to reveal him (Matt.
11: 27).]

That is what Scripture points out to us, when it says in so
many places that those who seek God will find him. It is not
this light we are speaking of, like the midday sun. We do not
say that those who seek the sun at midday, or water in the
sea, will find it. And so clearly the evidence of God is not of
such a kind in nature. It also tells us elsewhere: *Vere tu es
Deus absconditus.* [Truly, God is hidden within you. (Isa. 45:
15).]

645 How many beings which were unknown to earlier philosophers
have been revealed to us by telescopes. We boldly addressed
the holy Scripture on the great number of stars, saying: There
are only 1022 of them, we know.*

––––––––––

There are plants on earth, we see them; from the moon they
could not be seen. And on these plants there is down, and in
this down little creatures; but beyond that nothing else? What
arrogant men!

Compounds are made up of elements; but elements are not?
What arrogance! This is a delicate point. We must not say that
there are things that we cannot see. So we have to talk like the
others, but not think like them.

––––––––––

When we try to follow virtues to their extremes, vices appear from everywhere which mingle imperceptibly with them,* in their imperceptible ways from the infinitesimal end. And vices are there in crowds at the other end. The result is that we get lost in the vices and no longer see the virtues.

We are hostile to perfection itself.

Words arranged differently give a different meaning. And meanings arranged differently produce different effects.

Ne timeas, pusillus grex. [There is no need to be afraid, little flock (Luke 12: 32).] *Timore et tremore.* [With fear and trembling (Phil. 2: 12).]

Quid ergo, *ne timeas*, modo timeas. [Why then, fear not, provided that you fear.]

Fear not, provided you are afraid. But if you are not afraid, be fearful.

Qui me recipit, non me recipit, sed eum qui me misit. [Anyone who welcomes me welcomes not me but the one who sent me (Mark 9: 37).]

Nemo scit neque Filius. [Nobody knows it . . . nor the Son (Mark 13: 32).]

If there is ever a time when we ought to profess two opposites, it is when we are accused of omitting one. Therefore the Jesuits and the Jansenists are wrong to conceal them, but more so the Jansenists, because the Jesuits have been better at professing them both.*

M. de Condren:* There is no comparison, he says, between the union of saints and that of the Holy Trinity.

Jesus Christ says the opposite.

The dignity of mankind used to consist, in its innocence, in making use of and being master of creatures; but today in separating itself from them, and submitting to them.

Meanings. The same meaning changes according to the words which express it. Meanings gain their dignity from words instead of giving it to them. We must look for examples.

I believe that Joshua was the first of God's people to bear that name, as Jesus Christ was the last of God's people to do so.

Nubes lucida OBUMBRAVIT. [A bright cloud covered them with shadow (Matt. 17: 5).]

St John the Baptist was to convert the hearts of the fathers from the children, and Jesus Christ to make the division.
 Without contradiction.

The effects *in communi* and *in particulari* [in general, and in particular]. The semi-Pelagians are wrong to say *in general* what is only true *in particular*, and the Calvinists to say *in particular* what is true *in general* (it seems to me).*

XXXVIII

646 I take it as self-evident that, if everyone knew what was said about him, there would not be four friends in the world. This is clear from the quarrels which are occasioned by the indiscreet remarks which we sometimes make.

In this way I find an answer to all objections.

It is right that so pure a God discloses himself only to those whose hearts are purified.

Therefore this religion attracts me, and I find it already sufficiently justified by so divine a morality. But I find more in it than that: I find, effectively, that for as long as human memory can remember, a people more ancient than any other has existed. Human beings are constantly told that they are universally corrupt, but that a Redeemer will come. That it is not one person who says so, but countless persons and a whole people, prophesying explicitly for four thousand years. Their Books dispersed for four thousand years. Finally they themselves, without idols or king.

A whole people foretells him before his coming. A whole people worships him after his coming.

The more I examine that people, the more truth I find in them: both in what came before and what came after, and that synagogue which came before him, and the synagogue (*the number of Jews*) wretched and without prophets who came after him and who, being all hostile, are admirable witnesses to us of the truth of these prophecies in which their wretchedness and blindness are foretold.

The darknesses of the Jews, fearful and foretold: *Eris palpans in meridie. Dabitur liber scienti litteras, et dicet: Non possum legere.* [You grope your way at noontide (Deut. 28: 29). You give (a sealed book) to someone able to read and say, 'Read that.' He replies, 'I cannot, because the book is sealed' (Isa. 29: 11).]

_____

The sceptre still being in the hands of the first foreign usurper.

_____

The rumour of Jesus Christ's coming.

I find this sequence, this religion totally divine in its authority, its duration, its perpetuity, its morality, its conduct, its doctrine, and its effects. And so I hold out my arms to my Saviour, who, having been foretold for four thousand years, came to suffer and to die for me on earth, at the time and in the circumstances which were foretold. And through his grace I await death peacefully, in the hope of being eternally united with him, and meanwhile I live joyfully, either in the blessings which he is pleased to bestow on me, or in the afflictions which he sends me for my good and which he taught me to endure by his example.

647 It is an amazing thing to think about: that there are people in the world who, having renounced all God's and nature's laws, make up for themselves others which they strictly obey, as, for instance, Muhammad's soldiers, thieves, heretics, etc. And so do logicians.

It seems that their licence is without any bounds or limits, seeing that they have crossed so many just and holy ones.

648 Sneezing absorbs all the functions of the soul just as much as the sexual act. But we do not draw from it the same conclusions against man's greatness, because it is involuntary. Although we make it happen, it is nevertheless involuntarily achieved: it is not for the sake of the thing in itself but for another end. And so it is not a sign of man's weakness or his subjection to this act.

_____

It is not shameful for man to give in to pain, but it is shameful to give in to pleasure. This is not because pain comes to us externally while we are looking for pleasure; for we can look for pain and deliberately give in to it without this kind of contemptible behaviour. So why is it to reason's credit to give in to pain's efforts, and to its shame to give in to those of pleasure? It is because it is not pain which tempts and attracts us. It is ourselves who voluntarily choose it and want it to dominate us, so that we are in control of things, and in so doing it is man who gives in to himself. But in pleasure it is man who gives in to pleasure. But, only mastery and control create glory, and only subjection creates shame.

649* God
        created everything for himself,
        gave power of sanctions and blessings to himself.

_____

You can apply this to God or yourself.

_____

If to God, the Gospel is the rule.

_____

If to yourself, you will take the place of God.

_____

Since God is surrounded by people filled with charity, who ask of him the blessings of charity which are in his power, so . . .

_____

Know yourself then, and realize that you are only a king of concupiscence, and follow the paths of concupiscence.

_____

650 King, and tyrant.

_____

I too will have thoughts at the back of my mind.

_____

I will beware of every journey.

_____

Greatness of establishment, respect of establishment.

_____

The pleasure of the great is the power to make people happy.

_____

The proper function of wealth is to be distributed freely.

_____

The proper function of everything must be looked for. The proper function of power is to protect.

_____

When strength attacks the mask, when a simple soldier takes the square cap of the presiding judge and spins it out of the window.

_____

Martial's *Epigrams*. People like to be malicious, not against the half-blind or the afflicted, but against those who are contented and arrogant. Otherwise we are wrong. For concupiscence is the source of all our impulses, and humanity . . .

_____

We have to please those with human and tender feelings.

_____

The story of the two one-eyed people is useless, because it does not console them and only adds a very little shine to the author's reputation.

Anything written only for the author's reputation is worthless.

Ambitiosa recidet ornamenta. [He will strip off ambitious ornaments (Horace, *Art of Poetry*, 5. 447–448).]

XXXIX

653 *Fascinatio.*
Somnum suum.

Figura hujus mundi.
[Fascination, (Wisd. 4: 12). Sleeping their last sleep (Ps. 76: 5).
The world as we know it (1 Cor. 7: 31).]

EUCHARIST

Comedes panem TUUM/ panem NOSTRUM. [You will eat bread/ our (daily) bread (Deut. 8: 9., Luke 11: 3).]

Inimici Dei terram lingent [His enemies grovel in the dust (Ps. 72: 9)]: sinners lick the dust, that is, love earthly pleasures.

The *Old Testament* contained figures of future joy and the *New* contains the means of achieving it.

The figures were of joy, the means of penitence; and yet the paschal lamb was eaten *with bitter herbs, cum amaritudinibus* (Ex. 12: 8).

Singularis sum ego donec transeam. [While I go (Ps. 141: 10).] Jesus Christ before his death was almost alone in martyrdom.

Time heals pain and quarrels, because we change: we are no longer the same person; neither the offender nor the offended are the same. It is like a people whom we have angered and have come back to see after two generations: they are still French, but not the same.

If we dreamt the same thing every night, it would affect us as much as the things we see every day. And if a workman was sure of dreaming every night for twelve hours that he was king, I think he would be almost as happy as a king who dreamt every night for twelve hours that he was a workman.

If we dreamt every night that we were pursued by enemies and were disturbed by these painful apparitions, and spent every day in different occupations, as when we make a journey, we would suffer almost as much as if it were true, and we would dread going to sleep, as we dread waking up when we are afraid of actually encountering such misfortunes. And in fact it would create almost the same distress as reality.

But because dreams are all different, and there is variety within each one, what we see in them affects us much less than what we see when we are awake, because of the continuity. This, however, is not so continuous and even that it does not also change, though less abruptly, even if rarely, as on a journey, when we say: I think I'm dreaming. For life is a dream, if slightly less changeable.

_____

Are we to say that, because people said that justice had abandoned the earth, they had recognized original sin? *Nemo ante obitum beatus* [Call no man happy until he is dead (Ovid, *Metamorphoses*, 3. 135, quoted in Montaigne, *The Essays*, i 18)]: does this mean they realized that eternal and essential happiness begins at death?

_____

By knowing each man's ruling passion, we are sure of pleasing him. Nevertheless every man has fanciful ideas opposed to his own good, in the very idea he has of good. It is an idiosyncrasy that puts us out of tune.

_____

We are not satisfied with the life we have in ourselves and in our own being: we want to lead an imaginary life in the minds of other people, and so we make an effort to impress. We constantly strive to embellish and preserve our imaginary being, and neglect the real one. And if we are calm, or generous, or loyal we are anxious to let it be known so that we can bind these virtues to our other being, and would rather detach them from our real selves to unite them with the other. We would happily be cowards if that gained us the reputation of being brave. What a clear sign of the nothingness of our own being not to satisfied with one without the other, and to exchange one frequently for the other! For anyone who would not die to save his honour would be despicable.

XXXIX

655 There are three ways to believe: reason, custom, inspiration.* The Christian religion, which alone has reason, does not admit for its true children those who believe without inspiration. It is

not that it excludes reason and custom, on the contrary; but we must open our minds to the proofs, confirm ourselves in it through custom, yet offer ourselves through humiliations to inspirations, which alone can produce the true and salutary effect: *Ne evacuetur crux Christi*. [In which the crucifixion of Christ cannot be expressed (1 Cor. 1: 17).]

656 Incomprehensible that God should exist, and incomprehensible that he should not; that the soul should exist in the body, that we should have no soul; that the world should be created, that it should not; etc.; that original sin should exist, and that it should not.*

XL

661 For we must not misunderstand ourselves: we are as much automaton as mind. And therefore the way we are persuaded is not simply by demonstration. How few things can be demonstrated! Proofs only convince the mind; custom provides the strongest and most firmly held proofs: it inclines the automaton, which drags the mind unconsciously with it. Who has proved that tomorrow will dawn, and that we will die? And what is more widely believed? So it is custom which persuades us, it is that which makes so many Christians, that which makes Turks, heathens, professions, soldiers, etc. (There is also faith received at baptism by Christians in addition to that of the heathens.) In the end, we have to resort to customs once the mind has seen where the truth lies, to immerse and ingrain ourselves in this belief, which constantly eludes us. For to have the proofs always before us is too much trouble. We must acquire an easier belief, one of habit, which without violence, art, or argument makes us believe something and inclines our faculties to this belief so that our soul falls naturally into it. When we believe only through the strength of our convictions and the automaton is inclined to believe the opposite, that is not enough. We must therefore make both sides of us believe: the mind by reasons which only have to be seen once in a lifetime, and the automaton by custom, and by not allowing it to be disposed to the contrary.

Inclina cor meum, Deus . . . [Turn my heart, O God . . . (Ps. 119: 36).]

————

Reason works slowly, looking so frequently at so many principles, which must always be present, that it is constantly dozing or wandering off because all its principles are not present. Feeling does not work like that: it acts instantly and is always ready to act. So we must put our faith in feeling, otherwise it will always waver.

XLII. MATHEMATICS/INTUITION*

669 Mask and disguise nature: no more king, pope, bishop, but 'august monarch', etc. No Paris, 'capital of the realm'.

There are places where Paris must be called Paris, and others where it must be called capital of the realm.

————

The more intelligent we are, the more readily we recognize individual personality in others. The crowd finds no difference between people.

————

Different kinds of right thinking: some in a particular order of things, and not in other ways where they talk nonsense.

————

Some draw the right conclusions from a few principles, and that is one kind of right thinking.

Others draw the right conclusions from things where many principles are involved.

For example, some people fully understand the properties of water, which involve few principles; but the conclusions are so subtle that only an extremely accurate mind can reach them. For all that, these people might not be great mathematicians, because mathematics includes a large number of principles, and a mind may well be of the kind that can easily fathom a few principles in depth without being capable at all of penetrating things where many principles are involved.

There are therefore two sorts of mind: one penetrates quickly and deeply the conclusions of principles, and that is the accurate mind; the other can grasp a large number of principles without mixing them up, and that is the mathematical mind. The first is a powerful and precise mind, the other demonstrates breadth of mind. Now it is quite possible for one to work without the other, for a mind can be powerful and narrow, and can also be broad and weak.

XLIII. MATHEMATICS/INTUITION

670 *Difference between the mathematical mind and the intuitive mind.* In the one the principles are obvious, but far removed from common use, so that from lack of practice we have difficulty turning our head in that direction. But once we do so just a little in that direction, the principles can clearly be seen, and it would need a totally unsound mind to draw false conclusions from principles so blatant that they can scarcely be missed.

But with the intuitive mind the principles are in common use, in front of everyone's eyes. There is no need to turn our head or strain ourselves; we need only to be clear-sighted. But it must be clear, for the principles are so intricate and numerous that it is almost impossible not to miss some. But the omission of one principle can lead to error. So one needs to be very clear-sighted to see all the principles, and then to have an accurate mind so as not to draw false conclusions from known principles.

All mathematicians would, therefore, be intuitive, if they were clear-sighted, for they do not draw false conclusions from principles they know. And intuitively minded people would be mathematicians, if they could adapt their thinking to unfamiliar mathematical principles.

The reason, therefore, why some intuitive minds are not mathematical is that they cannot apply themselves to the principles of mathematics at all. But the reason that mathematicians are not intuitive is that they cannot see what is in front of them and, being used to the clear-cut, obvious principles of mathematics, and to draw no conclusions until they have properly understood and handled their principles, they become lost in matters which require intuition, where principles cannot be handled like that. Such principles can scarcely be seen, they are felt rather than seen; enormous care has to be taken to make them felt by people who cannot feel them themselves. These things are so delicate and numerous that it requires a very delicate and precise cast of mind to feel them, and to judge accurately and correctly from this perception. Most frequently it is not possible to demonstrate it logically, as in mathematics, because we are not aware of the principles in that way, and it would be an endless task to set about it. The truth must be seen straightaway, at a glance, and not through a process of reasoning, at least up to a point. So it is rare for mathematicians to be intuitive, and for the intuitive to be mathematicians, since mathematicians want to deal with intuitive things mathematically, and are ridiculous for wanting to begin with definitions, followed by principles: that is not the way to proceed in this kind of reasoning. It is not that the mind does not do it, but that it does it silently, naturally, and simply, for no one can give it expression, and only a few can feel it.

Intuitive minds, on the other hand, being accustomed to judge at a single glance in this way, are so astounded when they are faced with propositions they do not understand, and in order to understand them would have to start with such sterile definitions and principles which they are not used to looking at in detail, that they are discouraged and disgusted.

But unsound minds are never either intuitive or mathematical.

Mathematicians who are only mathematicians therefore reason straightforwardly, providing only that everything is explained clearly in definitions and principles; otherwise they are unsound and intolerable, because they reason straightforwardly only when principles are clearly established.

And intuitive minds which are only intuitive cannot have the patience to go to the heart of first principles of speculation and imaginative matters which they have never experienced, and which are quite out of the ordinary.

671 *Mathematics/intuition.* True eloquence has no time for eloquence. True morality has no time for morality—that is to say,

the morality of judgement has no time for the morality of the mind, which has no rules.

For judgement is what goes with feeling, as knowledge goes with the mind. Intuition is intrinsic to judgement, as mathematics is to the mind.

To have no time for philosophy is truly to philosophize.

Nourishment of the body comes gradually.
Ample nourishment, and little substance.

XLV. DISCOURSE CONCERNING THE MACHINE

680* *Infinity nothingness.* Our soul is thrust into the body, where it finds number, time, dimension. It ponders them and calls them nature, necessity, and can believe nothing else.

A unit added to infinity does not increase it at all, any more than a foot added to an infinite length. The finite dissolves in the presence of the infinite and becomes pure nothingness. So it is with our mind before God, with our justice before divine justice. There is not so great a disproportion between our justice and God's justice as there is between unity and infinity.

God's justice must be as vast as his mercy. But justice towards the damned is not so vast, and ought to shock less than mercy towards the elect.

We know that there is an infinite, but we do not know its nature; as we know that it is false that numbers are finite, so therefore it is true that there is an infinite number, but we do not know what it is: it is false that it is even and false that it is odd, for by adding a unit it does not change its nature; however it is a number, and all numbers are even or odd (it is true that this applies to all finite numbers).

So we can clearly understand that there is a God without knowing what he is.

Is there no substantial truth, seeing that there are so many true things which are not truth itself?

We therefore know the existence and nature of the finite, because we too are finite and have no extension.

We know the existence of the infinite, and do not know its nature, because it has extent like us, but not the same limits as us.

But we know neither the existence nor the nature of God, because he has neither extent nor limits.

But we know of his existence through faith. In glory we will know his nature.

Now I have already shown that we can certainly know the existence of something without knowing its nature.

Let us now speak according to natural lights.

If there is a God, he is infinitely beyond our comprehension, since, having neither parts nor limits, he bears no relation to ourselves. We are therefore incapable of knowing either what he is, or if he is. That being so, who will dare to undertake a resolution of this question? It cannot be us, who bear no relationship to him.

Who will then blame the Christians for being unable to provide a rational basis for their belief, they who profess a religion for which they cannot provide a rational basis? They declare that it is a folly, *stultitiam* (1 Cor. 1: 18) in laying it before the world: and then you complain that they do not prove it! If they did prove it, they would not be keeping their word. It is by the lack of proof that they do not lack sense. 'Yes, but although that excuses those who offer their religion as it is, and that takes away the blame from them of producing it without a rational basis, it does not excuse those who accept it.'*

Let us therefore examine this point, and say: God is, or is not. But towards which side will we lean? Reason cannot decide anything. There is an infinite chaos separating us. At the far end of this infinite distance a game is being played and the coin will come down heads or tails. How will you wager? Reason cannot make you choose one way or the other, reason cannot make you defend either of the two choices.

So do not accuse those who have made a choice of being wrong, for you know nothing about it! 'No, but I will blame them not for having made this choice, but for having made any choice. For, though the one who chooses heads and the other one are equally wrong, they are both wrong. The right thing is not to wager at all.'

Yes, but you have to wager.* It is not up to you, you are already committed. Which then will you choose? Let us see. Since you have to choose, let us see which interests you the least. You have two things to lose: the truth and the good, and two things to stake: your reason and will, your knowledge and beatitude; and your nature has two things to avoid: error and wretchedness. Your reason is not hurt more by choosing one rather than the other, since you do have to make the choice. That is one point disposed of. But your beatitude? Let us weigh up the gain and the loss by calling heads that God exists. Let us assess the two cases: if you win, you win everything; if you lose, you lose nothing. Wager that he exists then, without hesitating! 'This is wonderful. Yes, I must wager. But perhaps I am betting too much.' Let us see. Since there is an equal chance of gain and loss, if you won only two lives instead of one, you could still put on a bet. But if there were three lives to win, you would have to play (since you must necessarily play), and you would be unwise, once forced to play, not to chance your life to win three in a game where there is an equal chance of losing and winning. But there is an eternity of life and happiness. And that being so, even though there were an infinite number of chances of which only one were in your favour, you would still be right to wager one in order to win two, and you would be acting wrongly, since you are obliged to play, by refusing to stake one life against three in a game where out of an infinite number of chances there is one in your favour, if there were an infinitely happy infinity of life to be won. But here there is an infinitely happy infinity of life to be won, one chance of winning against a finite number of chances of losing, and what you are staking is finite. That removes all choice: wherever there is infinity and where there is no infinity of chances of losing against one of winning, there is no scope for wavering, you have to chance everything. And thus, as you

are forced to gamble, you have to have discarded reason if you
cling on to your life, rather than risk it for the infinite prize
which is just as likely to happen as the loss of nothingness.

For it is no good saying that it is uncertain if you will win,
that it is certain you are taking a risk, and that the infinite
distance between the CERTAINTY of what you are risking and
the UNCERTAINTY of whether you win makes the finite good
of what you are certainly risking equal to the uncertainty of
the infinite. It does not work like that. Every gambler takes
a certain risk for an uncertain gain; nevertheless he certainly
risks the finite uncertainty in order to win a finite gain, without
sinning against reason. There is no infinite distance between
this certainty of what is being risked and the uncertainty of
what might be gained: that is untrue. There is, indeed, an
infinite distance between the certainty of winning and the certainty of losing. But the uncertainty of winning is proportional
to the certainty of the risk, according to the chances of winning
or losing. And hence, if there are as many chances on one side
as on the other, the odds are even, and then the certainty of
what you risk is equal to the uncertainty of winning. It is very
far from being infinitely distant from it. So our argument is
infinitely strong, when the finite is at stake in a game where
there are equal chances of winning and losing, and the infinite
is to be won.

That is conclusive, and, if human beings are capable of
understanding any truth at all, this is the one.*

'I confess it, I admit it, but even so . . . Is there no way of
seeing underneath the cards?' 'Yes, Scripture and the rest, etc.'
'Yes, but my hands are tied and I cannot speak a word. I am
being forced to wager and I am not free, they will not let me
go. And I am made in such a way that I cannot believe. So
what do you want me to do?' 'That is true. But at least realize
that your inability to believe, since reason urges you to do so
and yet you cannot, arises from your passions. So concentrate
not on convincing yourself by increasing the number of proofs
of God but on diminishing your passions. You want to find
faith and you do not know the way? You want to cure yourself
of unbelief and you ask for the remedies? Learn from those
who have been bound like you, and who now wager all they

have. They are people who know the road you want to follow and have been cured of the affliction of which you want to be cured. Follow the way by which they began: by behaving just as if they believed, taking holy water, having masses said, etc. That will make you believe quite naturally, and according to your animal reactions.' 'But that is what I am afraid of.' 'Why? What do you have to lose? In order to show you that this is where it leads, it is because it diminishes the passions, which are your great stumbling-blocks, etc.

'How these words carry me away, send me into raptures,' etc. If these words please you and seem worthwhile, you should know that they are spoken by a man who knelt both before and afterwards to beg this infinite and indivisible Being, to whom he submits the whole of himself, that you should also submit yourself, for your own good and for his glory, and that strength might thereby be reconciled with this lowliness.

End of this discourse.

But what harm will come to you from taking this course? You will be faithful, honest, humble, grateful, doing good, a sincere and true friend. It is, of course, true; you will not take part in corrupt pleasure, in glory, in the pleasures of high living. But will you not have others?

I tell you that you will win thereby in this life, and that at every step you take along this path, you will see so much certainty of winning and so negligible a risk, that you will realize in the end that you have wagered on something certain and infinite, for which you have paid nothing.*

We owe a great deal to those who warn us of our faults, for they mortify us; they teach us that we have been held in contempt, but they do not prevent it from happening to us in the future, for we have many other faults to merit it. They prepare us for the exercise of correction, and the removal of a fault.*

Custom is natural to us. Anyone who becomes accustomed to faith believes it, and can no longer not fear hell, and believes in nothing else. Anyone who becomes accustomed to believing that the king is to be feared, etc. Who can then doubt that our soul, being accustomed to seeing number, space, movement, believes in this and nothing else?*

Do you believe that it is impossible that God should be infinite and indivisible? 'Yes.' I want to show you, then (*an image of God in his boundlessness*), an infinite and indivisible thing: it is a point moving everywhere at infinite speed.

For it is a single entity everywhere, and complete in every place.

Let this fact of nature, which previously seemed to you impossible, make you understand that there may be others which you do not yet know. Do not draw the conclusion from your apprenticeship that there is nothing left for you to learn, but that you have an infinite amount to learn.*

It is not true that we are worthy of being loved by others. It is unfair that we should want to be loved. If we were born reasonable and impartial, knowing ourselves and others, we would not incline our will in that direction. However, we are born with it. We are therefore born unfair. For everything is biased towards itself: this is contrary to all order. The tendency should be towards the generality, and the leaning towards the self is the beginning of all disorder: war, public administration, the economy, the individual body.

The will is therefore depraved. If the members of the natural and civil communities tend towards the good of the body, the communities themselves should tend towards another, more general body, of which they are the members. We should therefore tend towards the general. We are born, then, unjust and depraved.

No religion apart from our own has taught that man is born sinful. No philosophical sect has said so. So none has told the truth.

No sect or religion has always existed on earth, apart from the Christian religion.

Only the Christian religion makes men together both LOV-ABLE and HAPPY. We cannot be both capable of being loved and happy in formal society.

It is the heart that feels God, not reason: that is what faith is. God felt by the heart, not by reason.

The heart has its reasons which reason itself does not know:*
we know that through countless things.

I say that the heart loves the universal being naturally, and
itself naturally, according to its own choice. And it hardens
itself against one or the other, as it chooses. You have rejected
one and kept the other: is it reason that makes you love
yourself?

The only knowledge which is contrary to both common
sense and human nature is the only one which has always
existed among men.

XLVI. A LETTER TO FURTHER THE
SEARCH FOR GOD

681   ... Let them at least learn the nature of the religion they
attack, before attacking it. If this religion boasted that it had
a clear vision of God, and to have it plain and unhidden, it
would be attacking it to say that nothing can be seen in this
world which obviously proves it. But since, on the contrary, it
says that humanity is in darkness, estranged from God, that he
has hidden himself from its knowledge, that this is the very
name that he gives himself in the Scriptures: DEUS ABSCONDITUS
[the hidden God (Isa. 45: 15)]; and if, finally, it strives equally
to establish these two facts: that God has established visible
signs in the Church by which those who seek him sincerely
should know him; and that he has nevertheless hidden them in
such a way that he will only be perceived by those who seek
him whole-heartedly, what advantage can they derive when, in
their professed unconcern in seeking the truth, they protest
that nothing reveals it to them? For the darkness by which
they are surrounded, and with which they castigate the Church,
establishes simply one of the things the Church upholds, without affecting the other, and, far from destroying its doctrine,
confirms it.

In order to attack it, let them protest that they have made
every effort to seek it everywhere, even in what the Church
offers for their instruction, but without any satisfaction at all.
If they spoke like that, they would indeed be attacking one of

these claims. But I hope to show here that no reasonable person could speak like that, and I even dare to say that no one has ever done it. We know well enough how people in this state of mind behave. They think they have made great efforts to learn, when they have spent a few hours reading a book of the Bible, and have questioned some ecclesiastic about the truths of the faith. After that, they boast that they have consulted books and men unsuccessfully. But in fact I would tell them what I have often said, that such negligence is intolerable. It is not a question here of the passing interest of some stranger for us to treat it like this. It is a question of ourselves, and our all.

The immortality of the soul is of such vital concern to us, which affects us so deeply, that we would have to have lost all feeling in order to be indifferent to the truth about it. All our actions and thoughts must follow such different paths, according to whether there are eternal blessings to hope for or not, that it is impossible to take a step sensibly and discerningly except by determining it with this point in mind, which ought to be our ultimate aim.

In this way our primary interest and first duty is to enlighten ourselves in this matter, on which all our conduct depends. And that is why, among those who are unconvinced of it, I make an absolute distinction between those who strive with all their strength to learn about it, and those who live without bothering or thinking about it.*

I have nothing but pity for those who sincerely lament their doubting, who regard it as the ultimate misfortune, and who, sparing nothing to escape from it, make of this search their principal and most serious occupation.

But those who spend their lives without a thought for this final end of life and who, for the sole reason that they do not find the light of conviction within themselves, do not try to look for it elsewhere and examine closely whether this opinion is one of those which people accept out of credulous naïvety, or one of those which, though obscure in themselves, nevertheless has a very firm and unshakeable foundation; those I regard in quite a different way.

This indifference in a matter which concerns themselves, their eternity, their all, annoys me more than it fills me with

pity. It amazes and appals me: it strikes me as wholly monstrous. I do not say this with the pious zeal of spiritual devotion. I mean, on the contrary, that we ought to have this feeling
through the principle of human interest and self-love.* For
that we only have to see what the least enlightened see.

You do not need a greatly elevated soul to realize that in this
life there is no true and firm satisfaction, that all our pleasures
are simply vanity, that our afflictions are infinite, and lastly
that death, which threatens us at every moment, must in a few
years infallibly present us with the appalling necessity of being
either annihilated or wretched for all eternity.

Nothing is more real nor more dreadful than that. We may
put on as brave a face as we like: that is the end which awaits
the finest life on earth. Let us think about it, then say whether
it is not beyond doubt that the only good in this life lies in the
hope of another life, that we are only happy the closer we come
to it, and that, just as there will be no more unhappiness for
those who were completely certain of eternity, there is no hope
either of happiness for those who have no glimmer of it!

It is therefore certainly a great evil to have such doubt. But
it is at least an inescapable duty to seek when one does doubt.
And so someone who doubts and does not seek is both very
unhappy and very wrong at the same time. If in addition he is
calm and satisfied, let him proclaim as much, and be proud of
it, and let this very condition be the subject of his joy and
pride. I have no words to describe so deranged a person.

Where can we find the source of such feelings? What reason
for joy can we find in expecting nothing but hopeless wretchedness? What reason for pride to see ourselves cloaked in impenetrable darkness, and how can such an argument as this be
conducted in a reasonable man?

'I do not know who put me into the world, nor what the
world is, nor what I am myself. I am terrifyingly ignorant
about everything. I do not know what my body is, or my senses
or my soul, or that part of myself which thinks what I am
saying, which reflects on everything and itself, and does not
know itself any better than the rest. I see the terrifying ex-
panses of the universe which close around me, and I find
myself pinned to a corner of this vast space, without knowing

why I have been put in this place rather than in another, nor why the short time given to me to live is assigned to this moment rather than another in all the eternity which has preceded me and shall come after me.

'I see nothing but infinities on all sides, enclosing me like an atom, or a shadow which lasts only for a moment and does not return.

'All I know is that I must shortly die, but what I know least about is death itself, which I cannot avoid.

'In the same way that I do not know where I came from, neither do I know where I am going, and I know only that on leaving this world I either fall into nothingness for ever, or into the hands of an angry God, without knowing which of these two states will be my condition in eternity. Such is my state, full of weakness and uncertainty. And I conclude from all this that I must spend every day of my life without thinking of enquiring into what will happen to me. I could perhaps find some enlightenment among my doubts, but I do not want to take the trouble to do so, nor take one step to look for it. And afterwards, sneering at those who are struggling with the task, I will go without forethought or fear to face the great venture, and allow myself to be carried tamely to my death, uncertain as to the eternity of my future state.'

Who would wish to have as a friend a man who talked like that? Who would choose him among others in whom to confide his affairs? Who would turn to him in adversity?

And finally, to what purpose in life could he be put?

Indeed, it is a wonderful thing for religion to have for enemies people so lacking in reason (whatever certainty they have is a matter for despair rather than congratulation). And their hostility is so harmless that on the contrary it rather seems to establish the truths of religion. For the Christian faith is concerned almost wholly with establishing these two things: the corruption of nature and the Redemption of Jesus Christ. But I maintain that, if they do not serve to demonstrate the truth of the Redemption by the sanctity of their conduct, they do at least admirably serve to demonstrate the corruption of nature by such unnatural feelings.

Nothing is so important to man as his condition. Nothing is

so frightening to him as eternity. And so the fact that there are men indifferent to the loss of their being and to the peril of an eternity of wretchedness is not natural. They are quite different with regard to everything else: they fear even the most insignificant things, they foresee them, feel them, and the same man who spends so many days and nights in rage and despair over the loss of some office or over some imaginary affront to his honour is the very one who, without anxiety or emotion, knows he is going to lose everything through death. It is a monstrous thing to see in the same heart and at the same time both this sensitivity to the slightest things, and this strange insensitivity to the greatest.

It is an incomprehensible spell, a supernatural sloth, which points to an all-powerful force as its cause.

There must have been a strange upheaval in human nature for someone to rejoice in being in this state, in which it seems incredible that anyone at all could be. However, experience shows me such a large number of people like this that it would be astonishing, if we did not know that most of those who take part in it are pretending and are not really as they seem. They are people who have heard that clever behaviour demands excess of this kind. This is what they call throwing off the yoke, and they try to copy it. But it would not be difficult to make them understand how mistaken they are in courting esteem in this manner. That is not how to gain it, not even, I would say, among people of the world who judge things sensibly and who know that the only way to succeed is to appear honest, faithful, of sound judgement, and capable of helping their friend usefully, because by nature people care only for what can be useful to them. But what advantage is it to us to hear someone say he has thrown off the yoke, that he does not believe that there is a God who watches over his actions, that he considers himself alone the sole master of his behaviour, and that he intends to account for it solely to himself? Does he think that in this way he has henceforth brought us to have total confidence in him, and to expect consolation, advice, and help in all life's needs? Do they suppose they have given us pleasure by saying that they maintain that our soul is nothing but a puff of wind or smoke, and saying it moreover in a tone of pride and satisfaction? Is this something to say light-heartedly? Is it not rather something to say sadly, as the saddest thing in the world?

If they thought about it seriously they would see that this is so misguided, so contrary to good sense, so opposed to decency, and so far removed (in every way) from the civilized behaviour they are striving for, that they would be rather likely to reform than corrupt those who might have some inclination to follow them. And indeed, make them give an account of their feelings and the reasons they have for doubting religion: they will say such feeble and disgraceful things that you will be persuaded of the opposite. As someone aptly said to them one day: 'If you go on arguing like that,' he said, 'you will really convert me.' And he was right, for who would not be horrified to find himself sharing the feelings of such contemptible people!

In this way those who only affect these feelings would be miserable indeed if they were to coerce their nature in order to become the most insolent of men. If they are angry in their innermost heart at their lack of understanding, let them not hide it. Such an admission would not be shameful. The only shame is to have none. Nothing more surely underlines an extreme weakness of mind than the failure to recognize the unhappiness of someone without God. Nothing more surely betrays an evil mind than the failure to desire the truth of eternal promises. Nothing is more cowardly than to pit oneself against God. Let them then leave such impieties to those who are ill-bred enough to be genuinely capable of them: let them at least be honourable, even if they cannot be Christians! And let them realize, finally, that there are only two sorts of people who can be called reasonable: those who serve God with all their heart because they know him, and those who seek him with all their heart because they do not know him.

But as for those who live without knowing him and without seeking him, they consider themselves so unworthy of their own consideration that they are unworthy of the consideration of others, and we need all the charity of that religion they despise not to despise them to the extent of abandoning them to their foolishness. But because this religion obliges us always to look on them, as long as they live, as being capable of the grace which can enlighten them, and to believe that in a short while they can be filled with more faith than ourselves, and that we on the other hand can fall into the blindness where they are now, we must do for them what we would want others to do for us if we were in their place, and appeal to them to have pity on themselves and take at least a few steps to see whether they cannot find enlightenment. Let them apply to this reading a few of the hours they so uselessly employ on other things: with whatever reluctance they approach it, they will perhaps find something, and at least they will not lose a great deal. But for those who bring absolute sincerity to it and a real desire to find the truth, I hope they will be satisfied, and will be convinced by the proofs of so divine a religion which I have collected here, and in which I have followed more or less this order . . .

682 Before examining the proofs of the Christian religion, I find I must point out how wrong men are who live their lives indifferent to the search for truthfulness of something which is so important to them, and which affects them so closely.

Of all their faults, this is the one which most condemns them with their folly and blindness, and in which it is easiest to confound them with the first inklings of common sense and natural feelings. For it is beyond doubt that this life's duration is but an instant, that the state of death is eternal, whatever its nature may be, and that therefore all our actions and our thoughts must follow such different paths according to the state of that eternity that it would be impossible to take a sensible, well-thought-out step without measuring it against the aim of the point which must be our final objective.

There is nothing more obvious than this and so, according to the laws of reason, men's behaviour is quite irrational if they do not take another route. Let us therefore, on this point, judge those who live without reflecting about their final end of life, who, thoughtless and unworried, follow wherever their inclinations and pleasures take them, as if they could abolish eternity by keeping their minds off it, and think only of the happiness of the present moment.

Yet this eternity exists, and death, which must be its starting-point and which threatens them at every moment, must inevitably put them very shortly in the awful necessity of being either annihilated, or miserable in eternity, without knowing which of these two eternities has been prepared for them for ever.

This is a dilemma with terrible consequences. They are threatened with an eternity of wretchednesses; whereupon, as if the matter were not worth the bother, they omit to consider whether it is one of these opinions which the people accept with over-credulous ease, or one of those which, though obscure in themselves, have a very solid, though hidden, foundation. And so they do not know whether there is truth or falsehood in the matter, nor whether there is strength or weakness in the proofs. They have them in front of their eyes: they refuse to look at them, and in this ignorance they choose to do all that is required to fall into this state of misery, if it exists, to wait until death to test them, yet to be quite satisfied to remain in that state, to proclaim it, even to boast about it. Can we seriously think of the importance of this matter without being horrified by such outrageous behaviour?

This tranquillity in that ignorance is monstrous, and we must make those who spend their lives in this way feel the outrageousness and stupidity of it by pointing it out to them, so that they are overcome by the recognition of their folly. For this is how men argue when they choose to live in ignorance of what they are and without seeking enlightenment. 'I do not know,' they say . . .

'That is what I see and what troubles me. I look in every direction and everywhere I see only darkness. Nature offers me nothing that is not a source of doubt and anxiety. If I saw nothing there which indicated a divinity, I would settle on a negative answer; if I saw the signs of a creator everywhere, I would rest peacefully in faith. But seeing too much to deny and too little to affirm, I am in a pitiful state in which I have wished a hundred times that, if a God is upholding it, nature should proclaim him unequivocally; and that, if the signs it gives of him are deceitful, it should suppress them completely; it should say all or nothing, so that I could see which course I ought to follow. Instead of that, in the state in which I am, not knowing what I am or what I ought to do, I know neither my condition nor my duty. My whole heart longs to know where the true good lies in order to follow it. Nothing would be too high a price for eternity.

'I envy those of the faith whom I see living with such unconcern, and who put a gift to such poor use which I think I would use so differently.'

683 No other has known that man is the most excellent of creatures. Some who have fully understood the reality of his excellence have taken for cowardice and ingratitude the low opinions which men naturally have of themselves; others who have fully understood the truth of this low opinion have treated with ridiculous haughtiness the feelings of greatness which are also natural to man.

'Lift up your eyes to God,' say some. 'Look at him whom you resemble and who made you to adore him. You can make yourself like him. Wisdom will set you on a level with him if you want to follow him.' 'Lift your heads high, free men,' said Epictetus. And the others say to us: 'Lower your eyes towards the ground, miserable worm that you are, and look at the beasts whose companion you are.' What then will humanity become: will he be the equal of God or of the beasts? What a terrifying distance! What then shall we be? Who cannot see from all this that man has gone astray, that he has fallen from his place, that he seeks it anxiously and can no longer find it? And who will then guide him there? The greatest men have failed.

We cannot conceive of Adam's glorious state, nor the nature of his sin, nor the way it has been transmitted to us. These are things which took place in a state of nature entirely different from our own, and which pass our present understanding.

It would be of no use to us to know all this in order to escape. All that we need to know is that we are wretched, corrupt, separated from God, but redeemed by Jesus Christ. And that is what we have wonderful proofs of on earth.

And so the two proofs of corruption and Redemption are drawn from the ungodly, who live indifferent to religion, and from the Jews, who are its irreconcilable enemies.

684*<Self love, and because it is something of sufficient interest to us that we are moved by it, that we should be assured that after all the ills of life an inevitable death, which threatens us at every moment, must infallibly in a few years . . . in the horrible necessity . . .>

The three conditions.

This must not be said to be evidence of reason.

It is all a man could do if he were sure the news were untrue. Even so he ought not to be delighted about it but in despair.

Nothing matters but that, and that is what is neglected!

Our imagination so magnifies the present by dint of thinking about it continually, and so reduces eternity for lack of thinking about it, that we turn eternity into a void and a void into an eternity. And all this has such strong roots within us, that all our reason cannot save us from it and that . . .

I would ask them if it is not true that they confirm in themselves the foundation of the faith they attack, which is that man's nature is in a state of corruption.

685 Then Jesus Christ comes to tell men that they have no other enemies but themselves, that it is their passions which separate them from God, that he comes to destroy these passions and to give them his grace, in order to make of them all a holy Church.

That he comes to gather into this Church pagans and Jews, that he comes to destroy the idols of the first and the superstitions of the others. All men are opposed to this, not simply through the natural opposition of concupiscence, but above all the earthly kings unite to abolish this emerging religion, as it had been foretold (prophecy: *Quare fremerunt gentes . . . reges terrae . . . adversus Christum*). [Why this uproar among the nations? . . . kings on earth . . . against Yahweh and his Annointed (Ps. 2: 1, 2).]

All that is mightiest on earth unites: scholars, sages, kings. Some write, others condemn, others kill. And despite all this opposition, the simple, powerless people resist all these great ones and bring even these kings, these scholars, these sages to submission, and erase idolatry from the earth. And all this is done by the power that had foretold it.

686 Imagine a number of men in chains, all condemned to death, some of whom every day are slaughtered in full view of the others. Those who remain see their own condition in that of their fellows, and looking at each other in pain and without hope, await their turn!

687 After the Creation and the Flood, and God no more about to destroy the world than to create it anew, or to give those great signs of himself, he began to establish a people upon the earth, specially raised, who were to last until the people whom the Messiah should create through his own spirit.

XLVII. DISCOURSE CONCERNING CORRUPTION

688 *Antiquity of the Jews.* What a difference there is between one book and another! I am not surprised that the Greeks wrote the *Iliad*, nor the Egyptians and the Chinese their stories.

You only have to see how that arose. These writers of fables were not contemporary with the things they wrote about. Homer produced a story, which he offered as such and was accepted as such: for no one doubted that Troy and Agamemnon had existed any more than the golden apple. He did not think he was making a history of it, merely an entertainment. He is the only writer of his times, the beauty of his work makes it endure, everyone learns it and talks of it; it is something that has to be known, everyone knows it off by heart. Four hundred years later, the witnesses of these things are no longer alive; no one knows any longer from his own knowledge whether it is a fable or history: it has simply been learned from previous generations, it could pass for the truth.

Any history that is not contemporary is suspect. And so the Sibylline books and those of Trismegistus, and so many others which have enjoyed credence in the world, are false and have been found to be false in the course of time. It is not the same with contemporary authors.

There is a great deal of difference between a book created by an individual, and a book which itself creates a people. We can have no doubt that the book is as old as the people.

689 Without feelings something cannot be wretched: a ruined house is not. Only mankind is wretched. *Ego vir videns.** [I am the man familiar with misery (Lam. 3. 1).]

690 That if God's mercy is so great that he provides us with beneficent teaching even when he hides himself, what enlightenment should we not expect when he reveals himself?

Recognize therefore the truth of religion in the very obscurity of religion, in the little knowledge we have of it, in our indifference to understanding it.

The eternal Being exists always, if he once existed.

All the objections of both sides go only against each other, and not against religion. Everything the ungodly say.

And so the whole universe teaches man either that he is corrupt or that he is redeemed. Everything teaches him his greatness or his wretchedness. God's abandonment can be seen in the pagans, God's protection can be seen in the Jews.

Everyone errs all the more dangerously in that individually they follow a truth: their mistake is not in following a falsehood but in not following another truth.

It is therefore true that everything teaches man about his condition, but it must be properly understood: for it is not true that everything reveals God, but it is true that at the same time he hides himself from those who tempt him, and reveals himself to those who seek him, because humanity is at the same time unworthy of God and capable of God; unworthy through its corruption, capable through its first nature.

What shall we conclude from all our obscurities then but our unworthiness?

If there were no obscurity, we would not feel our corruption. If there were no light we could not hope for a remedy. And so it is not only just, but useful for us, that God should be hidden in part and revealed in part, since it is equally dangerous for man to know God without knowing his wretchedness, and to know his wretchedness without knowing God.

The conversion of the pagans was solely reserved for the grace of the Messiah. The Jews had spent so long fighting them unsuccessfully! Everything that Solomon and the prophets said about it was useless. Wise men, like Plato and Socrates, were unable to persuade them.

If no sign had ever appeared of God, that eternal deprivation would be ambiguous and could equally be attributed to the absence of any divinity, or to the unworthiness of man to apprehend it. But the fact that he appears sometimes, and not always, removes the ambiguity: if he appears once, he exists for ever. Thus the only possible conclusion is that God exists, and that men are unworthy of him.

They blaspheme against what they do not know. The Christian religion consists of two points. It is equally important for men to know them, and dangerous not to know them.

And it is equally owing to God's mercy that he gave signs of both.

And yet they venture to conclude that one of these points is not such that they could conclude the other from it.

Wise men who have said that there was only one God have been persecuted, the Jews hated, Christians even more so.

They saw by the light of nature that, if there is a true religion on earth, the conduct of all things must lean towards it, as to its centre.

(The whole conduct of things ought to aim at the establishment and the greatness of religion. Human beings ought to have within themselves feelings coinciding with what it teaches. In short it ought to be so truly the object and centre towards which all things lean, that whoever knows its principles should be able to explain both human nature in particular, and the whole conduct of the world in general.)

And on this basis they take the opportunity to blaspheme the Christian religion because they know it so badly. They suppose that it consists simply in worshipping a God considered to be great, powerful, and eternal: this is properly speaking deism, almost as far removed from the Christian religion as atheism, which is its complete opposite. From this they conclude that all things combine to establish the point that God does not manifest himself to us with all the clarity he might.

But let them conclude what they like against deism, they will conclude nothing against the Christian religion, which properly consists in the mystery of the Redeemer, who, uniting in himself the two natures, human and divine, saved men from corruption and sin in order to reconcile them with God in his divine person.*

So it teaches men both these truths: that there is a God of whom we are capable, and that there is a corruption in nature which makes us unworthy of him. It is equally important for us to know both these points, and it is equally dangerous for man to know God without knowing his own wretchedness, and to know his wretchedness without knowing the Redeemer who can cure him of it. Knowledge of only one of these points leads either to the arrogance of the philosophers, who have known God and not their own wretchedness, or to the despair of the atheists, who know their wretchedness without knowing the Redeemer.

And so, as it is equally necessary for us to know both these points, it is also equally due to God's mercy that he made us aware of them. The Christian religion does this, and it is indeed in this that it consists.

Let us examine the order of the world about this, and see whether all things do not tend to the establishment of the two main articles of our religion!

(Jesus Christ is the object of everything, and the centre to which everything tends. Whoever knows him knows the reason for everything.)*

Those who go astray only do so for lack of seeing one of these two things: one can then easily know God but not one's own wretchedness, and one's wretchedness without knowing God. But one cannot know Jesus Christ without knowing God and one's wretchedness both together.

And that is why I shall not undertake here to prove by reasons from nature either the existence of God, or the Trinity, or the immortality of the soul, or anything of that kind; not only because I would not feel sufficiently competent to find evidence in nature to convince hardened atheists, but also because such knowledge, without Jesus Christ, is useless and sterile. Even if someone could be persuaded that the proportions between numbers are intangible, eternal truths, dependent on an earlier truth in which they exist, called God, I would not consider that he had made much progress towards his salvation.*

The God of Christians does not consist of a God who is simply the author of mathematical truths and the order of the elements: that is the job of the pagans and Epicureans. He does not consist simply of a God who exerts his providence over the lives and property of people in order to grant a happy span of years to those who worship him: that is the allocation of the Jews. But the God of Abraham, the God of Isaac, the God of Jacob, the God of the Christians is a God of love and consolation; he is a God who fills the souls and hearts of those he possesses; he is a God who makes them inwardly aware of their wretchedness and his infinite mercy, who unites with them in the depths of their soul, who makes them incapable of any other end but himself.

All those who seek God outside Jesus Christ and whose search stops with nature, either find no light which satisfies them, or come to devise a way of knowing and serving God without a mediator. They therefore sink into either atheism or deism, two things which the Christian religion abhors almost equally.

Without Jesus Christ the world would not exist, for it would either have to be destroyed or it would be a kind of hell.

If the world existed to teach man about God, his divinity would shine in all parts of it in an incontestable way. But as it exists only through Jesus Christ and for Jesus Christ, and to teach men about their corruption and redemption, everything in it sparkles with proofs of these two truths.

What can be seen there indicates neither the complete absence, nor the obvious presence of divinity, but the presence of a God who hides himself. Everything carries this stamp.

Will the only one who knows nature know it only in order to be wretched?

Will the only one who knows it be the only one to be miserable?

He must not see nothing at all, and neither must he see enough to think that he possesses it, but he must see enough to know that he has lost it. For to know that one has lost, one must see and not see: that is precisely the state that nature is in.

Whatever course he takes, I will not leave him in peace.

The true religion would have to teach greatness and wretchedness, lead to self-respect and disgust with oneself, to love and hate.

LIII

705 There is nothing on earth which does not show either man's wretchedness or God's mercy, either man's helplessness without God or man's power with God.

706 God has used the blindness of this people for the benefit of the elect.

707 The vilest of human characteristics is his search for glory. But it is just this that is the greatest sign of human excellence; for whatever possessions we may have on earth, whatever health or essential commodities we enjoy, we are not satisfied unless other people think well of us. We put such a high value on men's reason that, whatever of earth's advantages he may have, he is unhappy if he does not also have a privileged position in peoples' esteem. This is the best position in the world; nothing can deflect us from this desire, and it is the most indelible quality in the human heart.

And those who most despise men and regard them as the equivalent of animals still want to be admired and believed by them, and contradict themselves by their own feelings, their nature, which is stronger than anything, convincing them more strongly of man's greatness than reason convinces them of their vileness.

708 As far as I am concerned, I admit that as soon as the Christian religion reveals this principle—that man's nature is corrupt and has fallen away from God—this opens eyes to see the nature of that truth everywhere. For nature is such that it points everywhere to a God who has been lost, both within man and elsewhere.

And a corrupt nature.

709 *Greatness.* Religion is so great a thing that it is right that those who would not want to take the trouble to seek it, if it is

obscure, should be denied it. So what is there to complain about if it can be found simply by looking for it?

LXI. FIGURATIVE LAW

737 *Figures*. To show that the Old Testament is—is only—figurative and that the prophets meant by temporal benefits other kinds of benefit, which are:

1. That it would be unworthy of God.
2. That their sayings express quite clearly the promise of temporal benefits, and yet say their sayings are obscure and that their meanings will not be understood: hence it seems that this hidden meaning was not the one they openly expressed, and consequently they meant to speak of other sacrifices, another Redeemer, etc. They say it will not be understood before the time is accomplished: *Jer*. 33, ult.*

The second proof is that their sayings are contradictory and nullify each other. So that, if we take it that they only intended by the words 'law' and 'sacrifice' anything other than what Moses said, there is an obvious and crass contradiction. Therefore they meant something else, sometimes contradicting themselves in the same chapter.

Now to understand an author's meaning . . .

Fine to see with the eyes of faith Herod's, or Caesar's story.

738 *Reason for figures*. <They had to address a carnal people and make it into the repository of a spiritual testament.>

In order to inspire faith in a Messiah there had to be earlier prophecies, and they had to be handed down by people above suspicion, who were conscientious, loyal, and widely known for their extraordinary ardour.

To succeed in all this, God chose this carnal people, to whom he entrusted the prophecies foretelling the Messiah as the saviour and provider of the carnal benefits which this people loved.

And so they had great enthusiasm for their prophets and handed on for all to see these books foretelling their Messiah, assuring all nations that he was to come in the manner foretold in the books they held open to all. And so this people, disappointed by the poor and humble coming of the Messiah, were his cruellest enemies. The result is that here, of all the people in the world the least suspected of favouring us, are the most scrupulous and zealous observers of its laws and prophets, which they maintain uncorrupted.

So those who rejected and crucified Jesus Christ, who for them was a source of scandal, are those who hand down the books which bear witness to him and say that he will be rejected and a source of scandal. So they have shown that he was the one by rejecting him, and that he was proved as such by the righteous Jews who accepted him as by the unrighteous who rejected him, both having been foretold.

That is why the prophecies have a hidden, spiritual meaning,* to which the people were hostile, beneath the carnal one they favoured. If the spiritual meaning had been revealed, they were not capable of cherishing it; and, unable to hand it down, they would have had no enthusiasm in preserving their books and ceremonies. And if they had cherished these spiritual promises and had preserved them uncorrupted until the Messiah's coming, their testimony would have had no strength, because they had cherished them.

That is why it was a good thing that the spiritual meaning was hidden. But, on the other hand, if this meaning had been so thoroughly hidden that it had not appeared at all, it could not have served as a proof of the Messiah. What then happened? It was concealed beneath the temporal meaning in most of the passages, and was so clearly revealed in a few; apart from the fact that the time and state of the world were foretold so clearly as to be clearer than daylight; and this spiritual meaning is so clearly explained in a few places that it would take the same blindness as the flesh imposes on the spirit when it is dominated by it for it not to be recognized.

This, then, is how God acted: this meaning is concealed beneath another in countless places, and revealed only rarely in others, but yet in such a way that the places in which it is concealed are ambiguous and can be relevant to both, whereas the places in which it is revealed are unambiguous and can concern only the spiritual meaning.

So that there was no reason for lapsing into error, and that there was only one people so carnal who could possibly misunderstand it.

For when benefits were promised in abundance, what prevented them from understanding as true benefits but their cupidity, which interpreted them as earthly benefits? But those whose only benefit was in God related them to God alone.

For there are two principles which divide man's will: cupidity and charity.* It is not that cupidity is incompatible with faith in God, and that charity is incompatible with earthly benefits. But cupidity makes use of God and delights in the world, whereas charity does the opposite.

Now the ultimate purpose is what gives names to things. Anything which prevents us reaching it is called an enemy. So creatures, though good, will be enemies of the righteous if they deflect them from God. And God himself is the enemy of those whose covetousness he disturbs.

Thus, the word 'enemy' depending on the ultimate purpose, the righteous took it to mean their passions, and the carnal people took it to mean the Babylonians. And so these terms were only obscure for the unrighteous. And this is what Isaiah says: *Signa legem in electis meis.* [I seal this revelation in the heart of my disciples (8: 16).] And that Jesus Christ will be *a stumbling-stone* (8: 16), but *Happy is the man who does not lose faith* in him (Matt. 11: 6).

Hosea, last verse, puts it perfectly: *Let the wise man understand these words. For the ways of Yahweh are straight . . . but sinners stumble* (14: 10).

And yet this testament, made to blind some and enlighten others, pointed out, in those very people whom it blinded, the truth which the others had to know. For the visible benefits they received from God were so great and so divine that it was quite clear that he was powerful enough to bestow invisible benefits and a Messiah.

For nature is an image of grace, and visible miracles are an image of invisible ones: *Ut sciatis, tibi dico: 'Surge'.* [To say (to the paralytic) 'Get up' (Mark 2: 10, 11).]

Isaiah. 51 says that the Redemption will be like the crossing of the Red Sea.

God therefore showed in the flight from Egypt, from the sea, the defeat of kings, in the manna, in the whole line of Abraham, that he was capable of saving, of making bread come from heaven, etc., so that this enemy people is the figure and representation of the same Messiah whom they do not know.

He has therefore taught us that all these things were only figures, and what *Truly free, True circumcision, True bread of heaven*, etc., means.

In these promises each man finds what lies in the bottom of his heart: temporal benefits or spiritual benefits, God or creatures; but with this difference, that those who seek creatures there find them, but with many contradictions; they are forbidden to love them, enjoined to worship only God and to love only him, which is just the same thing, and that in the end the Messiah did not come for them. Whereas those who seek God there find him, without any contradiction, with the command to love only him, and that a Messiah did come at the foretold time to bestow the benefits for which they ask.

Thus the Jews had miracles, and prophecies which they saw accomplished. And the doctrine of their law was to worship and love only one God; it was also perpetual. It therefore had all the marks of a true religion, and indeed it was. But we have to distinguish between the doctrine of the Jews and the doctrine of Jewish law. Now the doctrine of the Jews was not true, though it had miracles, prophecies, and perpetuity, because it did not have that further point of worshipping and loving God alone.

Kirkerus—Usserius.*

FRAGMENTS FROM OTHER SOURCES

739 People often take their imagination for their heart: and they believe they have been converted as soon as they start thinking of becoming converted.

740 The last thing one discovers in composing a work is what has to be put first.

(THE MEMORIAL*)

The year of grace 1654
Monday 23 November, feast of Saint Clement,
Pope and martyr, and others of the Roman Martyrology.
Eve of Saint Chrysogonus, martyr, and others.
From about half past ten in the evening until about
half past midnight.

Fire.

God of Abraham, God of Isaac, God of Jacob.
not of philosophers and scholars.

Certainty, joy, certainty, emotion, sight, joy
God of Jesus Christ.
Deum meum et Deum vestrum.[a]
Your God will be my God. Ruth.[b]
Oblivious to the world and to everything except GOD.
He can only be found in the ways taught
in the Gospel. Greatness of the human soul.

Righteous Father, the world did not know you,
but I knew you. John[c]
Joy, Joy, Joy and tears of joy.
I have cut myself off from him
Dereliquerunt me fontem.[d]
My God, will you forsake me?
Let me not be cut off from him for ever.

This is life eternal, that they might know you,
the only true God, and him whom you sent,
Jesus Christ[e]
Jesus Christ
I have cut myself off from him. I have fled from him, denied
him, crucified him.
Let me never be cut off from him.
He can only be kept by the ways taught in the Gospel.
Sweet and total renunciation.
Total submission to Jesus Christ and my director.
Everlasting joy for one day's tribulation on earth.
Non obliviscar sermones tuos.[f] Amen.

---

a My God and your God (John 20: 17).   *b* Ruth 1: 16.   *c* John 17: 25.
d They have forsaken me, the fountain [of living waters] (Jer. 2: 13).

743*The nature of self-love and of this human self is to love only self and consider only self. But what is it to do? It cannot prevent this object it loves from being full of shortcomings and wretchedness; it wants to be great and sees that it is small; it wants to be happy and sees that it is wretched; it wants to be perfect and sees that it is full of imperfections; it wants to be the object of people's love and esteem and sees that its shortcomings merit only their dislike and their contempt. This predicament in which it finds itself arouses in it the most unjust and criminal passion that it is possible to imagine; for it conceives a deadly hatred for that truth which rebukes it, and which convinces it of its shortcomings. It would like to crush it, and, being unable to destroy it as such, it destroys it, as best it can, in its consciousness and in that of others; that is to say that it takes every care to hide its shortcomings both from others and from itself, and cannot bear to have them pointed out or observed.

It is no doubt an evil to be full of shortcomings; but it is an even greater evil to be full of them and unwilling to recognize them, since this entails the further evil of deliberate self-delusion. We do not want others to deceive us; and we do not think it right that they should want to be esteemed by us more than they merit: neither, therefore, is it just that we should deceive them and want them to esteem us more than we deserve.

And so, when they reveal only the imperfections and vices which we actually have, it is obvious that they do us no wrong, since it is not they who are under scrutiny; and that they are doing us good, since they are helping us to escape from an evil, which is the ignorance of these imperfections. We ought not to be angry that they know them and despise us, it being just that they know us for what we are, and despise us if we are despicable.

These are the feelings which would spring from a heart full of equity and justice. What should we then say of ours, seeing in it a quite different disposition? For is it not true that we hate both the truth and those who tell it to us, and that we like them to be deceived to our advantage, and want to be esteemed by them as other than we really are?

---

e *This is life* . . . : Pascal's French is from the Louvain Bible.
f I will not forget thy word (Ps. 119: 16).

And here is a proof which horrifies me. The Catholic religion does not oblige us to reveal our sins indiscriminately to everyone. It allows us to remain hidden from all others; but it makes a single exception, to whom we are enjoined to reveal our innermost heart, and show ourselves for what we are. There is only this one person in the world whom we are enjoined to disillusion, and it lays on this person the obligation of inviolable secrecy, which means that this knowledge is known, but might as well not be. Can you imagine anything more charitable or more gentle? And yet people's corruption is such that they find even this law harsh; and this is one of the main reasons why a large part of Europe has rebelled against the Church.

How unjust and unreasonable the heart of mankind is, to resent the obligation to behave towards one person in a fashion that, in some ways, would be right to behave towards everyone! For is it right that we should deceive them?

There are different degrees in this aversion for the truth; but we can say that it is in everyone to some degree, because it is inseparable from self-love. It is this false delicacy which makes those who have to rebuke others choose so many devious ways and qualifications to avoid offending them. They must minimize our shortcomings, pretend to excuse them, combine them with praise and expressions of affection and esteem. Even then, this medicine still tastes bitter to self-love. It takes as little of it as possible, always with distaste, and often even with hidden resentment for those who offer it.

It follows from this that, if anyone has an interest in being loved by us, they shy away from rendering us a service they know we would find disagreeable. We are treated as we want to be treated: we hate the truth and it is kept from us; we want to be flattered and we are flattered; we like to be deceived and we are deceived.

This is why each degree of good fortune which takes us up in the world distances us further from the truth, because people are more afraid of offending those whose affection is more useful and whose dislike more dangerous. A prince can be the laughing-stock of all Europe and only he will not know it. I am not surprised: telling the truth is useful to the hearer but harmful to the teller, because they incur hatred. Now those who live with princes prefer their own interests to that of the prince they serve; and so they are careful not to procure an advantage for him by harming themselves.

This misfortune is no doubt greater and more common among those with large fortunes; but those less well-off are not exempt, because we always have some interest in being popular. And so human life is nothing but a perpetual illusion; there is nothing but mutual deception and flattery. No one talks about us in our presence as they do in our absence. Human relationships are founded only on this mutual deception; and few friendships would survive if everyone knew what their friend said about them when they were not there, even though the friend spoke sincerely and without passion.

Mankind is therefore nothing but disguise, lies, and hypocrisy, both as individuals and with regard to others. They therefore do not want to be told the truth. They avoid telling it to others. And all these tendencies, so remote from justice and reason, are naturally rooted in their heart.

DISCUSSION WITH MONSIEUR DE SACY*

11 'Epictetus,' he [Pascal] said to him, 'is one of the world's philosophers who has best understood man's duties. Above all he wants him to see God as his principal aim, that he should be convinced that God governs everything justly; that he should be whole-heartedly obedient to him, that he should follow him willingly in everything, as he does nothing except with great wisdom. This attitude will prevent all complaints and murmurings, and will prepare his mind to endure peacefully the most hurtful events. Never say, he says, "I've lost it"; say instead: "I've given it back." "My son is dead, I've given him back. My wife is dead. I've given her back." The same with possessions and all the rest. "But I'm being deprived by a wicked man," you say. Why are you being worked up because whoever lent it to you is now taking it back? While you have been allowed to enjoy it, take care of it, just as you would something that belongs to another, as a man on his travels does in an inn. You must not, he says, wish for things to happen as you would like; you ought to want them to be as they are.'

12 'Remember', he says elsewhere, 'that you are here as a player, and that you are playing whichever character in a play the director chooses to give you. If he gives you a small part, then play it accordingly; if he gives you a long one, then play it accordingly; if he wants you to act the beggar, you must do it with all the simplicity you can muster, and so on. It's your task to act well the character assigned to you; the choice is another's. Always keep at the front of your mind death and the ills which seem most unbearable, and you will never have base thoughts, and will not covet anything excessively.'

13 'He also shows in thousands of ways what man must do. He wants him to be humble, to hide his good resolutions especially when he has just made them, to carry them out secretly: nothing does them more harm than to show them off. He never tires

of repeating that all man's study and wishes must be directed towards recognizing God's will, and following it.'

14 'There, sir,' said M. Pascal to M. de Sacy, 'is the knowledge of this great thinker who has understood the individual's duty so well. I'm tempted to say he would deserve adoration, if he had also realized the individual's powerlessness, since he would have to have been God to teach men both these things. And since he was earth and ashes, after perfectly understanding what we owe, this is how he becomes lost in the presumption of what we are able to do. He says that God gave man the means to fulfil all his obligations; that these means are within our power, that we must look for happiness through things that we are capable of, since that is why God gave them to us; that we must find out what is free within us; that property, life, and esteem are not in our power and do not therefore lead to God. Our spirit cannot be forced to believe what is false, nor our will to love something which makes it unhappy. These two powers are, therefore, free, and it is through them that we can become perfect; man through these powers can know God perfectly, love, obey, and please him, cure himself of all his vices, acquire virtue, and thereby become saintly and God's friend. These wickedly proud principles lead man into other errors, such as that the soul is part of the divine being, that pain and death are not evils, that we can commit suicide when we are so afflicted that we have to believe God is calling us, and there are still more.'

15 'As for Montaigne, whom you also want me to discuss, sir; since he was born in a Christian country, he professes the Catholic faith, and there is nothing strange about that. But as he wanted to discover what morality reason should maintain without the enlightenment of faith, he took his principles from this supposition; and so, in considering humanity deprived of any revelation of faith, he argues like this.'

16 'He puts everything into a universal doubt, and this doubt is so widespread that it becomes carried away by its very self; that is to say, he doubts whether he doubts, and doubting even this last proposition, his uncertainty goes round in an endless and restless circle. He contradicts both those who maintain that all is

uncertainty and those who maintain it is not, because he does
not want to maintain anything at all. It is in this self-doubting
doubt, this ignorance which is unaware of its own ignorance,
and which he calls his master form, which is the keystone of his
thinking, that he could not express in any positive terms. For if
he says that he doubts, he betrays himself with saying at least
that he does so, which was strictly not his intention. He could
only explain his position by a question, so, not wanting to say:
"I don't know," he says: "What do I know?" he makes this his
motto,* and, putting it on the scales which, weighing all the
contradictions, are in perfect equilibrium. That is to say, he is a
straightforward Pyrrhonist.'

17 'It is on this principle that all his statements and all *The Essays*
depend; it is the only thing he attempts to establish properly,
although he does not always underline his intentions. He thereby
slowly undermines everything which seems to be taken as cer-
tainties by mankind, not in order to establish the opposite with
the single-mindedness of which he is the only antagonist, but
simply to show that, the arguments appearing equal on both
sides, we do not know to which one to give our support.'

18 'In this spirit he scoffs at all guarantees: for example, he takes
issue with those who have thought to establish in France a
major remedy against trial by the masses and supposed justice
of the law: as if you could cut through the root of doubts from
which the trials arise, and as if there were dykes which could
arrest the flood of uncertainty and fence in the conjectures. It is
there that, when he says it would be as worthwhile submitting
his case to the first passer-by as to judges armed with numerous
rulings, he is not claiming that the law and order of the State
should be changed, he is not as ambitious as that; nor that his
opinion is better, he does not believe any are good. It is only to
prove the lack of value of the most widely held opinions, demonstrating that getting rid of all laws would diminish somewhat
the number of differences which the multiplicity of laws only
serves to increase, that difficulties grow proportionally as they
are weighed, obscurities are multiplied by commentaries; the
surest method of understanding the meaning of a speech is not

to probe it but to accept it at first glance: however little one examines it, all its clarity is scattered.'

19 'And so he forms opinions at random of human actions and historical points, sometimes one way, sometimes another, freely following his first inclination and without constraining his thoughts within the rules of reason, which only have false guidelines. He is delighted to show by his own example the contradictions within a single mind. For in this spontaneous genius it is entirely the same to him whether he carries it into an argument or not, always having in one or another example the means of demonstrating the weakness of various opinions, and being so advantageously positioned in this universal doubt that he is equally strengthened both in success and defeat.'

20 'It is on this basis, wavering and shaky as it is, that he attacks the heretics of his time with unconquerable firmness over their claim to be the only ones to know the true meaning of the Scriptures, and on this basis, too, that he most vigorously crushes the terrible impiety of those who dare assert that there is no God.'

21 'In particular he tackles them in the *Apology for Raymond Sebond*; finding them wilfully bereft of any revelation and, left to their natural understanding, irrespective of faith, he questions them on what authority they base themselves in judging this sovereign Being, who by its own definition is infinite, while they themselves know completely not the least thing about nature! He ask them what principles they rely on, he urges them to make them plain. He examines all those they can produce, and delves into them so thoroughly, with the talent in which he excels, that he demonstrates the hollowness of all those which seem most likely, and soundly based. He asks whether the soul can know anything, whether it knows itself, if it is substantial or accidental, body or spirit, what each of these things are, and if there is anything which does not belong to any of these orders, whether the soul knows of its own body; he asks what matter is and if the soul can differentiate between the endless variety of effects which have been caused by it, how it can reason, if it is material and how it can be attached to a particular body and feel

its passions, if it is spiritual; when it came into being, at the same time as the body or beforehand; and whether it ends at the same time as the body or not; if it is ever mistaken; if it knows when it errs, given that the essence of misapprehension consists in not knowing it; if in its dimness it does not as firmly believe that two plus three makes six, then later knows it is five; if animals can reason, think, talk, and who can decide what time is, what space or distance is, what movement is, what unity is, which are all things which surround us and which are completely inexplicable; what are health, illness, life, death, good, evil, justice, sin, which we talk about all the time; if we have within ourselves principles of truth, and if those we believe in and which we call axioms or universal ideas, because they are common to all men, are consonant with universal truth, and since we only know through faith that an all-benevolent Being gave them to us as true, creating us to know truth, who will know without this enlightenment whether, being drawn up haphazardly, they are not dubious, or whether, being drawn up by a false and wicked being, he did not give them to us as false in order to beguile us; thereby showing us that God and truth are inseparable and if one is or is not, it is dubious or certain, the other is necessarily the same. Who therefore knows if common sense, which we take to be the judge of truth, accords with the nature of him who created it? In addition, who knows what truth is, and how can we be sure of possessing it without knowing it? Who can even know what being is, which is impossible to define since there is nothing more general, and in order to explain it to you would have first of all to use that very word, saying, "It is . . .", etc.? And since we do not know what is soul, body, time, space, movement, truth, good, nor even being, nor explain the idea we have of them, how can we be sure that they are the same for all men, given that we have no other sign than the uniformity of the consequences, which is not always a sign for that of principles? For they can very well be different and nevertheless lead to the same conclusions, everyone knowing that truth is often concluded from falsehood.'

22 'Finally, he examines all the sciences in great depth; mathematics, in which he shows the uncertainty of its axioms and in the

terms it does not define like area, motion, etc., physics in very many other ways, medicine in infinitely more detail, history, politics, moral teaching and jurisprudence, and so on, in such a way that we are convinced that we do not think better now than in some dream from which we only awaken when we die, and in the course of which we have as little grasp of the principles of truth as we do during normal sleep. In this way he so strongly and cruelly rebukes reason devoid of faith that, making it doubtful whether it is reasonable, and whether animals are reasonable or not, or more so or less, he topples it from the peak of excellence which it had assumed for itself and puts it mercifully on a plane with animals, not allowing it to leave that level until instructed by its very Creator of the rank of which it is unaware, threatening, if it complains, to put it beneath everything else, which is just as easy as the other way round, giving it, however, the only means of reacting by recognizing its weakness in sincere humility, instead of puffing itself up with witless insolence.'

[M. de Sacy's intervention occupies paragraphs 23–6. Pascal then continues.]

27 'I admit, sir, that I cannot see without delight the haughty reason of this author so invincibly crushed by his own weapons, and this bloodthirsty revolt of man against man, who, in God's circle in which he rose through the maxims of his own puny reason, thrusts him down to the level of animals. And I would have unreservedly loved, with all my heart, the instigator of such great vengeance if, being a disciple of the Church through faith, he had followed morality's rules by persuading the men, whom he had so usefully humiliated, not to anger with new crimes him who alone can uproot them from the ones he has convinced them not even to be able to recognize.'

28 'But he is acting, unlike this kind, as a pagan. From this principle, he says that without faith everything is uncertain, and considering carefully how many there are searching for truth and goodness with no progress towards peace of mind, he concludes that we must leave that task to others; we must remain, however, at ease, floating lightly over subjects in case we

become embroiled in them with too much prodding, taking truth and goodness at face value without close investigation, because they are so flimsy that, however lightly you squeeze, they disappear between the fingers, leaving you empty handed. That is why he follows the guidelines of the senses and widely held notions, because he would have to do himself an injury to deny them, and he does not know if he would win, being ignorant of where truth lies. And so he recoils from pain and death, because his instinct pushes him that way, and for the same reason he does not want to resist it. But he does not draw the conclusion that they are real evils, not believing strongly in these natural feelings of fear, since there are other, pleasurable ones which are said to be wicked, though nature tells otherwise. So there is nothing outrageous in his behaviour; he goes about his business like everyone else, and everything they do in the foolish belief that they are following the path of true goodness, he does from another principle, which is that the similarities are equal on both sides; example and convenience are the balancing factors which motivate him.'

29 'So he follows the customs of his country because habit demands it: he rides his horse as one who, not being a philosopher, puts up with it but without believing it to be his right, not knowing if the animal, on the contrary, ought really to be making use of him. He also goes out of his way to avoid certain vices; he even holds to fidelity within marriage because of the pain which results from licentious behaviour; but if what he accepts exceeds what he avoids, he remains at peace, the overriding rule for his actions being convenience and calm. He utterly rejects, therefore, that stoic virtue depicted with a severe expression, wild-eyed, hair on end, a frowning, sweat-drenched brow, standing painfully and warily apart in a cheerless silence, alone on the pinnacle of a rock: a spectre, as he says, likely to frighten children, and who does nothing but continually search for peace of mind, which never comes. His nature is unaffected, open, pleasant, sprightly, not to say playful; it pursues what it finds delightful and nonchalantly disregards what ever happens, good or bad, softly embedded within peaceful idleness, from where it demonstrates to men desperately seeking happiness

that it can be found only there, and that ignorance and lack of curiosity are two soft pillows on which to lay a sound head, as he himself says.'

30 'I cannot hide from you, sir, that, reading this author and comparing him with Epictetus, I have realized that they were certainly the two greatest apologists for the two most famous philosophical sects in the world, the only ones based on reason, since you can follow one only of these paths: that is, that there is a God, and that is where the soverign good is placed or else God's existence is uncertain, so then the true good is as well, since it is incapable of being situated.'

31 'I have derived huge pleasure in noting in these different arguments the ways in which they have all reached a certain point of agreement with the true wisdom they have been trying to understand. For while it is gratifying to observe nature's desire to paint God in all his works, where you can see some characteristics because they are images of him, how much better it is to consider in the productions of these minds the efforts they have made to imitate essential virtue even when running away from it, and to notice in what ways they come close and where they digress, which is what I have tried to do in this study.'

32 'It is true, sir, that you have just admirably shown me the little use that Christians can make of reading these philosophical works. Nevertheless, with your permission, I will not withhold what I think from you, though ready to discard every insight which does not come from you: I will have the advantage in this either of having come across the truth by luck, or of having received it from you with assurance. It seems to me that the origin of these two sects' errors lies in not knowing that man's present state is different from the one in which he was created, so that the one, seeing traces of his initial greatness and ignorant of his corruption, treated nature as healthy and in no need of a healer, which leads him to the pinnacle of pride, whereas the other, experiencing the wretchedness of the present age and unaware of the dignity of his inception, treats nature as inevitably weak and incurable, which pitches him into despair of attaining true good, and thereby into extreme laziness.'

33 'And so these two states which had to be considered together in order to know the whole truth, having been considered separately, inevitably lead to one of these two vices, pride or sloth. Before grace all men are infallibly sunk in one or other of them, since, if they do not remain in their disorders through laziness, they escape them through vanity. What you have just told me of St Augustine is so true, and I find of wide significance. "For in fact we pay homage to them in many ways."'

34 'It is therefore from this imperfect understanding that one, aware of man's duty and unaware of his powerlessness, becomes lost in reckless confidence, and the other, aware of the powerlessness but not the duty, sinks into laziness. From this it would seem that, since the two contained both truth and error, you would have a perfect morality by binding them together. But instead of this peace, the alliance would simply end up with war and general destruction: for with one establishing certainty and the other doubt, one man's greatness and the other his weakness, they destroy both the truth and the false position of the other. Thus they can neither stand alone because of their faults, nor unite because of their differences, and in so doing wreck and annihilate each other to leave the way open for the truth of the Gospel. It is this which brings together differences through a wholly divine skill, and, by uniting all truths and banishing all falsehoods, it combines them into a truly celestial wisdom in which opposites, incompatible in human doctrines, agree. And the reason for this is that these wise men of the world place opposites in the same subject, one attributing greatness to nature, the other weakness to the very same nature, two views which could not subsist together, instead of which faith teaches us to situate them in different subjects, with all weakness assigned to nature, all strengths to grace. That is the new and astonishing conjunction that only a single God could teach, that he alone could achieve, and which is merely the image and effect of the inexpressible marriage of two natures in the single person of Man—God.'

35 'Please excuse me, sir,' said M. Pascal to M. de Sacy, 'for having got so carried away before you in theology, instead of keeping to philosophy, which was my only theme; but it drew

me there by degrees, and it is difficult not to engage in it, whatever truth you are dealing with, because it is the kernel of every truth. It is perfectly apparent here, since it so obviously encloses all these truths which are to be fond in these opinions. And so I do not see why any of them could refuse to follow it. For if they are filled with the idea of man's greatness, how did they imagine that it would not yield before the Scripture's promises, which are none other than the worthy prize of a God's death? And if they enjoy the spectacle of nature's frailty, their idea is no longer on the level of sin's true weakness, whose cure was that same death. So everyone finds in it more than they wished for; and the wonderful thing is that they find themselves united in it, the same people who were unable to make an alliance in an infinitely inferior position.'

37 'As to the usefulness of this reading,' said M. Pascal, 'I will tell you quite simply what I think. In Epictetus I find an incomparable skill in disturbing the peace of mind of those people who seek it in external things, and in forcing them to recognize that they are genuinely slaves and wretchedly blind. They will find nothing but the errors and pain they are trying to escape if they do not unreservedly give themselves to God. Montaigne is incomparable in the way he confounds the pride of those people who, in their lack of faith, lay claim to true justice, in disabusing those who cling to their beliefs and think they have found unwavering truths in the sciences, and in so thoroughly convincing reason of its dearth of understanding and its deviations that it is difficult, when Montaigne's principles are properly observed, to be tempted to find anything repugnant in mysteries. For the spirit is so trampled upon by them that it is far from wanting to discover whether the Incarnation or the mystery of the Eucharist is feasible, something ordinary people only too often raise.'

38 'But if Epictetus overcomes laziness, he can lead to pride, with the result that he can be extremely harmful to those who are not convinced of the corruption of the most perfect justice outside faith. And Montaigne is completely harmful to those with some leaning towards impiety and vice. This is why reading these philosophers must be carefully and discretely monitored, and with consideration of the habits and circumstances of those to

whom they are recommended. It seems to me that only by joining them together can they succeed in doing no real harm, because one counterbalances the harm of the other: not that they can offer virtue, but they can discomfort vice, the soul being fought over by these two opposites, one chasing off pride and the other laziness, and being unable to settle into either of these vices through its reasoning, nor to escape them all.'

THE ART OF PERSUASION*

1 The art of persuasion is necessarily linked to the way in which men agree to what is suggested to them, and to the types of things we want them to believe.

2 No one is unaware that there are two ways by which opinions are received into the soul, which are its two principal powers: understanding and will. The most natural is by the understanding, for we ought never to consent to any but demonstrated truths; but the most usual, although against nature, is by the will. For every man is almost always led to believe not through proof, but through that which is attractive.

   This way is low, unworthy and alien, and so everyone refuses to acknowledge it. Everyone professes not to believe nor even to like anything which does not merit it.

3 I am not speaking here of divine truths, which I would take care not to include under the art of persuasion, since they are infinitely superior to nature. Only God can put them into the soul, and in the way he thinks fit.

   I know that he wanted them to enter from the heart into the mind, and not from the mind into the heart, in order to humiliate that proud power of reasoning which claims it ought to be the judge of what is chosen by the will, and to heal that feeble will which is completely corrupted by vile attachments. Hence, instead of speaking about human matters that they have to be known before they can be loved, which has become a proverb, the saints, speaking of divine matters, say that you have to love them in order to know them, and that you enter into truth only by charity, which they have made into one of their most useful pronouncements.

4 From this it appears that God has established this supernatural order, quite the opposite of the order which should have been natural to human minds in natural things—which they have nevertheless corrupted by acting with regard to profane matters as they should have acted only in sacred matters, because we

believe almost only in the things we like. Hence our estrangement from consenting to the truths of the Christian religion which are quite contrary to our pleasures. *Tell us the things we like and we will listen to you* (adapted, Exod. 20: 19), the Jews said to Moses, as if pleasure should regulate belief! So it is to punish this disorder by an order true to himself that God sows his illumination in people's minds only after quelling the rebellion of will by a totally heavenly sweetness which delights and overwhelms it.

5 I am only, therefore, talking about truths within our grasp; and about those I say that the mind and the heart are like gateways through which they are received by the soul, but that very few enter through the mind; instead they are prompted in great numbers by the headstrong whims of the will without the counsel of reasoning.

6 These powers each have their principles and the prime movers of their actions.

Those of the mind are natural truths, known to everyone, just as the whole is greater than its parts, apart from several particular axioms to which some are receptive and others not, but which, once allowed, are as powerful, though false, in engendering belief as the truest ones.

Those of the will arise from certain natural desires, common to everyone, such as the desire for happiness which no one is without, apart from several particular things which everyone follows in order to achieve it, and which, since they have the capacity to please, are powerful enough, though harmful in fact, to activate the will, as if they were achieving its true happiness.

That is what has to be said concerning the powers which lead us to consent.

7 But the qualities of the things we have to persuade people of are very varied.

Some things are inferred by necessary consequence from common principles and recognized truths. Those can infallibly persuade, for, by showing the relationship which they have with agreed principles, convincing people becomes necessarily inevitable.

There are some which have a strong link with objects of our satisfaction; and these are again accepted with certainty. For as soon as the soul is made to realize that something can lead it to what it loves above all, it is inevitable that it should joyfully embrace it.

But those things which have both these links, with accepted truths, and with the desires of the heart, are so sure of their effect that nothing in nature can outdo them.

As, obversely, what has no connection with either our beliefs or our pleasures is unwelcome, false, and completely foreign to us.

8 There is nothing to be doubted in all these encounters. But there are some where things we want to be believed are well founded on accepted truths, but which at the same time are opposed to the pleasures we enjoy most. And these ones are in great danger of demonstrating, in what is only too common an experience, what I was saying at the beginning: that this arrogant soul, which prided itself on acting only through reason, follows through a shameful, headstrong choice what a corrupt will desires, whatever resistance the only too enlightened mind can bring to bear on it.

It is then that there is an uncertain balance between truth and pleasure, and that the knowledge of the one and the feeling of the other creates a contest whose outcome is very uncertain, since, in order to judge it, we would need to know everything that happens in the deepest interior of a human being, who nearly never knows.

9 From this it appears that, whatever it is one wants to persuade people of, we must take into consideration the person with whom we are concerned, of whom we know the mind and heart, the principles admitted, and the things loved; and then we must take note, in the matter concerned, of the relationship it has with admitted truths or of the objects of delight through the charms we attribute to them.

So the art of persuasion consists as much in pleasing as it does in convincing, humanity being so much more governed by whim than by reason.

10 But, of these two methods, one of convincing, the other of pleasing, I will only give the rules for the first; and even then in the case of a person accepting the principles remaining firm in endorsing them: otherwise, I do not know if there is an art of accommodating proofs to the fickleness of our whims.

11 But the way of pleasing is incomparably more difficult, more subtle, more useful, and more admirable. And so, if I do not discuss it, it is because I am incapable of doing so; and I feel myself so unequal to the task that for me it would be absolutely impossible.

It is not that I do not believe that there are rules as reliable for pleasing as for demonstrating, and that whoever knows perfectly how to know and use them does not succeed as surely as making himself loved by kings and all sorts of people as he does by demonstrating the elements of geometry to those with sufficient imagination to understand the hypotheses.

But I consider, and perhaps it is my weakness which makes me believe it, that it is impossible to achieve. At least, I know that if anyone is capable of it, it is people I know, and that no one has such clear and abundant knowledge on this matter.

The reason for this extreme difficulty comes from the fact that the principles of pleasure are not firm and steadfast. They are different for everyone, and vary in each particular, with such diversity that there is no one more unlike another than themselves at different periods. A man's pleasures are not the same as a woman's: those of rich and poor differ; prince, soldier, merchant, bourgeois, peasant, the old, the young, the healthy, and the sick; all vary. The slightest mishap changes them.

12 But there is an art, and this is the one I am offering, of making clear the connection between truths and their principles, either true or pleasurable, provided that the principles once accepted remain firm and are never denied.

But as there are few principles of this kind, and as, apart from geometry which takes only very simple lines into consideration, there are almost no truths about which we remain in agreement, and even fewer objects of pleasure over which we do not hourly change our mind, I do not know if there is a way of laying down rules which would harmonize what we say with the fickleness of our whims.

13 This art, which I call the art of persuasion, and which is properly only the way of conducting perfect methodical proofs, consists of three principal parts: defining the terms to be used in clear definitions; proposing obvious principles or axioms to prove the point in question; and always mentally substituting in the demonstration the definitions for the things defined.

The reason for this method is obvious, since it would be useless to put forward something one wanted to prove and to undertake its demonstration, if one had not previously clearly defined all the terms which were not understood; and similarly, the demonstration must be preceded by demand for the obvious principles which are necessary. For if we do not ensure the foundations, we cannot be sure of the building; and in the end we must do this by mentally substituting definitions for the things defined, since otherwise we could misconstrue the various meanings which come together in the terms. It is easy to see that, looking at this method, we are certain to convince, since all the terms being understood and completely free from ambiguity on account of the definitions, and the principles agreed, if in the demonstration we always mentally substitute definitions for the things defined, the insuperable force of the consequences cannot fail to take full effect.

So a demonstration in which these circumstances have been kept can never have incurred the slightest doubt; and those where they have been missing can never be convincing.

14 Therefore it is important to understand them well and hold to them, and that is why, to make it easier and more immediate, I will give them all in a few rules which embrace everything one needs to know about the elaboration of definitions, axioms, and demonstrations, and, as a result, the whole method of mathematical proofs of the art of persuasion.

Rules for definitions

1. Do not try to define anything so obvious in itself that there are no clearer terms in which to explain it.

2. Do not allow any slightly obscure or ambiguous terms without definition.

3. Do not use any but perfectly well-known or already explained words in a definition.

Rules for axioms

1. Do not allow any of the necessary principles without having asked whether you agree with it, however clear or obvious it seems.

2. Do not ask of an axiom anything other than something perfectly self-evident.

Rules for demonstrations

1. Do not try to demonstrate anything which is so clearly self-evident that there is no simpler way of proving it.

2. Prove all slightly obscure propositions, and only use very obvious axioms, or previously agreed and demonstrated propositions, in their proofs.

3. Always mentally substitute definitions in place of things defined, so as not to mislead by ambiguity those terms which have been restricted by definitions.

15 These are the eight rules which contain all the precepts of solid, unalterable proofs. Of these, there are three which are not strictly necessary and which can be disregarded without error; which are indeed difficult and almost impossible to keep properly the whole time, although it is sounder to do so as far as possible. They are the first of each of the three sections:

For definitions

1. Do not define any term which is perfectly understood.

For axioms

1. Do not allow questioning of any perfectly obvious, simple axiom.

For demonstrations

1. Do not demonstrate anything which is clearly self-evident.

For there is no doubt that it is not a great mistake to define and explain things very clearly, however clear they are in themselves, nor to allow advance questioning about axioms which cannot be refuted where they are necessary, nor, finally, to prove propositions which one would accept without proof.

16 But the five other rules are absolutely indispensable, and cannot be discarded without incurring an essential deficiency, or often without error; and that is why I will repeat them here individually.

Necessary rules for definitions

    2. Do not allow any slightly obscure or ambiguous terms without definitions.

    3. Only use perfectly well-known or previously explained terms in definitions.

Necessary rules for axioms

    2. Only ask of an axiom things which are perfectly obvious.

Necessary rules for demonstrations

    2. Prove all propositions, using only in the proof obviously self-evident axioms, or already demonstrated or agreed propositions.

    3. Never employ ambiguity in the terms by failing to substitute mentally the definitions which circumscribe and explain them.

These are the five rules which form the essential basis for making proofs convincing, unalterable, and, to sum it up, mathematical; and together the eight rules make them even more perfect.

17 Now I pass on to the order of the rules, in which we must lay out the propositions so that they should be in an exact, mathematical sequence.

After establishing . . .

18 This is what the art of persuasion consists in, encapsulated in these two rules: define the names we prescribe; prove everything, substituting mentally the definitions for the things defined.

19 At this point I think it is timely to forestall three main objections which could be made. One, that this method is nothing new.

The next, that it is easily learned, without having to study the rudiments of mathematics, since it consists in these two statements acquired at the first reading.

And, lastly, that it is fairly futile, since it can practically only be used within mathematical fields.

20 For the first objection, which is that these rules are commonplace world-wide, that you have to define and prove everything, and that even logicians have included them in their maxims, I wish that it were so, and so widely known that I did not have to take the trouble of looking so carefully for the source of all the mistakes in reasoning which are truly commonplace. But it is so far from the truth that, if you exclude only mathematicians, who are so few that they are unique in whole communities over a long period, you find no one else who knows them. It would be easy to make those people understand, who have completely grasped the little I have said. But if they have not fathomed it completely, I admit they will have nothing to learn from it.

But if they have penetrated the spirit of these rules, and if the rules have made sufficient impression to take root and establish themselves, these people will realize how great a difference there is between what is said here, and what a few logicians have perhaps written by chance somewhere or another in their works, which approximate to it.

21 People who have a discerning mind know how much difference there is between similar words, depending on the context and circumstances which surround them. Do we truly believe that two individuals who have read and learnt by heart the same book equally understand it, if one knows it understanding all the principles, the strength of the consequences, the answers to the objections which can be made, the whole harmonious arrangement of the work; while for the other it consists of a dead language, and seeds which, though the same which have produced such fertile trees, have remained dry and unfruitful in the barren mind which absorbed them to no purpose?

22 All those who say the same things are not master of them in the
same way; and that is why the peerless author of the *Art of
Speaking** insists so carefully on making plain that we must not
judge a man's intellect by the appositeness of an overheard
witticism; but, instead of extending our admiration for a good
discourse to the one who delivers it, we should, he says, examine the mind from which it originates; we should find out if
he has it off by heart or if it is a happy accident; whether it
is received coldly and contemptuously, so as to discover if he
resents that what he says is not given the acclaim he thinks is its
due. More often than not he will be seen to withdraw it immediately, and they will be drawn away from the better ideas they
do not believe in to be plunged into another base and absurd
one. We have therefore to examine how the idea has come to its
author; how, in what way, and how deeply he understands it.
Otherwise a hasty judgement will be judged a rash one.

23 I would like to ask reasonable people if this principle: *Matter by
nature is naturally and invincibly incapable of thinking*, and this
one: *I think therefore I am*, are in fact the same thing in Descartes's
mind and in St Augustine's, who said the same thing twelve
hundred years earlier.

Actually I am very far from saying that Descartes* was not
the true author, even though he would only have discovered it
by reading that great saint. For I know how much difference
there is between writing something by chance without reflecting
longer and more deeply about it, and appreciating in this statement a valuable sequence of consequences which proves the
distinction between material and spiritual natures, and making a
firm principle from it supported by an entire physics, as Descartes
tried to do. For, without examining whether he effectively succeeded in his attempt, I am supposing that he did, and it is in
this supposition that I say that this maxim is as different in his
writings from the same maxim in other people's who put it in as
an aside, as is a dead man from a fully alive and vigorous one.

24 One man will say something of his own accord without understanding its profundity, where another will understand a wonderful set of consequences which makes us claim confidently
that it is not the same maxim, and that he does not derive it

either from the person he learnt it from, any more than a fine tree belongs to the person who had sown the seedling, thoughtlessly and unaware, in rich soil which would have nourished it anyway through its own fertility.

The same thoughts sometimes develop quite differently in another than in their author: infertile in their natural habitat, copious when transplanted.

25 But it happens much more often that a good mind produces by itself all the fruit that its own thoughts are capable of, and then later others, having heard them praised, borrow and parade them, but without realizing their worth; and it is then that the difference between the same statement in several mouths is the most apparent.

26 This is how logic has perhaps borrowed mathematical rules without understanding their strength. So putting them at random amongst the ones which belong to it, it does not therefore follow that they have become part of the mathematical spirit; and I would be very far, if they do not offer other signs than those said in passing, of putting them on the same level with that science, which teaches the true way of guiding our reason.

On the contrary, I would be very willing to exclude them, almost irrevocably. For having said it in passing, without taking care that everything is included in it, and instead of following these insights, getting endlessly lost in useless searches to run after what they offer yet cannot give, really shows that one is hardly clear-sighted, and even more so than if one had not missed following them because they had not been noticed.

27 The method of not erring is something everyone searches for. Logicians profess to point it out, only mathematicians attain it, and apart from their science and whoever imitates it, there are no true demonstrations. The whole art is enclosed in the sole precepts we have stated. They alone suffice. They alone provide proof. All other rules are useless or harmful.

I know this through long experience of all sorts of books and of people.

28 On this point I make the same judgement on those who say that mathematicians give them nothing new with these rules,

because in fact they had them, though mixed up with numerous other useless or false ones from which they could not distinguish them, like people who, searching for a valuable diamond amongst a great number of fakes and who could not tell the difference, would boast, holding them all together, of holding the real one, as much as the man who, not pausing over the worthless pile, puts his hand on the very stone being looked for, and for which the rest were not being thrown away. The flaw of false reasoning is an illness which is cured by these two remedies. Another has been composed of a huge quantity of useless herbs in which the beneficial ones are mingled and amongst which they are ineffectual, because of the noxious qualities of the mixture.

To remove all the sophisms and ambiguities from the specious arguments they invented arbitrary names which amaze everyone who comes across them; and, instead of being able to undo all the kinks of the complicated knot by pulling one of the ends earmarked by the mathematicians, they have marked out an extraordinary number of others in which those mentioned are included, without their knowing which is the right one.

And so, by showing us a number of different paths, which they say lead us in the direction we are pointed, although there are only two which actually go there, we have to know how to make them out individually. It will be claimed that mathematics, which marks them out exactly, gives only what the others have already given, because they gave, in fact, the same thing and more, careless of the fact that what was already there lost its worth through its abundance, that by adding to it, it subtracted from it.

29 Nothing is more widespread than good things: the only question is to recognize them; and they are certainly natural and within our grasp, and even known by everyone. But we do not know how to recognize them. This is universal. It is not in extraordinary and unusual things that excellence in whatever field is to be found. We make an effort to reach up to them and we fall away. More often we should stoop. The best books are those which the people who read them believe they could have written. Nature, which alone is good, is familiar and available to everyone.

30 I have no doubt, therefore, that these rules, being the true ones, ought to be simple, uncomplicated, and natural, as indeed they are. It is not *barbara* and *baralipton** which make up the argument. The mind must not be blinkered. Stilted, laboured ways fill it by some foolish presumption with an unnatural loftiness and a vain, absurd pomposity, instead of a solid, vigorous sustinence.

One of the main reasons which so put people off who are starting to penetrate the understanding of the right way they have to follow is the concept they first encounter that good things are inaccessible by being labelled great, mighty, elevated, sublime. That ruins everything. I would like to call them lowly, commonplace, familiar. These names befit them better. I hate these pompous words . . .

[WRITINGS ON GRACE]*

LETTER
[ON THE POSSIBILITY OF THE
COMMANDMENTS]*

1. [Beginning of the *Letter*: Detailed draft]

1 I have neither the time, the books, nor the competence to answer you as precisely as I would wish; I will do so however as well as I can at the moment so that, seeing these things I have often said to you written down, they will make a greater impression on you and you will not need me to repeat them to you.

2 You ask me to respond to these words of chapter 11 of the 6th session of the Council of Trent: *That the commandments are not impossible for the justified.* I will do what I can to satisfy you.

3 The proposition: *The commandments are possible for the justified*, has two quite different and separate meanings. This is not in this case a distinction of the schools; it is substantial and real, both in the nature of the argument and in the terms of the Council.

4 The first meaning which springs to mind and which you think is that of the Council in this instance, which you will find not to be the case, is that the justified man, considered in one particular moment of his justification, always has the proximate power to fulfil the commandments in the following one, which is the view of the rest of the Pelagians and which the Church has always repudiated, particularly in this Council.

5 The other meaning, which does not quite so readily spring to mind, and which nevertheless is that of the Council in this instance, is that the justified person, acting as such and with a movement of charity, can fulfil the commandments in the action he performs charitably. I know perfectly well that there are so few grounds for doubting that these charitably performed actions do not conform with the precepts, that it can scarcely be

believed that the Council wanted to define something so obvious; but when you think that the Lutherans formally upheld that the actions of the justified, even charitably performed, are necessarily always sins, and that concupiscence, which controls everything in this life, so strongly undermines the effects of charity that, however justified the men and whatever movements of charity motivate them, cupidity always plays such a large part that not only do they not fulfil the precepts, but they violate them, whatever the grace by which they may be aided, you will certainly see why it was necessary for the Council to pronounce against such an intolerable error.

6 You see how different these two meanings are; with one we clearly understand that the justified have the right to persevere in justice; with the other we clearly understand that the commandments are possible to charity, as it is in the justified in this life; and although these two meanings are put here into such different words, they can both still be expressed in these words: *The commandments are possible for the justified.*

7 But as this proposition is equivocal, you will not find it odd that it can be agreed with in one meaning and denied in the other. So there have been opposing heretics on both sides too.

8 The rest of the Pelagians maintain that the commandments are always possible for the justified, in the first sense; and the Church denies it.

9 The Lutherans maintain that the commandments are impossible, in the second sense; the Church denies it.

10 And so the Council, having to fight against such different errors (since it is as heretical to maintain that the commandments are always possible in the first meaning as to maintain that they are impossible in the second), as they are quite separate matters, refutes them separately. It fights against the Lutheran one in this eleventh chapter which is solely concerned with countering this heresiarch, and in the canons 18 and 25 against the semi-pelagian one in the thirteenth chapter, and in canons 16 and 22 which are formulated in it. And so its aim in chapter 11 is simply to point out that the justified, working through the love

of God, can perform works free from sin; and hence that he can observe the commandments if he is working through charity, and not that he always has the proximate power to keep that charity which makes them possible.

11 And its aim in chapter 13 is to declare that it is false that the justified always have the proximate power to persevere, anathematizing in canon 22, where it is formulated, those who say that the justified person has the power to persevere in justice without special help, and hence that it is not common to all the justified.

12 And although the Council thereby establishes that the justified not only do not have actual perseverance without special help, but they do not even have the power to persevere without special help, which is only another way of saying that the justified who do not have this special power do not have the power to accomplish the commandments in the next moment, since to persevere is nothing other than to accomplish the commandments in the next moments, nevertheless its decision is not contrary to chapter 11, *That the commandments are not impossible for the justified*, because of the different meanings of this proposition.

13 To prove what I am saying, you have only to translate the whole of chapter 11; and if you have it done, you will see the meaning of the Council clearly demonstrated. It first of all declares its proposition, *That the commandments are not impossible for the justified*, which are St Augustine's words. And to examine the meaning he implies, I ask you only to see the proof it gives of it, the conclusions it draws from the proof, and the canons it formulates from it. For if the proof it gives of it only has force in the first meaning, if the conclusion it draws is in univocal terms for that first same meaning, and the canons similarly purely in the first meaning, who can doubt the sense of the proposition?

14 Here is its proof: the commandments are not impossible for the justified, *since those who are God's children*, that is to say, the justified, *love Jesus Christ, and he said that those who love him keep his word*, that is to say, his precepts. This is an excellent proof for showing the possibility in the first meaning: for in order to

show that the commandments are possible through charity, this is an excellent proof: for Jesus Christ said that those who love him observe his commandments. But it cannot have any value in showing the possibility in the other meaning, that is for the future; for it is well said that those who love Jesus Christ at a present moment observe his commandments in the very moment at which they love him, but not that they will have the power to keep them in the future. And so the Council warns in the same part *that they can keep the commandments with God's help.*

15 Following this section, having quoted many passages from the Scriptures which call for justice and the observation of precepts, which would be absurd if human nature, even aided by grace, were absolutely incapable of it, it concludes in this way: from which it is established that those people repudiate the true faith who say that the justified man sins in all his good acts.

16 And consequently, the Council claiming that it has proved what it proposed, *That the commandments are not impossible for the justified,* when, through the use of this proof, *for those who love Jesus Christ keep his word,* it draws this conclusion: *therefore the justified does not sin in all his good acts,* can we deny that it claimed anything else in its proposition, that can be made equivocal than what it said in its conclusion, which cannot be interpreted in different ways, which is: *that the justified does not sin when he performs good acts and through the instigation of grace?*

17 That is made perfectly clear in the canons which it formulates, which are the substance, and as it were the soul, of the chapter. Here are all those it draws up concerning possibility.

18 **Canon 25**
If anyone says that a justified person sins venially in all good works, or, which is even worse, mortally, and that he thereby merits eternal suffering, and that he is not damned for the sole reason that God does not impute his works to him for his damnation: let them be anathema.

19 Is the meaning of the Council not clear?

20   Canon 18

If anyone says that observing the commandments is impossible for a man even if he is justified and constituted in grace: let them be anathema.

21 Is anything clearer than this? It seems that the Council was afraid that its expression would be misinterpreted and for that reason was not satisfied with saying: *if someone says that the commandments are impossible for the justified, let them be anathema*; but it said: *if it is said that the commandments are impossible for the justified person and that he is constituted under grace*; in order that we cannot believe that it was speaking of this Pelagian possibility; and that it was clearly understood that it was not fighting against those who say that the commandments are impossible for the justified person, even with grace and in the time he was constituted under grace, to use these terms: for the Council having said *justified* would not have added *and constituted under grace*, unless to make its intention even clearer and without any equivocal meaning, given that the canons are always produced in very short and compact terms.

22 I therefore leave you to judge how far those people are lacking in strength who look for equivocation in this chapter of the Council. And although this is sufficient to answer what you are asking me, I will add, however, another proof to satisfy you even further. These words: *The commandments are not impossible for the justified*, taken from St Augustine, who is quoted in the margin of the Council, must not be thought to have been used in a meaning opposite to St Augustine's; for it only introduced his words in order to introduce his meaning, since, otherwise, it would have been acting in bad faith.

23 Now, whether St Augustine ever implied anything else with those words, every time he used them, other than the way the Council does in this instance, you have only to glance at his writings to find out. I think he almost never said it without explaining it this way: that is, that the commandments are not impossible to charity and that they are impossible without charity; and that the only reason they are given is to make known the need we have to receive this charity from God. This is how he

puts it: *God, just and good, did not command impossible things—Aug. De natura et gratia, chap. 69*; which adverts us to do what is easy and to ask for what is difficult. For everything is easy with charity. And elsewhere: *De perfect. just., c. 10—Who is unaware that what is done through love is not difficult?*

[At this point a sheet of the manuscript which contained four lines of dots is missing.]

24 It would be no help to point out further passages. But, having shown you that the Council did not imply that the justified have proximate power to observe the commandments in the future, you will easily see that it could not have claimed it, and that not only did it not, but that it could not have done so.

25 This is what manifestly comes out of canon 22; for since it forbids, on pain of anathema, saying that all the justified have the power to persevere in justice, does it not necessarily imply that all the justified do not have the proximate power to observe the commandments in the next moment, since there is no difference between the power to observe the commandments in the next moment and the power to persevere in justice, since to persevere in justice is just the same as observing the commandments in the next moment?

26 This definition of the 22nd canon also necessarily implies that the justified do not always have the proximate power to persevere in prayer; for since the promises of the Gospel and the Scriptures assure us of the certainty of obtaining the necessary justice for salvation, if we ask for it through the spirit of grace and in the way we ought, is it not unquestionable that there is no difference between persevering in prayer, and persevering in the impenetration of justice; and hence, if all the justified have the proximate power of persevering in prayer, they also have the proximate power to persevere in justice, which cannot be refused to their prayer? This is strictly contrary to the decision of the canon.

27 Does this decision not also contain, as a necessary consequence, that it is not true that God never leaves the justified without proximately sufficient power to pray in the next moment, since

there is no difference between having proximate power to persevere in prayer; and hence, if all the justified have proximate
power to persevere in prayer, and, following on from this, they
all have proximate power to persevere in justice, against the
explicit terms of the Council, which declares that the justified
not only do not have perseverance, but even do not have the
power to persevere without special help, that is to say, that it is
not common to all?

28 From this you see how the necessary conclusion is that whilst it
it true in one meaning that God never abandons a justified
person if that person does not abandon him first, that is to say
that God never refuses his grace to those who pray to him as
they ought, and never distances himself from those who sincerely seek him, it is, however, true in another meaning that
God sometimes abandons the justified before they have abandoned him; that is to say that God does not always give proximate power to the justified to persevere in prayer. For since the
Council declares that the justified do not always have the power
to persevere, from which we have seen it can be necessarily
inferred that it would be to oppose the Council to say, of any
justified person at all, that God gave him proximate power to
pray in the next moment; does it not seem that there are justified people whom God abandons without this power while they
are still justified, that is to say before they have abandoned him,
even with no venial sin, since, if God refused none this proximate help who have committed no venial sin since their justification, it would follow that all the justified would receive with
their justification the proximate power to persevere through
general, not special, help?

29 From which we therefore conclude that, according to the Council, the commandments are always possible for the justified, in
one meaning; and in another meaning, the commandments are
sometimes impossible for them; that God never abandons a
justified person, if he does not abandon God, and in another
meaning, God sometimes abandons him first, and that one has
to be either quite blind or insincere to find a contradiction in
these propositions which coexist so easily. For it is only another
way of saying that the commandments are always possible to

charity, that all the justified do not always have the power to persevere: this is not contradictory. And that God never refuses what has been sincerely asked in prayer, and that God does not always grant perseverance in prayer. That is not contradictory in the slightest.

30 That is what I had to say to you on this subject, which I am glad to have investigated to make you understand that the propositions which in words are contradictory are not so in meaning. And as you have often thought you found contradiction in the things which I have been privileged to tell you, and because these days one comes across a number of people bold enough to suggest that there is a contradiction in St Augustine's thoughts, I cannot refuse such an opportune chance to explain fully the principles which reconcile so strongly the seemingly contradictory propositions which are, in fact, linked together in an admirable sequence.

31 We have only to realize that there are two ways in which individuals seek God; two ways in which God seeks individuals; two ways in which God abandons the individual; two in which the individual abandons God; two in which the individual perseveres; two in which God perseveres in doing good to the individuals, and so on.

TREATISE CONCERNING PREDESTINATION

2. [Beginning of the *Treatise*: Detailed draft]

1 It is an established fact that amongst men many are damned and many saved. It is also established that those who are saved wanted to be, and God wanted it too, for if God had not wanted it, they would not have been, and if they too had not wanted it themselves, they would not have been. He who made us without ourselves cannot save us without ourselves.

2 It is also true that those who are damned certainly wished to commit the sins which merited their damnation, and that God too wished to condemn them.

3 So it is obvious that God's will and man's concur in the salvation and damnation of those who are saved and damned.

4 And there can be no question about all these things.

5 If therefore we ask why men are saved or damned, in one sense we can say that it is because God wishes it, and in another that it is because human beings wish it.

6 But the question is knowing which of the two wills, that is the will of God or the human will, is the superior and dominant one, the source, principle and cause of the other.

7 The question is whether the human will is the cause of God's will, or whether God's will is the cause of the human will.

8 And the one which is dominant and superior to the other will be regarded as unique in some way; not that it is, but because it includes the concurring of the secondary will. And the action will be related to this primary will and not the other; although we cannot deny that it can also, in some sense, be ascribed to the secondary will; but it properly belongs to the superior will as its principle. For the secondary will is such that we can say in one sense that activity proceeds from it, since it concurs in it, and in one sense that it does not emanate from it because that will is

not the source; but the original will is such that we can say that activity proceeds from it, but in no way can we say that activity does not proceed from it.

9 And this is what St Paul says: *I live, not me, but Jesus Christ lives in me*. Certainly the first part of what he says: *I live*, is not wrong, for he was alive, and not only in body (which was not the point in that instance), but also spiritually, for he was in a state of grace, and elsewhere he says about himself several times: *We were dead, and he brought us to life* (Eph. 2: 5), etc. But though it was certainly true that he was alive, he denies it straightaway, saying: *I am not alive, 'Non ego vivo'*. The apostle was not a liar; it is true that he is alive, since he says: *I am alive*. It is also therefore true that he is not alive, since he says: '*Jam non ego, I am not alive*. And these two truths coexist, because his life, although it is his, does not come originally from him. He is alive only through Jesus Christ; Jesus Christ's life is the source of his.

10 And so it is true in a sense that he is alive, since he has life; it is also true in a sense that he is not alive, since he is only alive through another's life. But it is true that Jesus Christ is alive and it cannot be said that he is not.

11 This is what Jesus Christ says himself: *It is the Father, living in me, who is doing this work* (John 14: 10), and nevertheless he also says: *The same works as I do myself* (John 14: 12). Jesus Christ is not a liar and his humility does not damage the truth. We can therefore say, since he said it, that he did works and that he did not; but it is established that the divinity did them in him, and we cannot say that he did not do them.

12 The Prophet says this: *Yahweh, you are giving us peace since you treat us as our deeds deserve* (Isa. 26: 12). So the works are God's, since he did them, and the works are of us, since they are ours.

13 St Paul says this: *I worked, not through me, but the grace of Jesus Christ which is with me*. His words are not false. How can he have worked and not worked, unless it was the grace which was with him that worked, unless it was because his work can be called his own since his will concurred with it; and cannot be called his own since his will was not the source of his own desires? But God's grace is the one which can be said to have

worked, since it prepared his will, since it carried out within him the wish and the action, and it cannot be said of it that it did not work, since it was the origin and the source of his work.

14 He says this elsewhere: *Non ego, sed quod inhabitat in me peccatum* [It is no more I that do it, but sin that dwelleth in me (Rom. 7: 20)], speaking of the indeliberate movements of his will.

15 There are a number of examples in the Scriptures of these ways of speaking which make us see that, when two wills work together towards an end, if one is superior, dominant, and the infallible cause of the other, the activity can be attributed to the dominant one and cannot not be attributed to it.

16 So let us consider the dominant will as unique, although it is not, because it is unique to the one we can all attribute activity, and of which it cannot be denied. We attribute action to it. Following this line, the question is to know:

If the question whether there are damned and saved men proceeds from what God wishes or what human beings wish.

17 That is to say that:

The question is to know if God, submitting himself to human wills, had an absolute will to save some and damn others, and as a consequence of this decree, inclined to good the wills of the elect, and to evil the wills of the damned, in order to conform both to his absolute will to save or condemn them.

Or whether, submitting to the free will of men the use of his grace, he foresaw in some way how the ones and the others would want to use it, and following their will, he framed the will for their salvation or their damnation.

18 That is the question which is now being argued between people, and which is differently decided by three opinions.

The first are the Calvinists, the second the Molinists, and finally there are the disciples of St Augustine.

CALVINISTS

19 The opinion of Calvinists is:

That God, in creating men, created some to damn them and

others to save them, through an absolute will and without any foreseen merit.

That, in order to execute this absolute will, God made Adam sin, and not only allowed, but caused, his fall.

That in God there is no difference at all between *doing* and *allowing*.

That, God having made Adam sin and thereby all humanity in him, he sent Jesus Christ for the redemption of those he wished to save when he created them, and that he gives them charity* and salvation unquestionably.

That God abandons, and during the whole of their lives deprives of charity, those he decided to condemn when he created them.

20 That is the appalling opinion of these heretics, injurious to God and unbearable for men. These are the shameless blasphemies by which they establish in God an absolute will without foreseen merit or sin to damn or save his creatures.

MOLINISTS

21 Hating this abominable view and the excess in which it abounds, the Molinists took up not only an opposite opinion, which would have been enough, but an absolutely contradictory one.

This is that God has a conditional will generally to save all human beings.

That to achieve this Jesus Christ became incarnate to save them all, with no exception, and that,

His grace being offered to all, it depends on each individual to use it well or badly.

That God, having seen for all eternity the good or bad use which would be made of his grace, wanted to save those who would make good use of it and damn those who would misuse it, not having on his own part any absolute will either to damn or save any one man.

22 This view, contrary to that of the Calvinists, produces a quite different effect. It flatters the common sense, which the other one shocks. It flatters it and, making men masters of their salvation or damnation, excludes from God any absolute will, and

makes salvation and damnation derive from human will, whereas in Calvin's view both derive from divine will.

23 So these are the opposing errors between which St Augustine's followers, treading more slowly and more thoughtfully, base their view in this way:

FOLLOWERS OF ST AUGUSTINE

24 They examine two states of human nature:
   One is that in which it was created in Adam, sound, faultless, just, and upright, coming from God's hands from which nothing can emerge except what is pure, holy, and perfect.
   The other is the state into which it was reduced by sin and the first man's revolt, through which it became sullied, abominable, and detestable in God's sight.

25 In a state of innocence God could not justly damn anyone; God could not even refuse them sufficient grace for their salvation.
   In a state of corruption, God could justly damn the whole mass, and those who are still born today without being removed from that state by baptism are damned, and for ever deprived of the beatific vision, which is the greatest of ills.*

26 Following these two states which are so different, they come to two different views concerning God's will about the salvation of men.

27 They maintain that in the state of innocence, that is to say on the day of the Creation, God had had both a general and a conditional will to save all men provided they desired it, through the sufficient grace he would give them for their salvation, but which would not unfailingly lead them to persevere in good.

28 But that Adam, having through his own free will misused this grace and rebelled against God through a pure and simple movement of his will and with no prompting from God (which would be a hateful thought), and having corrupted and injected the mass of mankind with the result that they are rightly the object of God's anger and indignation, they make plain that God has divided that body of mankind, all equally culpable and which

deserve damnation, that he wanted to save a part of it through an absolute will based on his mercy alone, entirely pure and gratuitous, and that, leaving the other part in the state of damnation in which it was, and in which he could justly have left the whole mass, he either foresaw the individual sins which the individual would commit, or at least the original sin of which we are all guilty, and that, following this pre-vision, he willed to condemn them.

29 That to achieve this he sent Jesus Christ for the salvation of those only whom he chose and predestined amongst that body.

30 That it was only for their salvation that Jesus Christ died, and the others, for whose salvation he did not die, have not been spared universal and just damnation.

31 That nevertheless some of those who are not predestined are none the less called to the good of the elect, but that they do not persevere.

32 And consequently there are three sorts of people: those who never approach faith; others who approach it but, not persevering, die in mortal sin; and finally those who approach faith and persevere in charity until death.

33 For the first group, Jesus Christ did not die for them, and did not redeem them.

34 For the second group, Jesus Christ redeemed them, but for a while, and died for them, but not for their salvation.

35 For the last group, Jesus Christ died for their salvation.

36 That all persons on earth are obliged, on pain of eternal damnation and the sin against the Holy Spirit, incapable of remission in this world and the next, to believe that they are amongst the small number of the elect for whose salvation Jesus Christ died, and to believe the same of everyone who lives on earth, however wicked and ungodly they may be, for as long as they retain a second of life, leaving to God's impenetrable secrecy the distinction between the elect and the damned.

37 That is their view, from which it can be seen that God has the absolute will to save those who are saved, and a conditional will

based on pre-vision to condemn the damned; that salvation derives from God's will, and damnation from man's will.

38 And the followers of St Augustine, founded on the Scriptures, the Fathers, the Popes, the Councils, the unwavering tradition of the Church, use their tears directed to God and their attentions to human beings to make all know the truth, addressing both groups, and speaking to them in these terms:

39 'The Church is acutely distressed to see itself riven by contradictory errors which wage war against its holiest truths; but although it is right to complain about you, Molinists, and you, Calvinists, nevertheless it realizes that it receives fewer wrongs from those who, astray through their errors, remain within its bosom than from those who have left to erect altar against altar, with neither affection for its maternal voice calling them, nor deference for its decisions which condemn them.

40 'Molinist, if your error pains it, your submission consoles it; but, Calvinist, your error combined with your rebellion makes it cry out to God: *I fed the children and they have scorned me.* It knows, Molinist, that for you it is enough for it to speak through the mouths of its Popes and its Councils, that you hold the Church's tradition in veneration, that you do not undertake to give special interpretations to sacred texts, and that you follow those which have been determined by the crowd and by the Church's successive holy Doctors, Popes, and Councils.

41 'But as for you, Calvinist, your rebellion leaves it inconsolable. It has to behave with you as equal to equal, and, with no deference for its authority, has to use the arguments of reason. Nevertheless it calls everyone to it, and is ready to convince each of you according to your own principles.

42 'It is consoled in that your contradictory errors establish its truth; it is enough to leave you to your reasons to destroy you, and the arms you employ against it cannot harm it, and can only ruin you.

43 'It is not only in this encounter alone that it has experienced contradictory enemies. It has almost never been without this double battle. And as it experienced this contradiction in the

person of Jesus Christ, its head, whom some wanted to make solely a man and others solely God, it has felt the contradiction in all the other tenets of its belief. But, imitating its master, it holds out both arms to you to call you all and gather you together to form a joyful union.

44 'So it addresses itself to you and asks the subject of your complaints, firstly Molinists, to you as its children and . . .'

3. [Middle section: More detailed draft]

DOCTRINE OF ST AUGUSTINE

1 St Augustine distinguishes between the two states of men before and after sin, and has two views appropriate to these two states.

Before Adam's sin

2 God created the first man and in him the whole of human nature.
He created him just, sound, strong.
Without concupiscence at all.
With free will equally poised towards good and evil.
Desiring his beatitude and unable not to desire it.

3 God could not have created anyone with the absolute will to damn them.
God did not create individuals with the absolute will to save them.
God created human beings in the conditional will to save them all generally if they observed his precepts.
If not, disposing of them as master, that is to say, condemning them or granting them mercy according to his pleasure.

4 Innocent man emerging from God's hands could not, though strong, whole, and just, observe the commandments without God's grace.
God could not justly impose precepts on Adam and innocent men without giving them the necessary grace to accomplish them.

If at their creation men did not have the sufficient and necessary grace to accomplish the precepts, they would not have sinned by transgressing them.

5 God gave Adam sufficient grace, which is to say none other than that which was necessary to accomplish the precepts and remain just. By its means he could persevere or not, according to his pleasure.

So that his free will could, as master of this sufficient grace, make it void or efficacious, according to his pleasure.

God gave and allowed Adam's free will the good or wrong use of this grace.

6 If Adam, by means of this grace, had persevered, he would have merited glory, that is to say to have been eternally confirmed in grace with no risk of ever sinning; as the good angels merited it through the merit of a similar grace.*

And each of his descendants would have been born in justice, with the same sufficient grace as his, with which he could have persevered or not, according to his pleasure, and have merited or not eternal glory, like Adam.

Adam, tempted by the Devil, succumbed to temptation, rebelled against God, broke the precepts, wanted to be independent of God and to be his equal.

After Adam's sin

7 Adam, having sinned and made himself worthy of eternal death, for a punishment for his rebellion,

God left him with a love of created things.

And his will, which before had not been attracted at all with any concupiscence towards created things, found itself filled with concupiscence, which the Devil planted there, and not God.

8 Concupiscence therefore rose within his members and excited and titillated his will, pushing it towards evil, and darkness so filled his mind that his will, previously unconcerned by good and evil, understanding neither delectation nor titillation by either the one or the other but following, with no particular previous appetite, what he knew to be best for his happiness,

now finds himself affected by the concupiscence rising in his members. And his mind, very strong, very just, very enlightened, becomes dulled and deadened.

9 This sin having passed from Adam to all his descendants, who were corrupted in him like a fruit bred from rotten seed, all men descended from Adam are born into darkness, into concupiscence, guilty of Adam's sin and worthy of eternal death.

10 Free will has remained susceptible to both good and evil; but with this difference that, whereas with Adam there was no predilection towards evil, and he only had to know what was good to be able to follow it, now he shows complaisance and such a strong delectation in evil through concupiscence that he infallibly inclines towards it as if to his own good, and he voluntarily, and quite freely and joyfully, choses it as the object in which he experiences his beatitude.

11 As all human beings in this corrupt mass* are equally worthy of eternal death and of God's anger, God could justly abandon them without mercy to damnation.

However, it pleased God to choose, elect, and distinguish from within this equally corrupt mass, in which he saw only wickedness, a number of people of all sexes, ages, contradictions, disproportions, and from all countries, periods, and, in short, of every kind.

12 That God distinguished his elect from the others for reasons unknown to men and angels through pure mercifulness and without any merit.

That God's elect make up a universality, sometimes called *world*, because they are spread throughout the world, sometimes *all*, because they form a totality, sometimes *many*, because there are many of them, sometimes *few*, because they are few in proportion to the totality of those cast aside.

That those cast aside make up a totality which is called *world*, *all*, and *many*, and never *few*.

That God, through an absolute and irrevocable will, wanted to save his elect, in a purely gratuitous act of goodness, and that he abandoned the others to the evil desires to which he could have justly abandoned all men.

13 To save his elect, God sent Jesus Christ to carry out his justice and to merit with his mercy the grace of Redemption, medicinal grace,* the grace of Jesus Christ which is nothing other than complaisance and delectation in God's law diffused into the heart by the Holy Ghost, which, not only equalling but even surpassing the concupiscence of the flesh, fills the will with a greater delight in good than concupiscence offers in evil; and so free will, entranced by the sweetness and pleasures which the Holy Ghost inspires in it, more than the attractions of sin, infallibly chooses God's law for the simple reason that it finds greater satisfaction there, and feels his beatitude and happiness.

14 With the result that those to whom it pleases God to give this grace are brought themselves through their free will infallibly to prefer God to created things. And this is why it is said indifferently either that free will is said to be brought there of itself by means of this grace, because in fact it is brought in that direction, or that this grace carries free will there, because every time it is given, free will invariably is brought there.

15 And those to whom God pleases to give it infallibly persevere in this preference to the end, and so choosing unto death by their own will to fulfil the law rather than violate it, because they feel more satisfaction, they merit glory, both through the aid of this grace which has overcome their concupiscence, and through their own choice and the bidding of their free will, which voluntarily and freely moved in that direction.

16 And all those to whom this grace is not given, or not given until the end, stay so excited and delighted by their concupiscence that they invariably prefer to sin than not to sin, for the simple reason that they find more satisfaction in it.

   And so, dying in sin, merit eternal death, since they chose evil through their own free will.

17 With the result that men are saved or damned according to whether it pleased God to choose them to be given this grace amongst the corrupt mass of men in which he could justly abandon them all.

   All human beings being equally culpable for their part, when God made them.

OPINIONS OF THE OTHER PELAGIANS

18 The other Pelagians readily agree with St Augustine about the state of innocence, which is to say: that God created man just, with sufficient grace by which he could, if he wanted, persevere or not; and that in the creation God had a conditional will to save them all, provided that they used that grace well; that, the use being left to his free will, Adam sinned and in him all human nature; that he was punished for concupiscence and ignorance; that all his descendants are born worthy of damnation with the two scourges of ignorance and concupiscence. They agree with all these things. But they differ about God's conduct towards men after sin. This is their view:

19 That God would have been unjust if he had not wanted to secure all human beings (within the corrupted mass), and if he had not given to all sufficient help to save themselves.

That he could not without being invidious distinguish some from the rest, if, for their part, they had not somehow caused that distinction.

That God would have been unable, without damaging their free will, to will with an absolute will to act in such a way that they should fulfil his precepts through his grace.

20 And on these foundations they argue that God had a general, equal and conditional will to save all (within the corrupted mass) as in the creation; that is to say, provided they wanted to fulfil the precepts. But because they needed a new grace, because of their sin, that Jesus Christ became incarnate to merit for them and to offer to all, without any exception, and throughout their lives uninterruptedly, sufficient grace only to believe in God and to pray to God to help them.

21 That those who do not avail themselves of this grace, and who, despite this help, remain in sin until their death, are rightly abandoned by God, punished, and damned.

That those who, using this grace well, believe in God or pray to him, thereby give God the opportunity of distinguishing them from the others, and provide them with other help which some call efficacious and others simply sufficient, to save themselves.

22 With the result that all those who use this general and sufficient grace well obtain through God's mercy the grace to perform good works and reach salvation.

And those who do not use this grace well remain in damnation.

23 And so men are saved or damned according to whether they are pleased to render worthless or efficacious this grace given to all men to believe in God or to pray to him, God having on his part an equal will to save them all.*

CALVIN'S OPINION

24 Calvin has no conformity with St Augustine and differs from him in every way from start to finish.

25 He puts forward the view that God, having created Adam and all mankind in him, did not have a conditional will to save them when he did so. That the aim he intended in creating the noblest of his creatures was not ambiguous, but he created some with the absolute will to damn them, and others with the absolute will to save them. That God decreed it in this way for his glory. That consequently this decree is just, although we do not see how, since everything which glorifies him is just, it being just that he receives all glory.

26 That nevertheless, God being unable in his justice to damn them without sin, he did not allow, but decreed and ordained Adam's sin. That Adam, having necessarily sinned through God's decree, became worthy of eternal death. That he lost his free will. That he no longer had any tendency towards good, even with the most efficacious grace.

27 That Adam's sin was passed to all his decendants, not naturally, like the defect of a seed to the fruit it produces, but through God's decree by which all men are born guilty of the sin of their original father, without free will, with no inclination towards good even with efficatious grace, and worthy of eternal death.

28 That all men being guilty, God, as their master, disposed of them. That he only wished to save those he had created to save.

That he willed to damn those he had created to damn. That to effect this Jesus Christ became incarnate to merit the salvation of those who had been chosen from the mass which was still innocent before the prevision of sin.

29 That God gives them, and them alone, the grace of Jesus Christ, which they never lose once they have received it, which moves their will towards good (not making their will move towards it, but moving it despite its reluctance) like a stone, a saw, like dead matter in its action and with no capacity to be moved and to co-operate with grace, because free will has been lost and is completely dead.

30 With the result that grace operates on its own; and although it remains, and operates good works until death, it is not free will which performs them and which attracts it through choice; on the contrary, while grace is responsible in it for these good works, it merits eternal death. That Jesus Christ alone merits, and that, having none of the merits of the just, the merits of Jesus Christ are only ascribed and applied to them, and they are therefore saved.

31 And so those to whom this grace is once given are inevitably saved, not through their good works or good will, because they have none, but through the merits of Jesus Christ which are applied to them.

And those to whom this grace is not given are inevitably damned for the sins they commit, by God's command and decree, to which they are inclined for his glory.

32 So that human beings are saved or damned according to whether it pleased God to choose them in Adam at the moment of their creation and to incline them towards good or evil, for his glory.

All human beings being equally innocent for their part, when God distinguished between them.

EXPLANATORY NOTES

3 *Table of Liasse titles*: this table, in its two columns, is at the beginning of the manuscript. It is certainly by Pascal, and the copyist has treated it, no doubt wrongly, as if it were a *liasse* by itself.

Nature is corrupt: this *liasse* contains no fragments.

5 *Table of Liasse titles*: this *liasse* has been translated, like the rest of the first nineteen, in its entirety, but is of particular importance on account of the debate about its status. The table of *liasse* titles has been considered a projected chapter order for the unwritten apologetic, and this first *liasse* has been regarded as a table of its projected contents. See the Introduction, pp. xxi–xxii.

The Maccabees . . . Jesus Christ: the Maccabees were a distinguished Jewish family behind a revolution against the Hellenizing faction in the second century BC. The Books of Maccabees were not in the Hebrew canon, but two are in the Vulgate and a different one is in the Septuagint. Two others have little authority. The Massorah is a series of commentaries intended to assure the meticulous integrity of the text of the Hebrew scriptures.

The prophecies: Pascal was stimulated by the miraculous cure of his niece's lachrymal fistula at Port-Royal on 24 March 1656 to project an apologetic of the traditional type, based on the miracles of Jesus and the early Christian argument that he had fulfilled the Messianic prophecies of the Old Testament, in which he had also been prefigured.

Fascinatio nugacitatis: literally 'the enchantment of triviality'. The Latin phrase was commonly used in Port-Royal circles. See Fragment 653.

7 *Adam was the witness . . . Moses, etc.*: Pascal follows the traditional method of dating the world by the generations recorded in the Bible. Pascal thought the world about 6,000 years old. See Fragment 164.

The true nature of man . . . separately: the nature of man's true good, and the question of the chief virtue, had been much debated by French moralists of the late-sixteenth and early seventeenth centuries. There had notably been Christian adaptations of Seneca by Justus Lipsius, Epictetus by du Vair, and Epicurus by Gassendi, but there was confusion about Pyrrho, whom Pascal treats as a sceptic, and who is portrayed as one by Diogenes Laertius. See Fragment 25. Cicero, however, portrays him as an exaggerated stoic. Both in antiquity and in the late Renaissance there is an intrinsic connection between stoicism and scepticism, since the unknowability of the external world seemed to impose a moral stoicism.

7 *Two sorts . . . they might have*: Pascal, like all Christian apologists in the post-Renaissance era, is aware that valid Christian belief, necessary for salvation, cannot depend on high intelligence.

8 *Man does not know . . . impenetrable darkness*: much of Pascal's spirituality, as this fragment shows, is permeated with a recollection of Augustine's famous sentence from the *Confessions*, 'You have made us for Thee, and our heart is restless until it rests in Thee.' Augustine's use here of the word 'heart', like the Psalmist's 'Incline my heart, O Lord', is important for Pascal. See e.g. Fragment 661.

Solomon: the book of Ecclesiastes was commonly ascribed to Solomon.

9 *The stoics*: there had been a strong wave of Christian neo-stoicism in France during and after the Wars of Religion. The spirituality of Saint-Cyran and the theology of Jansen came to react strongly against everything they regarded as stoic.

Felix nihil admirari . . . Montaigne: Pascal here, and in 111, slightly misremembers Horace, who is correctly quoted by Montaigne.

False position of the philosophers . . . Montaigne: Montaigne writes that the philosophers who believe in immortality leave all discussion of eternal punishment to the poets (ii. 12).

This interior war . . . reject them: the war between reason and passion was a commonplace (see e.g. Fragment 514), but it had also become a commonplace to point out against the stoics that the passions were not false judgements but movements of the sensitive appetite, and could therefore not be eradicated. Des Barreaux (1599–1673) had a reputation for scepticism, but died repentant, remembered for a couplet contrasting the rules of reason and passion.

10 *Those who wish . . . Corneille*: the reference is to Pierre Corneille, *Médée*, ii. vi, first played in 1635, and published in 1639.

Wretchedness . . . to death: Pascal here touches on one of his major themes. Conversion depends for him on facing up to the terrifying condition in which all mankind is placed.

10 *We know ourselves*: 'know thyself', the inscription on Apollo's temple at Delphi, was considered the epitome of ancient wisdom. Montaigne is sceptical about the possibility of self-knowledge at the end of *The Essays*, iii. 9.

11 *god*: Pascal, careless about punctuation, selectively flouts modern typographical convention in spelling god with a lower-case initial even when he is clearly speaking of the Christian God.

Pyrrhonists: the Pyrrhonists are here taken to be those who believed in the impossibility of knowing the real world. [see also note to p. 28]

The machine: this signifies for Pascal that part of human activity which is automatic or uncontrolled. The argument that merely intellectual belief does not itself conduce to salvation is of primordial importance for Pascal. See Fragment 41.

13 *Perseus, king of Macedonia ... kill himself*: the incident in which Paulus Emilius sends word to Perseus that, if he wishes to avoid humiliation, he should kill himself, refers to Montaigne, *The Essays*, i. 20.

Grand Turk: Turkey was economically and politically important to France. Exotic Turkish themes had been popular since Georges de Scudéry's 1641 novel *Ibrahim, ou l'Illustre Bassa*.

A tip ... up in arms: reference to a notorious quarrel about the form of the Franciscan cowl.

16 *Imagination*: this fragment reverberates with reminiscences of Montaigne, one of whose chapters is devoted to the strength of the imagination, traditionally governed by the sensitive appetite, or capable of dominating it. The strength of the imagination, important for the Christian philosophy of Marsilio Ficino (1433–99) in Renaissance Florence, had been used by Pietro Pomponazzi (1462–1525) to develop a naturalistic explanation of apparent miracles. A list of such effects of the imagination was widely used by sixteenth-century authors to cast doubt on apparent miracles, and in Pascal's text the denunciation of the imagination as a source of error sits strangely in the context of a project to base a Christian apologetic on miracles.

19 *Dell'opinione regina del mondo*: the title means 'Opinion, Queen of the World', but the book is unidentified.

Possibility of a vacuum: Pascal's experimental work demonstrating against Descartes and others the existence of a vacuum must have been undertaken at least ten years earlier than this was written.

20 *Self-interest*: the word Pascal uses is *amour-propre*, here carrying its ordinary sense of self-esteem or self-interest. He will elsewhere use it as Jansen used Augustine's *amor sui*, as a state of non-justification incompatible with charity and grace. Both Jansen and Pascal, as also Nicole, play on the double meaning of an empirically discoverable psychological motivation and of a theological state excluding justification. La Rochefoucauld also feels the theological associations of the word, although he uses it in the sense of self-interest. Unlike self-interest (*intérêt*), *amour-propre* in La Rochefoucauld is never compatible with authentic virtue.

(*The chapter . . . begin with this.*): this sentence is added in the margin, presumably on a rereading by Pascal.

21 *The Swiss . . . high office*: in parts of Switzerland the nobility was suspected of being in league with the Habsburgs.

22 *proud reason humbled and begging*: as the celebrated fragment 'Infinity nothingness' (680) among many others makes clear, Pascal's view of reason is ambivalent. He will not abandon rationality as the highest human power, but recognizes that reason's pride can be an obstacle to belief, which is at least a precondition of justifying grace. This is one of a number of occasions on which he takes delight in the humiliation of reason. See also Fragments 142, 164, and *The Art of Persuasion*, §3.

impulses: the French word here, *inclinations*, was commonly used as a euphemism for 'passions' or, in the singular, 'infatuation'.

25 *King of England . . . King of Poland . . . queen of Sweden*: the references are to Charles I, beheaded 1649; John Casimir, briefly deposed in 1656; and Christina of Sweden, who abdicated in 1654.

26 *Pride*: the French word is *orgueil*, here used in its ordinary psychological sense. In the *Discussion with Monsieur de Sacy*, §§ 32–3, it will take on formal theological meaning.

27 *393*: this number, as also 395 and 399 which appear later in the fragment, all of which was crossed out by Pascal, refers to a page number in the 1652 edition of Montaigne used by Pascal.

28 *Pyrrhonists*: the Pyrrhonists, believing in the impossibility of knowing the external world, advocated the suspension of judgement, and naturally turned to stoic indifference as the only rational attitude towards that which it was not in their power to control. The close association between neo-stoicism and the sceptical suspension of judgement was inherited by Descartes.

30 *Fronde*: the Fronde to which Pascal refers is the earlier of the two,

the *Fronde parlementaire* of 1648–49, brought about essentially by the excessive pecuniary demands made by central government.

30 *The customs of our country*: the defensive principle of following the customs, and even the religion, in which we are born, until we discover a good reason for changing them, was much paraded during the religious wars. Pibrac devotes a famous quatrain to it, which Montaigne approvingly quotes, and it is part of the famous set of provisional moral rules adopted in the sevententh century by Descartes in the *Discours de la méthode*.

34 *Cannibals laugh at an infant King*: Pascal remembers a passage from Montaigne ('Des cannibales') which describes the reactions of a Brasilian in Rouen.

glory: the French term *gloire* had recently changed its meaning and no longer implied external recognition. *Gloire* could be the highest virtue, approaching in meaning self-esteem, a proper regard for personal dignity or merit. Pierre Corneille made it tragic in *Le Cid*.

35 *we cannot define . . . obscure*: Pascal is alluding to his own discovery that certain chiefly mathematical concepts elude definition by their very primordiality.

Members of the Academy: Plato's Academy, which in the third and second centuries BC is said to have become the radial point of a sceptical theory of knowledge.

by means of the heart: Pascal here, and perhaps in the *Pensées* only here, makes the heart the seat of forms of knowledge, including mathematical axioms, which are certain but which, unlike propositions, are felt rather than concluded. The *Art of Persuasion* confronts a similar difficulty. Pascal is clearly exploring the possibility that the heart is the seat of religious knowledge, which can be put into it by God. Because it would not simply be the term of a process of reasoning, it could also be virtuous. Merely rational belief, unsupported by the infusion by God of religious feeling in the soul, is without avail in the supernatural order of grace, justification, and salvation. Pascal is also remembering that any theory of faith must accept the religious authenticity of simple uneducated belief.

38 *A.P.R.*: it used to be assumed that 'A.P.R.' stood for 'A Port-Royal', and that this fragment, like 182, contained notes for the conference Pascal probably gave there in 1658. But Étienne Périer said Pascal had neither prepared nor thought in advance about any

conference, and Fragment 182 scarcely reads likes notes for a conference outlining a project for an apologetic based on miracles. See also Fragment 274.

42 *It is astonishing . . . understanding of ourselves*: Pascal here confronts the difficulties occasioned by his theology in their most acute form. They derive not only from the religiously intolerable notion that God continually creates individual souls knowing them to be destined to an eternity of suffering, conceived as endless time and generally still as physical pain, but also from the theological paradox which involved God in the creation of guilt. Pascal's view derives eventually from the late works of Augustine as they were understood at Port-Royal. Controversy occasioned by Augustine's legacy had been fierce for centuries. Pascal, however, who was not a trained theologian but who had developed an intense spirituality, was more interested in analysing the nature of human experience than in the strictly theological problems bitterly debated inside the scholastic tradition.

44 *Diversion*: the fourth chapter of the third book of *The Essays* is entitled 'Of Diversion'. Pascal is also thinking of Augustine's polarity *aversio/conversio*: the will can be averted from the true good which is its proper object and converted to a more immediate but sinful gratification.

I feel that I . . . infinite being: the ordinary scholastic doctrine held that each soul was directly created by God and infused into the foetus sixty or ninety days after conception, depending on gender. Pascal is not really arguing the 'existence' of God here. He is merely stating that the existence of any contingent being ultimately demands that there be a necessary and non-contingent reality on which it finally depends.

46 *Pyrrhus*: Pascal takes the reference to Pyrrhus from *The Essays*, i. 42. Pyrrhus' counsellor Cyneas kept asking him what he would do when he had conquered one territory after another until the whole was subject to him. Then he would rest at his ease. Why, asked Cyneas, did he not do that now, and spare himself all the fighting?

50 *Zeno himself*: Zeno was chiefly known to Pascal's period as the founder of the stoic school in the early third century BC.

three kinds of concupiscence: the three concupiscences referred to are pleasure, curiosity, and pride.

51 *There is a contradiction . . . like the plague*: Pascal is alluding to Jansen, who was being ironic at Seneca's expense.

51 *All men . . . hang themselves*: the allusion here is to Augustine, who shared the general classical view that all human beings sought happiness. Much of this fragment uses traditional material, no doubt recycled by the scholars of Port-Royal.

54 *Prosopopeia*: meaning 'personification', this is used of the two exhortations to humanity of divine Wisdom in the Book of Proverbs.

57 *God wanted to . . . has modified*: Pascal is here, as also often elsewhere, perilously close to suggesting that the recognition of divine truth depends on human disposition, a view which clashes with his theology in the *Writings on Grace*.

Sellier notes that the scored-out passage which follows begins on the second recto of a double sheet, which explains the number 2. Pascal then thought it would fit better in Fragment 274, but the copyist as usual retained it and scored it out. The copyist added in the margin that the continuation is to be found in the section 'Foundations of religion'.

58 *Heart. Instinct. Principles*: this is only one of the tripartite divisions of levels of human activity jotted down by Pascal for possible development. He did not use it systematically.

Atheism: the word 'atheism' was changing its meaning. In the late sixteenth century it had denoted any sort of moral as well as intellectual nonconformity, and in the seventeenth did not clearly refer only to the denial of any eternal and necessary being on which all other beings were contingent. Montaigne called Luther an 'atheist' without wishing to say that Luther did not believe in God. In the seventeenth century, doubters were known as *esprits forts* (literally, 'strong minds'). Pascal is punning.

59 *the soul is material*: Descartes had constructed his whole metaphysics in order to support belief in the immortality of the soul, which for him depended on its immateriality. Some of the Fathers of the first three centuries, as Voltaire was later gleefully to point out, had accepted the soul's materiality, and in the seventeenth century Gassendi (1592–1655), a committed believer and canon of Digne, also developed a metaphysic based on a corpuscular theory of the soul. It was no doubt on this account that, from the later seventeenth century, when Locke had rekindled interest in the possibility of thinking matter, the apologists relied more on Gassendi, as popularized by François Bernier (1620–88), than on Descartes.

60 *Said St Augustine*: in *The City of God*, xxii. 7.

60 *Mind and heart*: the use of the doublet is significant in view of *The Art of Persuasion*, §3.

St Augustine . . . submit: the view that there are matters beyond reason's range and before which reason can only 'submit' here comes from a letter of Augustine at his most speciously rhetorical (CXX. i. 3), also quoted in the *Logique de Port-Royal* (iv. 12), almost certainly written by Nicole, although generally attributed also to Arnauld. The scholastics held that the object of the intellect was the true. The difficulty for Pascal lies in seeing how the human mind could 'submit' without adducing evidence to show that such a submission was itself reasonable. Pascal clearly needed simultaneously to believe that there were things in which the Christian had to believe which surpassed or even contradicted human reason, and that reason was the highest spiritual power of human beings, imposing a responsibility which could never be abdicated. Many of the fragments of this *liasse* are concerned with the problem. See also e.g. Fragment 232.

61 *Jesus Christ . . . miracle*: in this fragment, as uncertain in date as all the rest, Pascal is plainly envisaging the abandonment of the project, probably of 1656, of basing an apologetic on miracles. He here considers the possibility of reducing the substantial proof of the truth of Christianity to the fulfilment of prophecies.

62 *Faith . . . against*: this fragment, like many others, derives from a reminiscence of the liturgy, here the eucharistic hymn, *Pange lingua*, known in the seventeenth century chiefly from being sung at matins on the Feast of the Exaltation of the Holy Cross, containing the words *Praestet fides supplementum / Sensuum defectui* ['may faith provide the supplement for what our senses are lacking']. Echoes of the psalms occur too frequently to be noted, but sometimes liturgical reverberations affect the translation. In Fragment 37, for instance, the translation of *toujours et partout et misérables* must include 'always and everywhere', as this is the standard English translation of the words Pascal is toying with, and which occur in all the *praefationes* opening the canon of the mass. The words are themselves a resonance of the famous criterion of the contents of Christian belief in the *Commonitorium adversus profanas omnium hareticorum novitates* written in AD 434 against Augustine by Vincent of Lerins: *quod ubique, quod semper, quod ab omnibus creditum est* ['what is believed everywhere, what always, and what by all . . .'].

64 *It is pitiful to see . . . soldier etc.*: Pascal is remembering the opening pages of Montaigne, *The Essays*, ii. 12, ostensibly devoted to the

defence of Raymond Sebond's *Theologia natualis*. There are many reasons for thinking that the title of that chapter should be translated as 'The Apologetic of Raymond Sebond', as Pascal seems here to think of it, instead of the more frequent 'for'.

64 *228*: this fragment, crossed out by Pascal, was written on the other side of the sheet containing Fragment 227, and was probably never destined for this *liasse*.

65 *H.5.*: it has been conjectured that the 'H' with or without a number, as also in Fragments 230 and 231, is a vestige of an intention to constitute a series of notes on *L'Homme*, with the meaning of 'mankind'.

66 *infinite sphere . . . circumference nowhere*: this metaphor of God, Neoplatonist in origin, is associated primarily with Nicholas of Cusa (1401–64) and was commonly used in the French Renaissance.

68 *De omni scibili*: 'of everything knowable': a phrase often used in connection with Renaissance efforts, sometimes associated with the tradition of Ramon Lull (1235–1315), to reorganize the whole field of the knowable into connected disciplines. It is not the title of a book.

69 *Of the principles of things, Of the principles of philosophy*: the attribution of the *De rerum principio* ('Of the origin of things') to Scotus (*c.*1266–1308) has been widely questioned, but has also been authoritatively defended. It exists in only one late fourteenth-century manuscript. The *Principia philosophiae* (1644) appeared first in Latin, and is by Descartes.

74 *or God would be unjust*: Pascal is turning round the ordinary argument that it would be an injustice on God's part to create human beings with such guilt attached to their natures that they deserve to go to hell. He explores the idea that human inclinations are such that only (inherited) guilt can explain God's justice in condemning those of the human race not specially chosen for predestination to salvation.

St Augustine: Augustine is replying to a remark by Cicero contrasting human incapacity with the divine spark in human beings.

Celsus and Porphyry: third-century opponents of Christianity, often linked together.

pride or sloth: the words for 'pride' and 'sloth' are *orgueil* and *paresse*, as in the *Discussion with Monsieur de Sacy*, §33. *Paresse* ordinarily means simple laziness, but in seventeenth-century France it acquired a different and theological connotation. Pascal depends on J.-F. Senault, who in 1641 makes *paresse* the chief of all the passive vices. For Pascal, here and in the *Discussion, paresse* is the vice which results in unconcern about the state of original sin in which we are born, which makes it one of the sources of vice. Its alternative, striving for virtue, results either in authentic virtue, which requires justifying grace, or its counterfeit, *amour-propre*, as denounced also by Senault and Nicole, which presents only the outwards apearance of virtue because inspired not by grace but by pride or *amour-propre*. The reverberations of Pascal's association between *paresse* and unconcern about justification is secularized but still clear in La Rochefoucauld. Pascal also uses *paresse* in a different technically theological sense to translate the technically theological vice of 'acedia', the sin of the desert fathers who gave up caring about spiritual matters, in the ninth *Lettre provinciale*.

74 *participation in the divinity*: according to the unanimity of scholastic theologians, beatitude must involve as well as created grace the bestowal of uncreated grace, that is the personal assumption of the individual into participation in God's divinity.

75 *241*: this fragment is inspired by Grotius, *On the truth of religion*.

figmentum malum: Pascal here takes the translation of Gen. 8: 21 from Vatable's translation from the Hebrew.

78 *sacrifice of the cross for all*: the fifth of the condemned Jansenist propositions in *Cum occasione* of May 1653 affirmed that Christ did not die for all human beings, while the Council of Trent had insisted a century earlier on the rigorous identity of the sacrifice of the mass with the sacrifice of Calvary. Pascal, who held the propitiatory nature of the redemptive sacrifice common to the Catholic Augustinian theological tradition in the seventeenth century, is not here distinguishing between the sacrifice of Calvary and that of each mass, and is obviously not limiting the potential beneficiaries of Christ's sacrifice to the liturgical assembly offering the sacrifice.

Miracles of Vespasian: Pascal refers to *The Essays*, iii. 8, where Tacitus (*Annals*, 4. 71) appears to believe in a miracle worked by Vespasian.

80 *Jesus, Christ's lineage . . . Ruth, etc.*: the allusion is to the genealogies of Jesus, especially those given at the beginning of their gospels by Matthew and Mark.

81 *God . . . absconditus*: a letter of Pascal to Charlotte de Roannez suggests that he was thinking primarily of the hidden presence of God in the eucharistic species.

82 *XXII. Perpetuity*: up to the end of the nineteenth *liasse* the whole text of C2 has been translated. *Liasses* XX and XXI ('Figurative Law' and 'Rabbinism') have been omitted, as containing notes whose concerns are more certainly limited to the projected apologetic, and which are more technical and repetitive.

States . . . dictated: this idea is taken from Montaigne, *The Essays*, i. 23.

83 *poets made up of a hundred different theologies*: during the Renaissance the view was widely taken up that poetry was the means by which truth was wrapped in fable and transmitted, and that the poets were early theologians. Much was made of the priestly or vatic function of the poet and of poetic inspiration in reaction to the late-medieval view of the poet as wordsmith.

84 *the circle in Montaigne*: possibly a mark made by Pascal on his copy of Montaigne.

the six ages: the six-part division of history, like the six days of creation, was commonplace.

86 *The infinite distance . . . supernatural*: the triad body–mind–charity suggests a comparison with the triad in Fragment 187

holy, holy, holy: allusion to the threefold repetition of *sanctus* sung during the early part of the canon of the mass.

87 XXVII. *Christian Morality*: the last two *liasses* are translated in their entirety.

88 *our members*: allusion to the church as the body of Christ, a doctrine developed in the early church from 1 Cor. 12: 12.

92 *I p. q. 113, a. 10, ad 2*: the reference can only be to Aquinas's *Summa theologiae*, Prima secundae, quaestio 113, articulus 10, reply to 2nd objection, but neither there nor elsewhere does the text of the *Summa* support Pascal's contention.

inclines their hearts: the psalmist's 'Inclina cor meum' reverberates in Pascal's mind as he again addresses the problem most succinctly expressed in Fragment 142.

93 *They judge with their hearts*: See previous note, and that to Fragment 142.

94 *Series*: the numbers at the head of sections from here on indicate the non-classified 'series' as opposed to the fragments classified into *liasses*.

103 *Non dicunt . . . praedicas*: the last Latin sentence is a comment by Pascal.

104 *The five propositions . . . the bull*: if Pascal is suggesting that the five propositions may have been correctly condemned, but that the Sorbonne, in stripping Arnauld of his doctorate, and Alexander VII, in declaring that the propositions were in the *Augustinus*, had gone too far, and had provoked a miraculous divine repudiation, there is a problem with dates. Arnauld lost his doctorate on 29 January 1656; the miracle of the thorn was on 24 March; and Alexander VII issued his constitution *Ad sacram beati Petri sedem* on 16 October.

105 *Molinists*: Pascal is using the term of the Jesuits in general. From the fifth *Lettre provinciale* it is clear that he regards Jesuit confessional practice as the cause of their doctrine of grace, against which, as developed by Lessius, Jansen had rebelled.

106 *Comminuentes cor . . . Corneille*: Pascal is using the Anvers 1572 Bible, and quoting Pierre Corneille's *Horace*. Both quotations have to do with holding individuals back from a danger it is their duty to face.

107 *between the two crosses*: the mother of the emperor Constantine had the hill of Calvary dug and discovered two crosses. The one which worked miracles was that on which Jesus had been crucified.

108 *St Athanasius*: the fourth-century Athanasius was the leader of the anti-Arian movement in early Christian theology, with whose beleagured position the defenders of Jansen's interpretation of Augustine frequently identified themselves. Anti-Arian orthodoxy won the power struggle, but the theological arguments were very finely balanced, seeming to allow only a choice of alternative heresies.

450: this fragment must be read in the context of the dispute with the Jesuits, whose self-congratulatory centenary publication of 1640, the *Imago primi saeculi*, is mocked in the *Lettres provinciales*. It was discussed among the Jesuits whether fully professed members of the Society were guaranteed salvation.

these people: the theologians associated with Arnauld.

prophecies . . . miracle: an indication that Pascal is putting weight here on miracles rather than the fulfilment of prophecies.

109 *Abraham, Gideon*: both the recipients of special divine signs. For Gideon, see Judg. 6: 36–40.

110 *454*: this fragment invites comparison with Fragment 94.

114 *The will . . . sees there*: on the role of the will in belief, see Fragment 142 and *The Art of Persuasion*, §5.

115 *opinion*: in seventeenth-century French 'opinion' means false judgement, under the control not of reason, but of passion.

dance on the tightrope... own: Pascal is remembering Epictetus, who had used the tightrope metaphor in *Diss.* 3. 12.

Desargues: a mathematician with an estate at Condrieu, where he produced particularly fine wines.

118 *Faith... lead there*: it is a recurring theme of Pascal's jotted notes that there is a distinction between intellectual belief, and the grace-inspired theological virtue of faith.

The self is hateful: the 1670 Port-Royal editors felt that this statement was too strong, and explained that by *moi* Pascal meant simply *amour-propre*.

120 *Casuists*: attacked by Pascal in the *Lettres provinciales*, but by no means confined to the Jesuits, the casuists were the authors of books of *cases of conscience* which put forward confessional situations requiring resolution by the confessor, and were intended as textbooks to ensure uniformity of confessional practice. In fact, whenever an apparently immutable law has to be applied to a real situation, the ordinary laws of human justice require a casuist solution, as, for instance, when the development in Europe of a mercantile economy rendered obsolete the apparently immutable prohibition of 'usury', or borrowing capital at interest. The casuists dissolved the loan contract into two legitimate contracts, a contract of sale now and a contract to purchase the same goods back at a higher price at a future date. Similar devices were employed by the Italian school of law which allowed the immutable precept of Roman law giving imperium to the emperor to stand, but only to the empire as a whole and not to any single part of it, so legitimizing *de iure* the *de facto* sovereignty of the Italian city-states. Both the British High Court and the US Supreme Court still use similar devices to allow changing public sentiment to affect the application of law.

121 *Sacerdos dei*: reference to letter 63 of Cyprian, in which Jesus is described as the priest of God the Father.

France... Pope: the question here was not about ordinary ecclesiastical jurisdiction, or the lucrative power of appointment to vacant prelacies, but about the church's teaching authority in its relationship to the theology faculties, to the French *parlements* or civil courts, to the king, who could suspend the jurisdiction of the civil courts, to the episcopacy of the universal church acting corporately, and to the papal curia. It is true that, with large parts of

Europe in schism, it was principally in France that Catholic opinion was still likely to favour the Gallican possibility of an appeal to a general council over the head of the pope. The regent, Anne of Austria, and the young Louis XIV could not, however, politically afford to alienate the curia in more than more or less trivial ways. A French schism on the Anglican pattern was a serious possibility in the late seventeenth century.

121 *an upright person*: see note to Fragment 532, p. 127.

122 *There can be . . . this*: Pascal here comes to one of his principal concerns. If the human soul is immortal, then what happens in this life is trivial in comparison to the soul's unending eternal state, and if behaviour on earth can influence our eternal fate, ethical norms must be defined in terms of the pursuit of eternal ecstasy. In the last line of the fragment Pascal notes that the Aristotelian philosophy of the scholastics, making knowledge dependent on the experience of senses which decompose after death, has always made the defence of immortality more difficult. The advantage of the Aristotelian perspective lay historically in its ability to account for the role of perception in knowledge.

charity as cupidity: 'cupidity', understood like *amour-propre* as a counterfeit of charity, the exterior forms without the interior grace, is the term derived from Augustine and Bernard and used here ambiguously for the psychological motive or interior state of those who keep the appearances of virtue while deprived through the absence of grace of its reality. One of the several distinctions made by Augustine in the *City of God* (xiv. 28) between the heavenly and earthly cities is that one is based on the love of God taken as far as contempt for self, and the other on the love of self taken as far as contempt for God. But the outward appearances of self-love for both Senault and Nicole are the same as those of charity. Pascal certainly depended on Senault, as did Nicole, but the established dates make it uncertain whether Pascal depended also on Nicole. See also the immediately following fragments, especially 510, and also 738.

124 *520*: this fragment derives directly from Montaigne, *The Essays*, i. 41.

A simple being . . . dejection: derived from Augustine's anti-Manichaean *De duabus animabus* repudiating an eternal principle of evil via Montaigne's *The Essays*, ii. 1.

126 *p. 184*: of the 1652 edition of Montaigne, *The Essays*, i. 41.

127 *Honnête homme*: *honnête* denotes a degree of social rank and

sophistication, and generally implies adherence to some code of honour. The difficulty comes from its occasionally deliberate non-reference to religious virtue. 'Upright' as a deliberate archaism is often an acceptable translation.

127 *Montaigne . . . about himself*: in 1580 Montaigne pretended, not without affectation, to have written a self-portrait. That was in fact a way of cloaking his intimate monologue under the guise of an elevated literary form used notably by Augustine and Petrarch, but Montaigne was immediately criticized for it, notably by the lawyer Étienne Pasquier (1529–1615) in a letter to the financial adminstrator Claude Pellejay (1542–1613).

128 *Man is neither . . . the beast*: this play on the orders of being, with humanity between the angels and the beasts, is taken from Montaigne, *The Essays*, iii. 13.

Mademoiselle de Gournay: Marie Jars de Gournay (1566–1645), learned but self-taught admirer of Montaigne, whose adoptive daughter she became. This fragment contains phrases and page numbers from Pascal's edition of Montaigne.

129 *Abstine et sustine . . . follow nature*: both commonplaces of stoic origin.

130 *Proper to mankind*: another commonplace, but this time taken from Pierre Charron (1541–1603).

131 *It is not . . . there*: Pascal adapts a famous phrase of Montaigne, *The Essays*, i. 35.

Montalte: the pseudonym used by Pascal for the *Lettres provinciales*.

133 *Mohatra*: the name of the double contract of present sale and future repurchase into which the casuists resolved the loan at interest. In this fragment Pascal is thinking of an attack on the recent generals of the Jesuit order.

135 *So the daughters of Lot . . . children*: this idea is taken from Augustine, *Against Faustus*, xxii. 43.

Liancourt . . . intellect: a story attributed to Liancourt relating how frogs attack the eyes of pikes to protect themselves appeared in *Un recueil de faits médicaux mémorables . . .* (Trèves, 1628).

Truth . . . know it: taken from Augustine, *Contra Faustum*, xxxii. 18, and frequently quoted at Port-Royal.

136 *Salomon de Tultie*: anagram of Louis de Montalte, the name used by Pascal for the *Lettres provinciales*.

137 *630*: this fragment, which does not exist in Pascal's autograph, is

inserted into C2, and appeared in 1678 with the *Maximes* of the marquise de Sablé, whom Pascal had occasionally visited, and at whose home his aphorisms were discussed. Its argument appears in Nicole's dispute with Racine.

139 *644*: this fragment implies the consideration of a structure for the apologetic different from those considered elsewhere.

portrait: Montaigne introduced *The Essays* as a self-portrait.

140 *1022 of them, we know*: according to Ptolemy.

141 *When we try . . . imperceptibly with them*: this idea is common to Montaigne and La Rochefoucauld. Like them, Pascal is drawing here on a stock of commonplace moral aphorisms.

Jesuits . . . both: Pascal is noting that the Jesuits are better than the Jansenists at stating both sides of a case in the interests of showing that their own view is the correct one. Pascal attempts something similar in the *Writings on Grace*.

M. de Condren: Charles de Condren (1588–1641) became General of the Oratory in 1629 in succession to Bérulle.

142 *The effects . . . to me*: Philippe Sellier points out that this fragment must refer to the scholastic distinction between justification in general and in particular. Pascal suggests that some place may be found for human initiative in the justification of the individual but not, as the semi-Pelagians believe, of the whole race, whereas the Calvinists are right to attribute to God the whole process of justification, but wrong to deny the validity, for instance, of the prayer of the individual.

144 *649*: Fragments 649 and 650 are probably for a document for the education of the duc de Chevreuse (1646–1712), Luynes's son. Louis Lafuma deduces from the paper used by Pascal that the fragments were written in the summer of 1660 in Auvergne.

147 *three ways to believe . . . inspiration*: the three orders of belief in this fragment can no doubt be related to Pascal's other psychological triads. See e.g. Fragment 187.

148 *Incomprehensible . . . should not*: Pascal here states the difficulty in dichotomies which could support the doctrine of original sin as transmitted guilt, justifying the damnation of the majority of members of the human race.

149 *XLII: Mathematics/Intuition*: Fragments 669 and 670 are linked to the *De l'esprit géométrique*, of which *The Art of Persuasion* is part. The original French of the title 'Mathematics' is *Géométrie*.

152 *680*: this is the most important of the longer fragments, known as

'the wager'. It is written on a single sheet, folded once to give four sides, two outside and two inside, which was once kept in Pascal's pocket. Many of the constitutent paragraphs or sentences are written between lines or paragraphs, themselves separated by dashes, with some remarks written vertically or obliquely in the left-hand margins, and twice upside-down at the top of the page. Some remarks are scratched out. It is possible that the additions do not belong to the sequential text, but were later jotted on to a corner or a margin of the piece of paper Pascal happened to have in his pocket. On this occasion, however, we can deduce with certainty the movement of Pascal's thought, since the marginal notes and additions must have been written after the main text, and a probable order between them can be established. Far too much uncertainty remains, however, for any attempt to reconstruct the fragment as a straight augmented and emended text. See the Introduction, p. viii.

153 *Who will then blame . . . accept it*: this paragraph, which lapses into dialogue form, is an addition to the sequential text at the bottom of the second of the four sides.

154 *to wager*: Pascal's interest in probability theory asserts itself at this point.

155 *this is the one*: end of sequential portion of third side of manuscript. The paragraph of dialogue 'I confess it . . .' is written in the margin of the *second* side.

156 *But what harm . . . you have paid nothing*: these two paragraphs are written in the margin of the third side. The last two lines of the fragment—'The only knowledge . . .'—is squashed alongside the marginal addition, and is in a different ink, strongly suggesting that not all this fragment was written at the same time.

We owe . . . a fault: this paragraph belongs to the main body of the second page of text.

157 *Custom . . . nothing else*: from main body of fourth side of text.

infinite amount to learn: end of main body of text. The next two paragraphs—'It is not true . . .' and 'The will is therefore . . .'—are written obliquely in the margin of the fourth side. The paragraphs 'No religion . . .', 'No sect . . .', and 'Only the Christian religion . . .' were written higher and higher up the page in the left-hand margin, and from the miscalculation of line lengths in that order.

158 *The heart . . . not know*: this most famous sentence of all is written upside-down at the top of the fourth side, as if Pascal despairingly

refuses to abandon rationality in his quest for religiously valid and grace-inspired faith.

159 *In this way . . . about it*: Pascal here comes up against the fundamental difficulty concerning the value of human effort and the relationship between intellectual conviction and the theological virtue of faith.

160 *Self-love*: here has its ordinary meaning as a psychological motivation.

167 *684*: editions which start a new series with Fragment 684 overlook a correction made to C1 text. C2 emphasizes that the series is not interrupted at this point.

169 *Ego vir videns*: the Latin text is familiar from Tenebrae, the name given to matins on the last three days of Holy Week.

171 *But let them . . . divine person*: Pascal here assumes a theory of the redemption different from the propitiation he presupposes elsewhere.

(*Jesus Christ . . . everything.*): written in the margin of the manuscript.

172 *Even if someone . . . salvation*: the frequency with which Pascal makes notes about any possibile relationship between faith and belief shows how central it was to his concerns.

174 *Jer.* 33, ult.: Pascal's reference is mistaken. He seems to be thinking of the last verse of Jer. 30: 24.

175 *spiritual meaning*: traditionally, and in order to harmonize scriptural teaching with Christian doctrine, each text of scripture could have one or more of three interpretations in addition to the literal meaning, allegorically drawing the religious lesson, tropologically teaching a moral doctrine, and anagogically conveying a mystical meaning. As the rhyme put it:

> Littera gesta docet; quid credas allegoria;
> Moralis, quid agas; quid speres, anagogia.

176 *cupidity and charity*: see Fragment 508.

177 *Kirkerus—Usserius*: Conrad Kircher and Jack Usher were authors of biblical commentaries.

178 *The Memorial*: there exist two texts of this document, one in the hand of Pascal on paper found sewn into the lining of his jacket after his death, and a second, sworn, exact copy of text on parchment, itself lost, which covered the paper and was sewn into the jacket with it. The parchment text adds the last three lines and the

scripture references. The *Memorial* follows as closely as possible the layout of the parchment version, which is slightly longer than the paper copy it protected when sewn into Pascal's jacket.

A special receipt for the *Mémorial* was issued when it was deposited on 25 September 1711 in the library of Saint-Germain des-Prés, demonstrating that it was considered a document apart from the fragments now known as the *Pensées*. The document, presumably written within hours of the experience it records, captures the moments of a movement of profound spiritual exaltation.

179 *743*: La Rochefoucauld's famous text on *amour-propre* was first published anonymously in the third part of the *Recueil de pièces en prose . . .*, edited by the publisher Charles de Sercy with an *achevé d'imprimer* of 13 December 1659. It is virtually certain that Mme de Sablé knew La Rochefoucauld's text before it was published. Pascal was a visitor to her small gatherings, where the discussion of moral aphorisms and gourmet table fare were staple subjects of conversation.

182 *Discussion with Monsieur de Sacy*: on this document, see the Introduction, 'Pascal's Texts'. It is included here for three principal reasons: partly because it shows Pascal arguing in extended prose to indicate, as he so often elliptically states in the fragments, how two opposite excesses could have complemented one another; partly to show his attitude to two writers on whom he drew extensively, Epictetus and Montaigne; and partly for the view that, while no moral effort, that is sloth, certainly leads to damnation, moral effort itself is not enough, but can result in pride counterfeiting charity with the appearance of virtuous behaviour as well as authentic grace-inspired virtue itself. Fontaine drew up the document in the last years of the century. It is likely to reproduce the argument, and even the terminology, of Pascal himself, but, if it does, Pascal may well have derived from Nicole the dilemma between the appearance of virtue, based on *amour-propre*, and its reality, based on grace.

184 *What do I know*: Montaigne did take 'What do I know?' as his motto, but he was not 'a straightforward Pyrrhonist', and more typical of him is the motto on the medal he had struck in 1576, taken from Sextus Empiricus, 'I suspend judgement'. Charron, on the other hand, much used by Pascal, had inscribed on his door lintel an answer to Montaigne, 'I don't know.'

193 *The Art of Persuasion*: this document, part of *De l'esprit géométrique*,

is included for two principal reasons: it shows that there is in Pascal's mind a constant distinction between purely rational proof and a persuasion which involves a submission of the whole human being; and it shows how Pascal adapts the traditional division of the disciplines into those based on authority, and those based on rational investigation and discourse. His insistence on the need both for rational belief and for meritorious grace-inspired faith leads him to try to overcome the old scholastic distinction between the operative faculties of the soul, intellect, and will, which precluded the possibility of any act which proceeded jointly from both, and to equivocate by making the heart the seat both of rational conviction and religious faith. If God illuminates the mind by delighting the will, it is difficult to see how the resulting act of faith can be rational, and guided by evidence towards truth. Since virtuous faith in any individual human being depends on a divine initiative, the rules for persuasion as laid out by Pascal cannot help towards salvation. See Fragment 142.

201 *Art of Speaking*: Montaigne, 'De l'art de conférer' (*The Essays*, iii. 8).

Descartes: the argument of Descartes, 'I think, therefore I am', could have been based on at least three passages of Augustine, and several twelfth- and thirteenth-century authors. Descartes is not ordinarily thought to have based himself consciously on any predecessor here.

204 *barbara and baralipton*: medieval mnemonics for transposing syllogisms between definite ('all'), indefinite ('any'), positive, negative, and conditional forms.

205 [*Writings on Grace*]: Jean Mesnard's reconstruction of the unfinished *Writings on Grace* provided in 1991 the first working text to become available, and this is the first translation of its major parts. Pascal tries to present his view as Augustinian, orthodox, and steering a middle path between what he regards as the heresy of 'Molinism' and that of Calvinism. Even if he were accurate, his view would leave each human being incapable of himself of any act which could in any way conduce to his eternal salvation, and Pascal must therefore regard every human being as deserving of eternal torment. On the underlying theological and religious problems, see the Introduction.

Letter . . . Commandments]: this document is a detailed draft of the beginning of the letter.

216 *charity*: charity is here used in the sense of justifying or sanctifying

grace. Those who die in the state of justification it bestows are eternally saved.

217 *deprived of . . . ills*: technically salvation consists in the 'vision of God', the communication of created and uncreated grace which enables the soul intellectually to perceive what the will is enabled to embrace as its supreme good.

221 *as the good angels . . . grace*: Pascal's theology becomes confused here. Angels, as pure spirits, could not, in scholastic theology, merit or choose. Their moral determination had to be instantaneous and permanent at the moment of their creation.

222 *corrupt mass*: see Fragment 164 on the transmission of original sin.

223 *To save his elect . . . grace*: Pascal's interpretation of Augustine here avoids Jansen's point that Adam's original state must have contained the aspiration to and exigence of fulfilment in the supernatural order. Grace, as medicinal, first restores lost powers of self-determination. Augustine is interpreted as having taught that grace then exercises its irresistible attraction through a greater 'delectation' in the psychological order than that offered by concupiscence. Both Augustine and Jansen do write, perhaps metaphorically, of a double delectation.

225 *And so men . . . them all*: for Pascal here, it is Pelagian to allow any autonomous human power of self-determination to good.

THEMATIC INDEX

The figures refer to page numbers

abêtir xxiv; translated 'according to your animal reactions' 156;
abjectness, need for 8
Abraham, Messiah to be born of stock of 5; as prophet 7; Jews blessed in 77; surrounded by idolators 83; and miracles 109; took nothing for himself 120; God of 172, 178
Academy, Plato's and scepticism 35, 231; sect of 74
Adam, nature and grace of before fall xi, xxxii, 166, 217; transmission of guilt of xxiv, xxx, xxxiii, xxxvi; use of will by 217; sin of, according to Calvin, derives from divine will 216–17; and promise of Saviour 6; and Jesus Christ 78
ad sacram beati Petri . . ., papal bull 238
affliction, *see* wretchedness
ages, the six 84
agitation: fragment title 10; quest for 46; *see also* distraction
Alexander VII, Pope, and the five propositions 238
Alexander the Great, youthful desire of to conquer 21
ambiguity between theological states and psychological order 240; about God removed by signs 170, 172; and figures 175; *see also* Introduction
amour-propre (*amor sui*) use of term in Saint-Cyran and Augustine xii; in Senault, La Rochefoucauld, Nicole, and Pascal xii, 230, 236, 245; allusion to 58; note in 1670 edition on 239; analogous to cupidity 240; *see also* self-love

angels, we are not on same level as, or as beasts 38, 128; psychology of 247
Annat, François (1590–1670), Jesuit and royal confessor, attacked by Pascal vii
Anne of Austria (1601–66), Spanish infanta, wife of Louis XIII, and curia 240
Antichrist, miracles of foretold 95; will speak against Christ 98; deceptions of 104
anxiety, and man's condition xxviii, 14
Apollo, and Delphi inscription 229
apologetic, Pascal's project for, and nature, purpose, change, and abandonment of vii, ix, xvi, xix, xx, 234; and miracle of thorn xvi; and theory of grace xx–xxi; and possibility of non-apologetic work xxii; draft sketched in *Discussion with M. de Sacy* and *Art of Persuasion* xxx
A.P.R., *liasse* title 3, 52, 231–2
Archimedes, and public recognition 86
Aristotle, upright and light-hearted 112
Arnauld, Antoine (1612–94), and Port-Royal, Jansen, and Saint-Cyran xi; and theology of xii, xix, xxv, xxxii; and *Lettres* of 1655 xiv–xv; and *Lettres provinciales* xvi; signs second formulary xviii, xxxiv; uncle of Le Maître de Sacy xxix; and *Art of Persuasion* xxxi; work of on Pascal's manuscript xxxix; and *Logique de Port-Royal* 234; condemnation of 238

Art of Persuasion, mentioned x; and
two ways of knowing truth xii;
and *The Mathematical Mind* xv;
written before the fragments xx;
on conviction, proof, persuasion,
and submission xxiv; analysis
of xxx, xxxi

ataraxia of Pyrrhonists and stoics 28

Athanasius, Saint, anti-Arian
theology of and Jansenist
identification with 108, 238;
controverted in his day 119

atheism(t), limited strength of 58;
and materiality of soul 59;
objections of 82; fragment title
and position of 104–5; change of
word's meaning 233

Augustine, Saint, theology of
interpreted by Jansen xi; and
amour-propre xii, 240; Pascal and
xxiii–xxxvi *passim*; quoted 25, 63,
72, 74, 233, 241; alluded to 79;
and miracles 60; and submission
of reason 60; and order of
charity 85; and law of
probabilities 116; and early use of
Descartes's argument 201, 246;
and middle path between
Molinists and Calvinists 217–23;
Pascal and 228, 232; *aversio/
conversio* in 232; and quest for
happiness 233; and Vincent of
Lerins 234; and Cicero 235; and
cupidity 240; and Montaigne 241;
see also *Writings on Grace* passim

Augustinus (1640): date of xi; and
Saint-Cyran xii; the five
condemned propositions and xv,
xxxiv; submitted to judgement of
Church xxv; attempt to prevent
publication of xxxiii;
condemnation of 238; *see also*
Jansen

Augustus, youthful desire of to
conquer 21

automaton, as instinctive part of
human beings 148; *see also* custom

axioms, nature of 197–9; *see also*
principles

baptism, necessity of for salvation
217

baroque, and cultural optimism in
France xxviii

baseness, not unique state of
humanity 8; shown in submission
to beasts 22; and human
greatness 37; *see also* wretchedness

beasts, human submission to 22;
humanity and level of 38, 43, 54,
128; renunciation of reason makes
us 99; *see also* angels

beauty, model of 117–18

beginning, *liasse* title 3, 57

belief, role in salvation xx, xxxvi;
distinction between faith and xxi,
12, 229, 231, 239; salvation and
xxx, xxxiv, xxxvi, 11, 36; reason
as obstacle to xxxi, xxxv; in heart
without study 36, 92–3; and
superstition and licentiousness
61–2; will, organ of 113–14; three
ways of 147–8; two ways of
believing 193; *see also* faith

Bernard Saint, quoted 64, 76; on
cupidity 240

Bernier, François (1620–88),
popularizer of Gassendi 233

Bérulle, Pierre de (1575–1629),
founder of Oratory, Neoplatonism
of xi; spirituality of xxviii;
succeeded by Condren 242

binding and loosing, fragment title
134

blame, inappropriateness of 8

blind: 'To blind, to enlighten',
fragment title 79

blindness, proves God 59; inspires
fear 65; reasons for 79; inflicted
by Jesus 94; of unconverted Jews
99; types of 123; of world 128;
human state of 140; of doubters
163–4; used by God 173

blood, circulation of 135

body, *see* machine

boredom, and anxiety xxviii; *liasse* title 3, 28; and distraction 10, 16, 46; man's condition 14; inevitability of 47, 123

Caesar, too old to want to conquer 21

Calvin, Jean (1509–64) and Calvinism, theory of grace of xxiv; and of predestination xxviii, xxxiv, and 246; opposed to semi-Pelagians 142; and Pascal's exposition of 215–16, 225–6, 242; and attitude of followers of Augustine to 219; see also *Writings on Grace* passim

cannibals, reference to Montaigne on 231

Carthusians, obedience of not military 88

Casimir, John, king of Poland 230

casuists 120, 239

causes and effects, *liasse* title 3, 29; of love 10, 20, 65; fragment titles 31, 32, 33; law of 35

Celsus 74, 235

certainty, and doubt xxviii; quest for 8, in *Memorial* 178; *see also* uncertainty

change, obstacle to belief 11

charity, image of in concupiscence 37; order of 85, 86, 87; not figurative 102; victor over concupiscence 113; and in cupidity 122, 176, 240; required not to abandon unbelievers 163; reprobate deprived of by God 216, 246; in body–mind–charity triad 237

Charles I, king of England 230

Charles II, king of England, and dating of fragments xx

Charron, Pierre (1541–1603), division in 139; borrowing from 241; motto of 245

Chevreuse, duc de (1646–1712), son

of Luynes xviii; fragments written for 242

Christianity, belief in depends on miracles 60; is demanded by reason 61, 161; few true Christians 61; proved by prophecies 66; alone able to resolve pride–sloth dichotomy 74, and greatness–corruption dichotomy 171; unique 82; characteristics of 82–4, 171; against nature, common sense, and our pleasures 84; unique in making lovable and happy 157; happiness of Christians 88; explains corruption and redemption 161; between atheism and deism 170

Christian morality, *liasse* title 3, 87

Christina, Queen of Sweden 230

Church as body of Christ 237

Cicero, quoted 24, 27, 30; and Pyrrho 228; and Augustine 235

City of God, The, of Augustine, and *amour-propre* xii

Cleopatra, references to xxvi; nose of 10; and love 20, 65

Clermont-Ferrand and Pascal family xiii; Pascal takes waters at xviii

cognition, attributed to heart xxxi, xxxv

commencement, status of *liasse* entitled xxii

conclusion, *liasse* title 3, 92; mathematics and conclusions 149

concupiscence, punishment of sin xxxiii, 221–2; harms others 27; with force, basis of all human actions 32; and moral order 35, 37, 75, 76; should be hated 38; three sorts of found in three sects 50–1; true religion must explain 53; cannot be used for common good 75; should be reined in 89; linked to superstition 90; has become our second nature 122; does not bring pleasure 134; we follow paths of 144; Augustine taught nature created without 220; without grace, leads to damnation 223; is threefold 232

Condren, Charles de (1588–1641), Oratorian, spirituality of xi; contradicted by Jesus Christ 141; General of the Oratory 242

contradictions, *liasse* title 3, 37, and fragment title 26; lead to religion 8, 169; within us 39, 40, 46, 51, 54, 55; must be resolved by religion 53; bad indication of truth 61; in grandeur-wretchedness dichotomy 74–6, 124; contrary reasons 116; in conflict of reason and passion 123; Jansenist and Jesuit attitudes to 141; John the Baptist and 142; and prophets 174

contrition, role of in sacrament of penance 135

conversation, fragment title 128

conversion, nature of 92

Copernicus 59

Copies of the fragments xxii, xxxviii–xli

Corneille, Pierre (1608–84), optimism of xxviii; alluded to 10, 228; quoted 106; and glory 231

corrupt(ion), *liasse* title 3; of nature 10, 11, 73, 74, and *liasse* 73–7; argument from 42, 173; ignorance of 50; importance of knowledge of 74; series title 168; proof of God from 166; justifies reprobation 217

cowl, dispute about 13, 229

creation, our uncertainty about 40; signs of everywhere 165

Cromwell, Oliver (1599–1658), trivial cause of downfall of 136–7

Cross, as key to Christian religion 99; and submission 148

Cum occasione, Papal bull of 1653,

promulgation of xiv; contents of 236

cupidity, mirror image of charity 122, 240; and its opposite 176

curiosity, as vanity 28

Cusa, Nicholas of (1401–64), theologian 235

custom, power of xxxv; our subservience to 15; following those of own country 23, 231; and justice 24–5; contrasted with might 31; power of 39, 64, 156; and justice 110; one of three ways to believe 147; inclines the automaton 148; Montaigne and 188; *see also* machine

cycloid, competition on problems posed by xvii

Cyneas 232

Cyprian, Saint 239

damnation, eternity and immutability of ix; most of human race condemned to xxxvi; distraction leads to 10; condemnation to by own reason of damned 60–1; world not created for 106; concurrence of divine and human will in 213–15; cause of for Calvinists 215–16; and Molinists 216–17; and followers of Augustine 217–20; God's absolute decree of for Calvin 225

darkness, and light xxviii, 82; impenetrable 8; outside Jesus Christ inevitable 10; and sin 53; and light 56–7, 79, 81, 95–6, 137; of hidden God 158

David, and circumcision of heart 82; and inclining our hearts 92

death, our nearness to 7; alone to be found 8; knowledge of through Jesus Christ 10; preferred to peace or war 15; terror in idea of 49; eternal consummation in 52; connected to sin 53–4; last act of play 59; Montaigne on 128–9;

uncertain date of 134; appalling
alternatives imposed by 160,
161–2; eternity of 164
definitions, rules for 197–9; *see also*
principles
delight (delectation) of will xxxi, 223
Delphi, Apollo's temple at 229
Democritus, quoted 68
demonstrations 197–9
Desargues, Gérard (1593–1662) 115,
239
Des Barreaux, (1599–1673) 9, 228
Descartes, René (1596–1650), calls
on Pascal xii; optimism of xxviii;
and Epictetus xxix; and
psychology of faculties xxxi;
philosophy of 29–30; useless and
uncertain 105; projected attack on
115; originality of basic premiss
of 201, 246; and vacuum 229;
and suspension of judgement 230;
and *Principia* of 235
Deschamps brothers, and Pascal's
father xi; and Pascal xi
desires, inability to satisfy effect of
fall 8
Desmolets, Père, and text xl
devil, Adam tempted by 221; *see also*
Satan
dialogues, consideration of form of
11
Discussion with Monsieur de Sacy, as
introduction to Pascal's thought
ix; occasion and date of xiv, xx;
on Montaigne xxvii; composition
of xxix–xxx
disproportion of man, fragment
title 66
distraction: happiness not to be
found in 9; sign of wretchedness
in quest for 10, 12; and boredom
16; and sound opinions 33; desire
for 45–6; fragment title 48, 49;
see also diversion
diversion, divert: *liasse* title 3, 44;
analysis of human desire for xxiii,
47–8; blame for those who seek 8;

projected letter on 9; sign of
unhappiness 26; and incapacity to
stay quietly in one room 44;
fragment title 44, 49; and
Augustine 232; *see also* distraction
diversity, fragment title 25; extent
of 115
divinity, human participation in
43, 74, 236; signs of in nature
165
doctrine, among proofs of religion 8;
and relationship to miracles 94,
97, 100
dogma(tism/t), and proof 9; and
quest for God 11; ignorance of
dogmatists 27; strength of
arguments of Pyrrhonists and of
dogmatists 41–2; *see also* reason
Domat, Jean (1625–96), refuses to
sign second formulary xviii
Dominican Order, and grace
disputes xxxiii
doubt, and certainty xviii; need for
and limits of 60; those who
lament doubting 159; in
Montaigne 183–4; *see also*
judgement (suspension of);
Pyrrho
dream, translating both 'songe' and
'rêve', and reality 146–7; we know
we do not 35, 41
droit, question de xv, xviii
du Vair, Guillaume (1556–1621),
and Epictetus xxix, 227–8, and
Descartes xxix

écoles (petites) de Port-Royal, and
solitaires xii; Pascal writes for
xvii; *Discussion with Monsieur de
Sacy* for xxix; no emulation at 25
Écrits des curés de Paris,
circumstances of xvi; Pascal's
authorship and xvi
Écrit sur la signature of Pascal; not
extant xix
education, seventeenth-century
reform of xxxi

efficaciousness, of grace 224
Egyptians, idolatry of and belief in
  magic 82; stories of 168
eloquence, as painting 117; merely
  relative importance of 127; *see also*
  style
end, final, God alone 7
Enoch, example of Old Testament
  saint 83
Epictetus, Pascal's views on
  xxix–xxx, 245; and neostoicism
  xxix; and anger 32–3; and what is
  in our power 33; advice of 49–50;
  and Christians 51; and ambiguity
  82; style of 136; human greatness
  exaggerated by 166; Christian
  adaptation of 227; see *Discussion
  with M. de Sacy* passim
epicureans, sect of 74; Gassendi's
  adaptation of Epicurus 227
error, and imagination 16; and
  illness 19–20; corrected by grace
  20; in ancient and contemporary
  Church 84
Escobar y Mendoza, Antonio
  (1589–1669), Jesuit, and moral
  values 128, 131 *esprit géométrique,
  de l'*, see *Mathematical Mind, The*
esprits forts 233
esteem, for soul 9; for ourselves 37;
  and presumptuousness 38; by
  others 50; absent from animals
  129; our need for 173; and
  amour-propre 179
eternity, contemplation of 164–5
Eucharist, fragment title 146;
  stupidity of disbelief in 60; and
  impiety 62; hidden reality of 78
evil(s), civil war worst of 32; as
  'ills' 133; and free will 222
experience, and instinct 39; tricks
  us 52
experiment, science and xxxi

fable, and relationship to theology
  237
faculties, psychology of xxxi

fait, question de xv; and *question de
  droit* xviii
faith: relationship with grace xx,
  placed in heart xxxv, 12, 36, 157;
  upright man and 11–12;
  relationship to proof 12; necessary
  for knowledge of good 51; and for
  happiness 51; reference to 62;
  above but not against senses 62;
  consists in Jesus Christ and Adam
  78; gift of God, not reasoning
  118, 157; not in our power 133;
  felt in heart 157; see also notes
  239, 243–4; *see also* belief
fall, of human race 6, 221; see
  Writings on Grace passim
falsehood, guilt in making believed
  7; and imagination 16; human
  principles of 20
falseness of other religions, *liasse*
  title 73; fragment titles 73
fantasy, and feeling 112
fear, and confidence xxviii; of not
  believing 5, 12; of immensity of
  space 26, and its eternal silence
  73; does not derive from divinely
  implanted religion 60; inspired by
  contemplation of universe 65–7;
  need to fear and not to fear 141;
  inspired by contemplation of
  eternity 162
feeling(s): principles felt in heart 36;
  and instinct 36; our surrender to
  112; and fantasy 112; fragment
  title 127; and reason 127, 137,
  149; and perception 130; tender
  145; God felt by heart 157
Fermat, Pierre de (1601–65),
  mathematician, and Pascal xiii;
  letter to xviii
Ficino, Marsilio (1433–99),
  neoplatonist philosopher, on
  imagination 229
figure(s), fragment titles 6, 80;
  figurative law 3, 174; predict
  Jesus Christ 5; among proofs of
  religion 8; only some conclusive

76; of future joy 146; reason for figures 174; series title 174

Filleau de la Chaise, Jean (*c.*1630–93), on Pascal's conference xvi–xvii; source for apologetic nature of Pascal's projected work on religion xix

flies, power of 13, 21

folly, base of might of kings 14; of original sin in human eyes 132

force, and justice 29, 30; basis for human actions 32

formulary (*mandement*), signature imposed xviii; new formulary xviii; and Mazarin xix; refusal to sign of Pascal and others xxxiv

foundation(s), *liasse* title 3, 78; projected chapter on 78

François de Sales, Saint (1567–1622), canonization of and Molinist theory of grace xxv; optimism of xxviii

Fronde wars, Pascal family moves to escape xiii; nature of xiii; injustice of 30; reference to 230–1

gambling, pastime of 28; references to bets, wagers, gaming 35, 45; and boredom 47; and stakes 58; playing piquet and analogy of human condition 59; *see also* wager

Gassendi, Pierre (1592–1655), philosopher 227, 233

Gideon, and miracles 109, 238

glory, fragment title 25, 129; change in meaning of 231

God, hiddenness of xxviii; hiddenness and revelation of 7, 78, 81, 140, 158, 172, 236; holiness of 7; temptation not to think of 7; our happiness alone in 8; knowledge of through Jesus Christ alone 10, 62, 63, 64; nature does not prove 11; projected letter on seeking 11; need to listen to 42; diversion and thoughts of 44; need to postulate infinite being 44; our true good 52; words in mouth of wisdom of 53; ultimate happiness only in knowledge of 54; unity with only through grace 55; universe of overwhelms imagination 66; meeting-point of both infinities 69; opposition between us and 92; gift of to love him 92; mutual obligation between us and 99; aphorisms concerning 144; incomprehensibility of existence and non-existence of 148; knowledge of, and faith 153–8; human attitudes to 163; and nature 165; possibility of equality to 166; signs of 170; of love and consolation, not simply of mathematical principles 172, 178; involvement in creation of guilt 232; vision of 246–7; *see also Writings on Grace*

gods, human desire to become 9, 11, 22

good, sovereign, *liasse* title 3, 51; true 7, 52, 166; sorts in Montaigne 9

good sense, fragment title 21

Gournay, Marie Jars de (1566–1645) 128, 241

grace xxiii–xxxiv; gratuity of ix, xxxvi; eradicates errors 20; puts religion in heart 60; human capacity to receive and lose 88; movements of 133; created and uncreated 236; *see also Writings on Grace*

greatness: and wretchedness xxviii, xxx, 36–7, 38, 39, 52–3, 173; *liasse* title 3, 34; and man's state 8; fragment titles 9, 35, 37, 153; and excess 129; involuntary acts do not detract from 144

Greeks, false deities of 83; quest for wisdom of 95

Grotius (Huigh de Groot, 1583–1645), Pascal draws on 236

Habsburgs 230
happy/happiness, quest for 8; Solomon and 8; not in distraction, but in esteem for soul, and sorts of 9; in Jesus Christ 10; with God 11; our condition not 26; only with God 27, 51–2, 59; capacity for 38; and diversion, and quest for 44; lack of and incapacity to stay in one room 44; not in esteem of others or external objects 50; not in ourselves 54; in Christians 88; in desire, not nature 126; possibly in ignorance 130; begins at death 147
hateful, self is 118
heart, organ of spiritual knowledge and seat of virtue xii, 231; and will xxxi; organ of cognition, volition, and faith xxxv; not in our power 33; and knowledge of truth 35–6, which is felt 36, 92, 93; hollow, full of filth 49; in triad with instinct, principles 58; religion implanted in through grace 60; seat of belief 61; circumcision of 82, 85; has its order 85; faith of simple people inspired in 92; need for purity of 142; feels God 157; has its reasons, loves universal being or itself 158; seeks true good 166; each finds what lies at bottom of 177; and imagination 177; unjust and unreasonable 180; deception rooted in 181; mind and 234
heel, fragment title 15, 39
heresy, nature of xix
Homer, quoted 115; see also *Iliad*
honnête homme, fragment title 127; meaning 240–1; *see also* upright
Horace, quoted 9, 14, 28, 145, 228

Huguenots, exodus of xxviii
humble (humility, humiliation), allows knowledge of God 7; humbling of reason 36, 193; achieved through penitence 55; appearance of 56; pride needs humbling 79; speeches about 127; need for humiliations 148; in Jesus Christ 214
Huyghens, Christiaan (1629–95), visited and written to by Pascal xviii

ignorance, and knowledge xxviii; sorts of 29; not absolute 70; monstrous tranquillity in 165
Iliad 168
illness, cause of error 19; effects of 125
illusion, universal 31; in sleep 40
imagination, fragment title 16; mistress of error 16–20; feats of 24; reliance on 30; limits imposed by 36; and infinity of creation 66, 72; exaggerations of 111, 112, 115; capability of 139; and effort to impress 147; dangers of 167; often confused with heart 177; Pascal on 229
immateriality, of soul 37, 59; for Descartes 233
immortality, Pascal's assumptions about viii; and philosophers 9; and happiness 44; of primordial importance 59, 159; determines our ethics 121; knowledge of, useless without Jesus Christ 171; and immateriality 233; philosophical difficulty raised by 240
Incarnation, and greatness in wretchedness 88; single person of Man-God 190; purpose of, according to Molinists 216, 224; and to Calvinists 226
incomprehensibility, and postulation of original sin 43; projected

explanation of 52; fragment title 55; that God exists and that he does not 148; of God 153; insensitivity to most important concerns 162

inconstancy, fragment titles 13, 22; of human condition 14; and pleasures 27

inequality, inevitability of 114

infinite, double infinity of greatness and smallness xxxv, 66–72; of space 26, 73; of distances between body, mind, and charity 86; of movement 129; considerations on 152–6; fragment title 152

injustice, projected letter on 12; fragment titles 26, 27, 124; of Fronde 30

innocence, human condition in state of 42; state of according to Augustine 217; see also *Writings on Grace* passim

insensitive, to matter of chief concern to us 5; to great things 124, 162

inspiration, one of three ways to believe 147

instinct, fragment title 9; principle of animal behaviour 34; in doublet with heart 36; and with experience 39; human secret instincts 46; leads us outwards 50; in triad with heart and principles 58, 233; which lifts us up 125

intellect, faculty of: distinguished from will xii; inadequacy of xxxv; kingdom of 23; acts of not volitive 246; see also reason

intuition (intuitive knowledge) 35–6; series title 149; intuitive mind and mathematical mind 150–2; use of word 242

Isaac, retained faith 83; God of 172, 178

Isaiah, on blinding unbelievers 94; on works 214

Jacob, prophecy of concerning Messiah's lineage 5–6; retained faith 83; God of 172, 178

Jansen, Cornelius (1585–1638) and Jansenists, author of *Augustinus*; theology of and relationship with Saint-Cyran 230; five condemned propositions of 104; and Jesuits 141 and 242, and stoics 228; ironic about Seneca 232

Jesuits, Pascal's hostility to xv; and grace disputes xxxiii; centenary *Imago primi saeculi* of 108; possibility of miracle among 110; and Jansenists 141, 242; referred to as Molinists 238; see also Molinists

Jesus Christ: Pascal's use of that form of name xxvi; proofs of, *liasse* title 3, 85; and scripture 5, 10, 79, 98; subject of prophecy 6, 8, 11, 63, 78, 80, 93, 94, 98, 99, 123, 143; our wretchedness without 10, 35; foundation of self-knowledge 10; and unique way to knowledge of God 10, 62–4, 140; witnesses to 11; our happiness in 35; as the Way 50; divinity of probative 60; and miracles 61, 84, 97, 98, 99, 101, 102, 109; Muhammad and 74, 75; inspires neither pride nor despair 76; for all 77; sacrifice of for all 78; prophecies of unclear 78; unrecognized by contemporaries 78, 103; role in faith 78; purposes of 79, 85, 86–7; came to blind and sanctify 80, 94; two natures in 81; and order of charity 85, 102; lowliness of 87; Christians members of body of 91; and Cross 95; and Antichrist 95; and Moses 97; and Saint Peter 114; and accomplishment of mystery 114; state of men before 131; last of prophets 142; mankind redeemed by 166; moral teaching of 167; object of universal knowledge 171; mediator and centre 172; no knowledge without 172; and Jews 175; in *Memorial* 178; source of life 214; and works 214; died only for few 218; Calvinist doctrine of 226; sacrifice of and Mass 236; priest 239; *see also* Messiah; Redeemer

Jews, and prophecies 6, 61; state of 12; no redeemer for 78; reason for creation of 80; differ from Muslims 81; true Jews and true Christians 84–5; demand for miracles by 94; dispute among 98; opposite of Christians 122; before and after coming of Jesus Christ 143; enemies of religion 166; Jesus Christ came to gather 167; antiquity of, fragment title 168; and pagans 169–70; had miracles and prophecies 177

Job, and human wretchedness 8, 26; and Solomon 26, 27

Joshua 142

joy, a feeling 127; figures of and means to 146; intensity of, in *Memorial* 178

Judah, Redeemer to be born of line of 5–6

judgement, Pyrrhonist suspension of 28, 245; preference for own 33; relativity of 111; opinion and false judgement 239

justice, uncertainty about 15, 20, 23; relativity of according to place 23; determinants of 24; fragment titles 25, 34; and laws 26; obeys force 29, 30; and strength 34; and established laws 126; abandonment of and original sin 147; *see also* injustice

justification xxiv, xxx, xxxii

Kirkerus 244

knowledge, and ignorance xxviii, 29; and volition xxxv; folly of 9; and

faith 12; not dependent on reason alone 35; clouded by passion 38; and love of God 56; limits of 65, 140; distance between knowing God and loving him 92; *see also* belief; faith; heart; intellect; proof; reason

Koran, not by Muhammad 74; foundation of Muslim religion 81

lâcheté, Pascal's use of term xxx

Laertius, Diogenes, and Pyrrho 228

Lafuma, Louis, editor of *Pensées* xxxix, 242

Lamech 83

La Rochefoucauld, François VI, duc de (1613–80), and *amour-propre* xii, 230, 245

law(s): Old Testament 6; relative to place and time 23–4; and injustice 26; projected consideration on 28; and force 29; Old and New 84–5; and circumcision 90; and Holy Spirit 90; corruption of 128; *see also* justice

laziness, *lâcheté* xxx; and wretchedness 189; and pride 191–2; *see also* sloth

Lessius, Leonard, Jesuit theologian 238

letter (form) considered 9, 11, 12

Lettres provinciales by Pascal vii, x, xvi, xxiii, xxxi, xxxiv, xxxvi; Pascal's comment on title 105

Liancourt, Roger du Plessis, marquis de (1599–1674), refused absolution xiv; mentioned 135, and *see* note 241

liasses vii–xli *passim*

life, brevity of 15, 26; dissatisfaction with our 147

light, and darkness xxviii, 56–7, 79, 81, 95–6, 137, 158

Lipsius, Justus (1547–1606), neostoic philosopher 222

Livy, quoted 15

Locke, John (1632–1704), English philosopher 233
Lot, daughters of 135
Louis XIII, king of France xi
Louis XIV, king of France, and Jansenism xiv; and the curia 240
Lull, Ramond (*c.*1235–1315) 235
Lutherans, held all actions sinful 206, 233
Luynes, Louis-Charles d'Albert, duc de (1620–90) xviii

Maccabees, and prophets 5, 227
machine, meaning and power of xxiii–xxiv, xxxv–xxxvi, 11; obstacle to reason's quest for God 12; yields to respect and terror 14; series title: Discourse concerning the machine 152, 155–6; *see also* custom
madness, extent of our 9; punishment by God 12; might of kings based on 14; errors of imagination not confined to 18; of kings in Plato and Aristotle 112; original sin in eyes of men 132; derangement of those complacent in doubt 160; of those who neither know nor seek 163
marriage, Pascal on xvii
Martial, quoted 145
Massorah 3, 227
mathematics, Pascal writes on x; need for mathematical quality 60; profundity of 132; series title 149; and intuitive mind 149–52; definitions confined to 200; Montaigne on 186–7; concepts of 231, 242
The Mathematical Mind, date of xv
Mazarin, Jules (1602–61), and Papal bull *cum occasione* xv; and *parlement* xvii
members, martyrs as our 88; fragment title 90; Church as body of thinking 90–2
Memorial, nature and importance of

document and experience xiii, xx, xxi; text of 178, 244–5
memory, Pascal's xxix; and sciences of xxxi; is a feeling 127; necessary for reason 127
Menjot, Antoine (1615–94), book by, sent to Pascal xviii
Méré, Antoine Gombaud, chevalier de (1610–84), and Pascal xiii
Mesnard, Jean, editor of Pascal's works, and the *Writings on Grace* xv, xxxi; and the first *liasse* xxii; and the text xl, 246
Messiah, prophecies of vii; and *liasse* 'Order' xxii; prophesied 5, 61, 82, 84; law of 6; prefigured by Noah 83; and true and false Christians and Jews 84; Jesus Christ proved he was by miracles, not prophecies 101; Jews raised in view of 168; and pagans 169; need for prophecies of 174; prophecies of partly hidden 175; rejection by Jews 177
might, *see* power
mind, easily distracted 21; confused with bodies 72; has order different from heart's 85; distance of from body, charity 86; dignity above non-cognitive things 87; and will 114; we are as much automaton as 148
miracles, apologetic to have been based on vii, xv–xvi; abandoned as its basis xvi, 234; of flood 6; among proofs of religion 8; and for Augustine 60; and prophecies 61; make disbelief sinful 62; unbelievers accept miracle of Vespasian 78; serve to condemn 92; and doctrine 94; demanded by Jews 94; considerations on 94–110; and imagination 229; and fragment 182, 232
misery, *see* wretchedness
Mitton, Damien (*c.*1618–90), and Pascal xiii; and hateful self 118; and corruption of nature 126

Mohatra, double contract of present
sale and future re-purchase 241

Molina, Molinists: theology of xxvi;
condemnation of 105; see *Writings
on Grace* passim and 246; doctrine
of opposed to Calvinists 216–17;
Church's attitude to 219; term
used of Jesuits 238; *see also* Jesuits

Montaigne, Pascal and *The Essays* of
xxvii–xxx; edition used by Pascal
xli; quoted 9, 14, 15, 24, 25, 30,
44, 50, 70, 115, 129, 147, 237,
240, 241; dilemma of philosophers
in 9; naïvety of 31, 116;
mentioned 84; on custom 110;
style of 127, 136; faults of 128–9;
reply to remark in 131; confusion
in 139; see *Discussion with
Monsieur de Sacy* passim 228, 229,
231, 233, 234–45, 236, 237, 241,
242, 245, 246

Montalte, fragment title 131, 241

morality, *liasse* title 3, 87; among
proofs of religion 8; knowledge of
laws of 14; and concupiscence 35,
37, 75; through scripture and
Jesus Christ 63; in workings of
concupiscence and grace 78;
fragment title 89; dependent on
immortality 121–2; corruption
of 128; divisions of ethics 129;
Escobar's 131; and religion 142;
of judgement and mind 151–2

Moses, proofs of *liasse* title 3; and
prophecies of Messiah 6, 7;
uniquely concerned with one
people 77; miracles of 78; and
lineage of Jesus Christ 79; and
circumcision of heart 82, 85;
fidelity of 83; chronological
proximity to Adam 84; and
miracles 94

Muhammad, bears witness to
himself 10; not author of Koran
74; false prophet 74; difference
from Jesus Christ 75; absurdity
of 76–7; foundation of Muslim
religion in 81

Muslims, and earthly pleasures 53;
religion of founded in Muhammad
and Koran 81

mystery, of original sin 43; religion
must contain 60; accomplishment
of by Jesus Christ 114

Nantes, revocation of Edict of xxviii

nature, spiritual concept of xi;
relationship with grace xxiii, xxv,
xxxii; corruption of in *liasse* title
3, 73; knowledge and loss of 7;
corruption of, fragment title 10,
126; confusion of without
scripture 10; progress not
constant in 14; our nature capable
of good 37; custom, instinct,
experience and 39; differ within
us 39; Pyrrhonists and 40;
infinity of 66; double infinity
of 66–72; human beings weakest
reeds in 72; makes us unhappy
126; consists in movement 126;
truths of self-contained 129;
copies itself 132–3; signs of God
in 165; states of in Augustine
217; *see also* grace

Nicole, Pierre (1625–95) xii, xvi,
xviii, xxv, xxix, xxxix, 230, 234,
240, 242

Noah, and promise of Saviour 6;
prefigures Messiah 83;
chronological proximity to Adam
84

nobility, appearances of rank and
power 14, 18, 34; and self-
deception 47

nothing(ness), spirituality based on
nature as xi; as absence of object
of quest 11; and everything,
humanity midway between
66–72; knowledge of our 127–8;
and infinity 152

occupation(s), fragment titles 16, 39

Olier, Jean-Jacques (1608–57), and
refusal of absolution to Liancourt
xiv

omnibus service, inaugurated by
 Roannez and Pascal xix
opinion, unnatural 15; and
 imagination 19; can be
 manipulated 30; and
 understanding 31; and truth 31;
 unsound 32; 'Sound opinions of
 the people', erased *liasse* title 3,
 and fragment titles 32; the people
 have sound opinions 33; exploited
 by power 115; meaning of 239;
 see also people
oracles, pagan 81
order, possible arrangements of
 fragments x; and first *liasse* xxii;
 liasse title 3, 10; fragment titles 5,
 11, 12, 85, 129, 132; three 'orders'
 of body, mind, charity 85, 86, 87;
 of Jesus Christ 87; why Pascal
 writes without 112, 177; of
 thought 123; ordered and
 disordered lives 132; three orders
 of belief 242
orgueil, Pascal's use of xxx, 235; *see
 also* pride
originality, to be hidden 31; *see also*
 imagination
original sin, theology of xi, xxiv,
 xxxiii, xxxvi; necessary hypothesis
 of 42; transmission of guilt of 43;
 occurrence and effects of 53–5;
 we are born with guilt of 74; folly
 in men's eyes 132; recognition of
 147; incomprehensibility of 148;
 doctrine of, and Montaigne, and
 Epictetus 189; see *Writings on
 Grace* passim 235, 242
Ovid, quoted 147

pagans, salvation of xxv; religion of
 77, 81, 84; Jesus Christ light to
 77; Jesus Christ comes to gather
 167; and Messiah 169
paresse, Pascal's usage of term xxx,
 235
parlement de Paris, and formulary,
 xvii; and powers of 239
parrot 35

Pascal, Étienne, father of Blaise xii,
 xiii
Pascal, Jacqueline xii–xiv, xviii
Pasquier, Étienne (1529–1616) 241
passions, avoiding harm from 5; war
 with reason 9, 123, 228;
 immateriality of soul from
 subjugation of 37; clouds truth
 38; pull us outwards 50;
 dominated passions become
 virtues 120; collision between
 138; each man's ruling 147; and
 inability to believe 155; separate
 from God 167
Paul, Saint, on grace and works 214
Paulus Emilius 13, 37
Pelagius, Pelagianism, heresy of
 xxxi–xxxii; see also *Writings on
 Grace* passim
Pellejay, Claude (1542–1613) 241
Pensées, use of as title vii; editions
 of vii, x, xvii; 1670 preface xx
people, sound opinions of, 'Sound
 opinions of the people', erased
 liasse title 3, and fragment titles
 32; deception of 25; ordinary and
 clever 29; language of 31; opinions
 of 31; have sound opinions 33;
 three kinds of 59; Christian
 religion lifts up 77; and laws 110
Périer, Étienne, son of Gilberte xvii,
 xix, xxi, xxxviii–xxxix, 231–2
Périer, Gilberte, Pascal's sister xiii,
 xv, xviii–xix, xxxix
Périer, Jacqueline, daughter of
 Gilberte, Pascal and proposed
 marriage of xvii
Périer, Louis, nephew of Pascal
 xxxix
Périer, Marguerite, daughter of
 Gilberte, cure of at Port-Royal
 xv–xvi
perpetuity, *liasse* title 3, 82;
 fragment titles 5, 82, 84;
 references to 61, 78, 90; sign of
 religion 106; as continuity 84;
 quest for 134
Perseus 13, 37, 229

perseverance, theology of xxx,
xxxii–xxxiii, xxxvi; special grace
of 207; gratuitous in state of
innocence 217–18; within Adam's
power 221; predestined 223
persuasion, *see also* machine;
Introduction and *The Art of
Persuasion* passim; and proof
xviii, xxiv, xxx–xxxi, 148, 246;
and machine xxiii; and apologetic
xxxiv; and salvation xxxvi
Petrarch 241
Petronius, quoted 128
Philo, on monarchy 90
Philosophers, philosophy, *liasse* title
3, 49; fragment titles 50; failures
of 7, 9, 28, 53–4, 72; folly of 9;
imagination outweighs reason even
in greatest of 17; irony at expense
of 27–8; worthlessness of 30;
have subdued passions 37; agree
up to a point with Christians 82;
have made vices holy 92; have
shown vanity of possessions 124;
to have no time for is truly to
philosophize 152; to be balanced
against one another 191
Pibrac, Guy du Faur de (1529–84) 231
piety, and superstition 61; impiety of
disbelief in Eucharist 62
Pirot, Georges (1599–1659) xvi
Plato, personal normality of 112; to
attract to Christianity 122; and
ethical principles 129; unable to
move pagans 170, and the
Academy 231
pleasure, and devotion of others 7;
vanity of 8; inauthenticity of 27;
originates outside body 35; always
unattainable 126; concupiscence
precludes 134; shameful to give in
to 144
poetry: poetic beauty 117–18;
relationship to theology 237
Pomponazzi Pietro (1462–1525), on
imagination 229
Pope, and council 121; and scholars

128; fragment title and
powerlessness of 134
Porphyry 74, 235
Port-Royal and Port-Royal-des-
Champs, *see* Introduction
possessions, equality of endorsed 29
power, of kings 14; founded on
appearance 18; projected chapter
on misleading powers 20;
foundation of 24; and usurpation
25; number of retainers sign of
32; Epictetus on what is within
our power 33; and Justice 34;
does not lead to happiness 45;
mistress of world 115; and the
powerless 167; *see also* force
praise, of man blameworthy 8
predestination, *see* Introduction,
Writings on Grace 213–23; *see*
reprobation
preface, fragment title 63; to first
part, to second part 139
present, our inability to envisage
20–1
presumption, extent of our 38, 53,
68; and pride 88; accompanies
wretchedness 124; arrogance 140
prevision, of God, according to
Molinists 216, 218
pride, blinds xxxv; and
wretchedness 26; fragment title
28; human weakness 55; produced
by ignoring Jesus Christ in
approach to God 63, 64;
alternative to sloth 74, 190–1;
leads to presumption 88, 230,
235; wickedness becomes 113;
extent of 124; knowledge of
greatness leads to 189; see also
orgueil; vanity
principles, knowledge of 36; natural
39; of truth and goodness 40; in
triad with heart, instinct 58, 233;
ultimate 68; existence of a single
principle 73; principles and their
contraries both true 123;
deduction from 149–50

prison, analogy of man in, hour before execution 59; of universe 66; of men in chains in 168
probability, laws of 116; 243
proof xx–xxi, xxiii–xxiv, xxx–xxxi, xxxiv; liasse titles 3, 85; of God 11; projected letter on usefulness of 11; different from faith 11; as instrument of faith 12; of Christian religion 21, 164–5; and feeling 35–6; by zeal of seekers and blindness of others 59; limits and necessity of 60; those who believe without 93; not conclusive 95–6, 98; by Jesus Christ 101; metaphysical proofs of 139–40; persuasion and 148; impossibility of, and need to wager 153; *see also* belief; persuasion
prophecies, prophets, and projected apologetic vii, xvi, 227; *liasse* title 3; universality of 5; of Jesus Christ 5; of Messiah 6; among proofs of religion 8; and miracles 61, 101 2; prove divinity of Jesus Christ 63; proofs of Christianity 66; of Jesus Christ as hidden God 78; proof in fulfilment of 80, 84; testify to God's spirit 93; not cogent during life of Jesus Christ 98; and miracles 102; the Jews and 143–6; nature of 174
propitiation, theories of redemption based on xxx, 236, 244
propositions, proved not felt 36; become feelings 127
prosopopeia 233
psalms, over whole earth 10
Ptolemy 242
Pyrrho, Pyrrhonism, Pyrrhonist 229, 230; and truth 9; and search for God 11; considerations on 15, 41–2; and stoicism 28, 227–8; fragment title 35; cannot attack heart's knowledge 35; strengths of 40; need for 60; obstinacy of 105; cure for disbelief 106; fragment

titles 108, 112, 131; partly true 108, 131; and order 112; speeches about 127; helps religion 128; vanity of 132; Montaigne straightforward Pyrrhonist 183–4; *see also* doubt; judgement
Pyrrhus 46, 232

Rabbinism, *liasse* title 3
Racine, Nicole's quarrel with 242
reason(s), sciences of xxxi, humiliation of xxxi, 22, 36, 42, 193, 230; grandeur of xxxv; *liasse* title 3; and passions 9, 20, 228; and beasts 9; not contrary to religion 12; imagination, enemy of 16–17; corrupted 24; inadequacies of 27; our behaviour betrays 33–4; not unique path to certainty 35, 36; human distinctive feature 36; of different order from instinct 36; repudiated by dogmatism 42; shocked by doctrine of original sin 42–3; and unbelievers 57; force of 60; Augustine on submission of 60; limits of 62; thought is source of human dignity 73, 123, 137; order of 85; and feeling 112, 127, 148–9; and faith 118, 243–4; depends on memory 127; and original sin 132; in triad with custom, inspiration 147–8; works slowly 149; heart and 158; submission of 234; *see also* belief; faith; heart; intellect; proof
Recueil original xxxviii–xxxix
Redeemer, proved by scripture 11; grace of 75; not for pagans 78; prophecy of 142; need for knowledge of 171
redemption, theology of xxv–xxvi, xxxiii; proof of 166; Christian religion consists in 171; nature of, and Mass 236; *see also* propitiation
reed, thinking, fragment title 36;

human being only a, but thinking 72, 73

religion(s), *liasse* title 3; knowledge of inseparable from that of man's true nature, good, and virtue 7; proofs of 8; contradictions lead to true 8; project to show as venerable, rational, lovable 12; conditions for truth of 53; in mind and heart 60; must contain mysterious, supernatural 60; existence of opposing 65; fragment titles, falseness of other religions 73; criteria for truth of 73, 94, 106; must command love of God 76; other religions more popular 77; *liasse* 77–8; true religion discernible 80; perpetuity of 82–4; contains two kinds of men 90; wise and foolish 99; and man's obligation to receive 99; and self-love 122; purity of 131; difficulty of 131; justified by morality of 142; teaches man born sinful 157; truth in obscurity of 169

reprobation ix, xxiii, xxxiv; *see also* predestination

republic, fragment title 90; Christian and Jewish have only God as master 90

respect, machine yields to 14; implication of 15; meaning of 29; and originality 31

Retz, Jean-François-Paul de Gondi (1613–79), Cardinal de, and resignation of Paris See xiv

Richelieu, Armand-Jean du Plessis, Cardinal-duc de (1585–1642) xi

Roannez, Charlotte de (1633–75), Pascal's relationship with xiii; Pascal's letter to 236

Roannez, Arthus Gouffier, duc de (1627–96) xiii–xix; and *Writings on Grace* xxxi

Roberval, Gilles Personne de (1602–75), and cycloid prize xvii

Romans, false deities of 83

Rouen, Pascal family house at xi

Ruth 80

Sablé Madeleine de Souvré, marquise de (1599–1678), Pascal writes to xviii; and Pascal 242, 245

Sacy, Isaac Le Maître de (1613–84), Pascal's discussion with xiv; Pascal's director xxix; *Discussion with Monsieur de Sacy* 182–92, 245

Saint-Cyran, Jean Duvergier de Hauranne, abbé de (1581–1643) xi–xii, xix, xxviii, 228

Salomon de Tultie, style of 136, 241

salvation, theology of ix, xviii, xxv, xxx, xxxii, xxxiv; and belief 36; *Writings on Grace* 213–19, 225–6

scholastics, faculty psychology of xxxi

sciences x; classification of xxxi; fragment title, vanity of 14; two extremes of 29; abstract 130

Scotus, Duns 235

Scripture, and cognition in heart xxxi; versions used xli; necessary for knowledge 10; proof of Redeemer 11; and original sin 43; quoted without comment 60; has no order 85; ambiguity of 98; and hiddenness of God 140; permits avoidance of wager 155; four meanings of 244

Sebond, Raymond, Montaigne's chapter on xxvii, 185–6, 235; mentioned 79;

self, consists in our thinking 44; hateful 118; nature of 130–1; love of 179

self-interest, need to break power of xxxv; blinding effect of 20; and search for sovereign good 27; see also *amour-propre*

self-knowledge, through Jesus Christ 10

self-love, and self-hate 38, 91, 118–19, 122–3; natural 158; demands concern for immortality 160; and death 167; effects of 179–81; located in heart 181, 244; *see also amour-propre*

Sellier, Philippe, editor of *Pensées* xxii, xxxix–xl, 242; notes of 233, 242

semi-Pelagian, meaning and usage of term xxxii; and Calvinists 142

Senault, Jean-François (1601–72), and *amour-propre* xii, 240; and *paresse* 236

Seneca, quoted 24, 51; Christian adaptation of 227; Jansen ironic at expense of 232

senses, and error 19; and projected chapter on misleading powers 20; and reason 20, 54; relationship to faith 62; can perceive nothing extreme 69

Sercy, Charles de 245

Sextus Empiricus 245

Shem, as prophet 7

sins, frightful consequences of 131; indeliberate 215; *see also* original sin; *Writings on Grace* passim

Singlin, Antoine (1607–64), spiritual director of Port-Royal and of Pascal xiii

six, fragment on lists of six 84

sloth, and pride 74, 190; supernatural 162; *see also* laziness

sneezing, absorbs all functions of soul 144

Socrates 170

solitaires, at Port-Royal xii; at Port-Royal-des-Champs xiv

Solomon, and wretchedness 8, 26; Job and 26, 27, and authorship of *Ecclesiastes* 228

soul, philosophers and immortality of 9; happiness and esteem for 9; contradictions within 22; nobility of 27; self-knowledge of 28; immateriality of 37; importance of

immortality of 59, 121–2, 159–61; range and agility of 129; site of self 131; incomprehensibility of 148; nature of 162; creation of 232

sovereign good, *liasse* title 3, 51; everything becomes 7, 124; Montaigne's agnosticism about 9; self-interest and search for 27; opinions on 27–8; God alone is 52–4; not found by philosophers 53, 54; sought by heart 166

space, infinity of 26; terrifying silence of 73

Spartans, noble deaths of 88

stoics, and peace 9; and Pyrrhonists 28, 228; propose what is difficult and worthless 50; fragment title 51; among sects 74; conclusions of wrong 123; vanity of lives of 132; and passions as false judgements 228; aphorisms of 241

strength, and justice 34; fragment title 134; *see also* force; power

style, Pascal's xxix, xxxvi; reflections on his 125; natural, power of 127, 128, 136; fragment title 128; and arrangement of materials 132, 141

submission xxi, xxiii; sciences involving xxxi; necessary for salvation xxxiv; *liasse* title 60; need for 60; Augustine on 60; can be superstitious 62; to Jesus Christ and director 178

sufficient, of grace 224

supernatural, order of xxxii–xxxvi; in religion 60

superstition, and belief 61; differs from piety 61; and submission 62; to trust in formalities 89; and concupiscence 90

Swiss 21, 230

Tacitus, quoted 24, 70, 236

Terence, quoted 30

Thamar 80

theatre, dangers of 137–8
Theresa, Saint, mutability of
  judgements on 119
Thomas Aquinas, Saint, on riches
  13, 237
transition from knowledge of man to
  knowledge of God 3, 64
tree, does not recognize its
  wretchedness 36
Trent, Council of xxxii–xxxiii; see
  also *Writings on Grace* passim
truth, of religion, and fear 5, 12;
  and falsehood 7; desire for 8; and
  pyrrhonism 9; human incapacity
  for 14; and imagination 16; and
  justice 20; reason and search for
  27; and opinion 31; known by the
  heart 35; human capacity for 38;
  need to rely on faith for 40; not
  to be found in ourselves 54; no
  excuse for those who dislike 61;
  absence of contradiction no sign
  of 61; this not land of 97; we do
  not have 106; knowledge and
  maintaining of 135, 136; itself not
  the same as true things 153; of
  wager calculation 155; hatred of
  179; divine, excepted from laws of
  persuasion 193; different ways of
  knowing sacred and profane 193;
  apparent contradictions in 214;
  wrapped in fable 237
Turk Grand 13, 19
tyranny, fragment title 22; nature
  of 22–3

uncertainty, human state of 8; of
  unknown goal 34; leads to Jesus
  Christ 79; of religion 116; and
  use of probability 116; prompting
  wager argument 152–8; reason for
  searching for God 158–64; of
  perseverance 218; *see also* doubt
unfairness, in devotion to self 7;
  self-love makes us 157
uprightness (*honnêteté*), fragment
  title, universal quality 127; people
  not taught to be 138

Urfé, Honoré d' (*c.*1568–1625),
  optimism of xxviii
Usher, Jack 244

vacuum, possibility of 19
vanity, *liasse* title 3, 12–22 *passim*;
  fragment titles 13, 14, 15, 20;
  Pascal's use of term xxx; shown
  by phenomenon of love 10, 65;
  and appearances 32; and esteem
  of five or six 38; alternative to
  despair 74; anchored in heart
  124; examples of 124; of all
  conditions 132; alternative to
  laziness 189–90; *see also* pride
Varro, quoted 25
Vatable, François (*c.*1493–1547) 236
Vespasian 78, 336
Virgil, quoted 9, 28, 234
virtue xxx, xxxiii, xxxv; true virtue
  12; excess of, and vices 129, 141
volition, *see* will
Voltaire (Arouet, François-Marie,
  1694–1778) 233

wager, fragment 'Infinity
  nothingness' known as 152–8;
  manuscript and argument of viii,
  xxxv, 242–3; need for 154;
whims, their importance in our
  affairs 65
will, divine 213–20 *passim*
will, human faculty of, distinguished
  from intellect xii; and heart xxxi;
  and concupiscence 76; motivation
  of more than of mind 79;
  unsatisfiable 89; analogy of
  hypothetical autonomous will of
  limbs 91, 92; organ of belief
  113–14, 238; adding machine
  without 136; depraved 157; belief
  depending on, and heart 193–4;
  indeliberate movements of 215;
  in state of innocence 220; in
  Adam 221; and freedom, grace,
  and concupiscence 222–4; Calvin
  and 225; acts of not intellectual
  246

wisdom, human we are not in state
    of 15; and stoics 50
witnesses, quality of 11
works, of Jesus 214; and of
    ourselves 214; in Paul dependent
    on grace 214–15; *Writings on
    Grace* passim
wretchedness, Pascal's preoccupation
    with xxviii; and analysis of xxxv;
    and greatness xxx, 36–7, 38, 39,
    52–3, 171, 173; *liasse* title 3, 22;
    human 8, 166; Solomon and Job
    on 8; titles of fragment 10, 26;
    and distraction 10, 12, 49;
    without Jesus 10; witnesses to
    Jesus Christ in state of 11; of
    men without God 11; and pride
    26; in what it consists 42, 45;
    known through Jesus Christ 62,
    63, 64, 228; inspires fear 65; leads
    to despair 88; instinct lifts us
    above 125; threat of eternity
    of 165
Writings on Grace x, xv, xix–xx, xxi;
    analysis of xxxi–xxxiv

yoke, consequences of throwing off
    162

Zeno, vices of 50; and stoics 232

The Oxford World's Classics Website

www.worldsclassics.co.uk

- Browse the full range of Oxford World's Classics online

- Sign up for our monthly e-alert to receive information on new titles

- Read extracts from the Introductions

- Listen to our editors and translators talk about the world's greatest literature with our Oxford World's Classics audio guides

- Join the conversation, follow us on Twitter at OWC_Oxford

- Teachers and lecturers can order inspection copies quickly and simply via our website

www.worldsclassics.co.uk

American Literature

British and Irish Literature

Children's Literature

Classics and Ancient Literature

Colonial Literature

Eastern Literature

European Literature

Gothic Literature

History

Medieval Literature

Oxford English Drama

Poetry

Philosophy

Politics

Religion

The Oxford Shakespeare

A complete list of Oxford World's Classics, including Authors in Context, Oxford English Drama, and the Oxford Shakespeare, is available in the UK from the Marketing Services Department, Oxford University Press, Great Clarendon Street, Oxford OX2 6DP, or visit the website at www.oup.com/uk/worldsclassics.

In the USA, visit www.oup.com/us/owc for a complete title list.

Oxford World's Classics are available from all good bookshops. In case of difficulty, customers in the UK should contact Oxford University Press Bookshop, 116 High Street, Oxford OX1 4BR.

A SELECTION OF OXFORD WORLD'S CLASSICS

HONORÉ DE BALZAC — **Père Goriot**

CHARLES BAUDELAIRE — **The Flowers of Evil**

DENIS DIDEROT — **Jacques the Fatalist**

ALEXANDRE DUMAS (PÈRE) — **The Count of Monte Cristo**
The Three Musketeers

GUSTAVE FLAUBERT — **Madame Bovary**

VICTOR HUGO — **Notre-Dame de Paris**

J.-K. HUYSMANS — **Against Nature**

PIERRE CHODERLOS DE LACLOS — **Les Liaisons dangereuses**

GUY DE MAUPASSANT — **Bel-Ami**
Pierre et Jean

MOLIÈRE — **Don Juan and Other Plays**
The Misanthrope, Tartuffe, and Other Plays

JEAN RACINE — **Britannicus, Phaedra, and Athaliah**

ARTHUR RIMBAUD — **Collected Poems**

EDMOND ROSTAND — **Cyrano de Bergerac**

JEAN-JACQUES ROUSSEAU — **Confessions**

MARQUIS DE SADE — **The Misfortunes of Virtue and Other Early Tales**

STENDHAL — **The Red and the Black**
The Charterhouse of Parma

PAUL VERLAINE — **Selected Poems**

JULES VERNE — **Twenty Thousand Leagues under the Seas**

VOLTAIRE — **Candide and Other Stories**

ÉMILE ZOLA — **L'Assommoir**
La Bête humaine

	Eirik the Red and Other Icelandic Sagas
	The German-Jewish Dialogue
	The Kalevala
	The Poetic Edda
LUDOVICO ARIOSTO	Orlando Furioso
GIOVANNI BOCCACCIO	The Decameron
GEORG BÜCHNER	Danton's Death, Leonce and Lena, and Woyzeck
LUIS VAZ DE CAMÕES	The Lusiads
MIGUEL DE CERVANTES	Don Quixote
	Exemplary Stories
CARLO COLLODI	The Adventures of Pinocchio
DANTE ALIGHIERI	The Divine Comedy
	Vita Nuova
LOPE DE VEGA	Three Major Plays
J. W. VON GOETHE	Elective Affinities
	Erotic Poems
	Faust: Part One and Part Two
	The Flight to Italy
E. T. A. HOFFMANN	The Golden Pot and Other Tales
HENRIK IBSEN	An Enemy of the People, The Wild Duck, Rosmersholm
	Four Major Plays
	Peer Gynt
LEONARDO DA VINCI	Selections from the Notebooks
FEDERICO GARCIA LORCA	Four Major Plays
MICHELANGELO BUONARROTI	Life, Letters, and Poetry

A SELECTION OF **OXFORD WORLD'S CLASSICS**

LUDOVICO ARIOSTO — Orlando Furioso

GIOVANNI BOCCACCIO — The Decameron

MATTEO MARIA BOIARDO — Orlando Innamorato

LUÍS VAZ DE CAMÕES — The Lusíads

MIGUEL DE CERVANTES — Don Quixote de la Mancha
Exemplary Stories

DANTE ALIGHIERI — The Divine Comedy
Vita Nuova

BENITO PÉREZ GALDÓS — Nazarín

LEONARDO DA VINCI — Selections from the Notebooks

NICCOLÒ MACHIAVELLI — Discourses on Livy
The Prince

MICHELANGELO — Life, Letters, and Poetry

PETRARCH — Selections from the *Canzoniere* and
Other Works

GIORGIO VASARI — The Lives of the Artists

A SELECTION OF   **OXFORD WORLD'S CLASSICS**

PETRARCH   **Selections from the Canzoniere and Other Works**

J. C. F. SCHILLER   **Don Carlos and Mary Stuart**

JOHANN AUGUST STRINDBERG   **Miss Julie and Other Plays**